masters of music

conversations with Berklee greats

Mark Small and Andrew Taylor

Edited by Johathan Feist

BERKLEE PRESS

Director: Dave Kusek

Managing Editor: Debbie Cavalier

Marketing Manager: Ola Frank

Senior Writer/Editor: Jonathan Feist

Contributing Editor: David Franz

A special thank you to Sherry McAdams of Wilkins Management.

Creative Consultation by Kristen Schilo,
Gato & Maui Productions

Design by Lisa Vaughn,
Two of Cups Design Studio

PHOTO CREDITS:

Page 8 by Hideo Oida.
Page 20 by Joel Marion.
Page 50 by David Redfern.
Page 60 by Bob Kramer.
Page 68 by David Bassett.
Page 88 by David Redfern.
Page 98 by Gene Martin.
Page 108 by James Hamilton.
Page 122 by Mark McCarthy.
Page 142 by Terri Bloom.
Page 152 by Jim Hagopian.
Page 162 by Gene Martin.
Page 174 by Greg Norman.
Page 184 by Bob Kramer.
Page 194 by Gene Martin.
Page 204 by Gene Martin.
Page 214 by Jim Hagopian.
Page 226 by Jana Leon.
Page 258 by Gene Martin.
Page 268 by Frank Ockenfellas.
Page 280 by Jim Hagopian.
Page 292 by Kevin Ellsworth.
Page 304 by Gene Martin.
Page 316 by Jim Hagopian.
Page 328 by Gene Martin.

ISBN: 0-634-00642-8

DISTRIBUTED BY

HAL•LEONARD®
CORPORATION

1140 Boylston Street
Boston, MA 02215-3693 USA
(617) 747-2146

Visit Berklee Press Online at:
www.berkleepress.com

7777 W. BLUEMOUND RD. P.O. BOX 13819
MILWAUKEE, WISCONSIN 53213

Visit Hal Leonard Online at:
www.halleonard.com

table of contents

Preface   5

Andrew Taylor

Mark Small

Preface

DURING THE SEVEN YEARS that I have been editor of *Berklee Today*, I have fielded many phone calls from people hoping to procure a back issue to reread the interview with Arif Mardin, Paula Cole, Quincy Jones, or any of the 28 other luminaries who have been featured on the cover. There are few back issues, so many callers have been disappointed. *Masters of Music* will fill that need and go a little further. This volume includes all 31 cover stories printed during *Berklee Today's* first decade. Since the book does not have the space limitations the magazine has, where possible, the original transcripts of the interviews were consulted, and some great dialogue that had to be cut appears here for the first time.

Berklee Today made an auspicious debut in the summer of 1989 with a cover story on Beatles' producer George Martin. Among the many "firsts" of his fruitful career, Martin owns the distinction of being the only non-alumnus to be featured on a *Berklee Today* cover. Some might argue that he is an alumnus of sorts though; he was awarded an honorary doctor of music degree at Berklee's 1989 Commencement. All of the other cover personalities share the mutual experience of having attended Berklee in their formative years.

Andrew Taylor, the magazine's first editor, working closely with President Lee Eliot Berk and others, created a unique publication that is a hybrid alumni/trade magazine. When Andrew left the post in 1992 to pursue his master's degree, I interviewed for his job after receiving a nudge from President Berk to do so. Although I had lots of experience as a freelance writer, I had none in desktop publishing and the myriad tasks involved in the production of a magazine. I shall be ever grateful to Andrew for showing me the ropes, and also to Lee Berk for his encouragement when I wasn't sure that I could do the job.

I have often been amazed to think that it is actually my job to visit and speak with some of the brightest lights of the music industry and to have license to ask them about any aspect of their careers. It has been illuminating to learn how they got their breaks and what challenges they face now.

For me, the best preparation for an interview comes from making an emotional connection with the music my subjects have produced. I have typically immersed myself in their music until I could feel the heartbeat of their artistry and under-stand exactly why they are widely acclaimed as greats. The picture has come fully into focus on those occasions when I have been able to follow these master musi-cians into their own world in the studio or to the concert hall and then ask them afterwards how or why they did certain things.

It was an education to sit in the control room during scoring sessions for *The Simpsons* with Alf Clausen, listening back to cues he composed that ran the gamut from orchestral grandeur to tongue-in-cheek satire. It was a much differ-ent thrill when Brad Whitford took me backstage to talk shop and show me his arsenal of amazing guitars before an Aerosmith concert.

I am grateful that these people, some of the industry's busiest musicians, have made time for Andrew Taylor or me to come to their homes, to phone in from the road, or to show up at the *Berklee Today* office for an interview. In preparing these stories for this book, I see now that they have a slightly different character than those these same artists have given to *Rolling Stone, Musician, Down Beat*, or another commercial magazine.

Perhaps it is because these conversations frequently stirred youthful memories of times when life was simpler, and there was so much that was unknown that lay ahead. Most have shared valuable life lessons they learned along the way that they wish they knew beforehand. These factors contribute to giving these inter-views—some conducted 10 years ago—enduring qualities. I hope that in reading them, you will find these pieces helpful and that they will leave you with the feeling that you have just spent a few minutes catching up with an old friend from college.

—Mark Small

George Martin

beyond the beatles

Thoughts on the past, present, and future of music from a man who helped define them.

EVERYONE HAS HEARD THE LEGEND: a frustrated but resolute band manager, a record label chief with an open mind, and a young group of four Liverpool boys that no other label would touch.

"The recording, to put it kindly, was by no means a knockout," George Martin later reflected on the demo in his book *All You Need is Ears* (St. Martin's Press). "I could well understand that people had turned it down. But there was an unusual quality of sound, a certain roughness that I hadn't encountered before...I thought as I listened: Well, there just might be something here." To put it mildly, he was right.

Although signing, producing, and advising the Beatles may be George Martin's most quotable claims to fame, he's made a lifetime of sound judgements, unusual choices, and unusually wonderful music. In 1989, he was awarded an honorary degree, doctor of music, at Berklee's commencement ceremonies. It was one recognition in a string of honors that have included the title of Commander of the British Empire in 1988 and induction into the Rock and Roll Hall of Fame ten years later.

In October, 1998, MCA Records released what the 72-year-old Martin promised would be his last album as a producer, *In My Life*. The album of electric cover versions of Beatles hits is a fitting capstone to Martin's career as a record producer, composer, arranger, performer, film composer, record label chief, and chairman of a remarkably successful production company. But even that doesn't quite cover it.

George Martin was born in 1926 in London and was drawn to music at an early age. His family obtained their first piano when he was just six years old, and the instrument became an instant source of fascination to him.

He played and composed from his early years through his service with the Royal Air Force during World War II. After the war, Martin attended the Guildhall School of Music studying composition, piano, and oboe. That was followed by a short stint as a freelance oboe player and an even shorter stint as a clerk at the BBC music library. In September of 1950, George Martin was offered a position as assistant to Oscar Preuss, head of a small label in the EMI group, Parlophone. Martin took the job—helping Mr. Preuss with administrative chores, assisting the label's artists, and supervising studio sessions. He was a fast learner. When Oscar Preuss retired in 1955, Martin was offered the position of head of Parlophone. He was only 29 years old.

Martin immediately began searching for an untapped market where Parlophone could make its mark. He found that market in comedy records. His recordings of Peter Sellers, Spike Milligan, Flanders & Swann, and Beyond the Fringe (a young troop including such talents as Dudley Moore, Peter Cook, and Jonathan Miller) set new precedents in the industry, and are considered classics today. From there, Martin expanded Parlophone's classical and jazz presence and, by 1962, began looking for an opening in the pop market. Enter the Beatles.

With the immense success of the Fab Four, Martin branched out to other pop soloists and groups. Gerry and the Pacemakers, Billy J. Kramer and the Dakotas, Cilla Black, and David and Jonathan all made appearances on Parlophone. But it was the Beatles that took most of his time. Each album grew more complex and creative; each demanded more of him and the band. *Help!*, in 1965, contained Martin's first arrangements for instrumentalists other than the band, the string ensemble on "Yesterday," and each following recording contained more and more orchestration, studio experimentation, and sound manipulation. As George Martin and the Beatles grew and experimented, the role of the producer also grew. The collaboration reached one of its highest points in 1967 with the release of *Sgt. Pepper's Lonely Hearts Club Band*. With one release, the vinyl LP was transformed from a medium into an art form.

By 1965, Martin had become disenchanted with EMI. Although he had built Parlophone into a successful label and produced one of the most popular bands of all time, he was still being paid a relative pittance. Martin and a group of colleagues left Parlophone to form a collaborative production company, Associated Independent Recording (AIR), where he continued to explore and produce up to his recent farewell recording.

His production credits have included albums with Paul McCartney, America, Jeff Beck, Sea Train, Paul Winter Consort, John McLaughlin, Jimmy Webb, Neil Sedaka, the Bee Gees, Cheap Trick, and Ultravox. He also has written scores for many films including the Beatles' *A Hard Day's Night* and *Yellow Submarine*, *Pulp* starring Michael Caine, and *Live and Let Die*, for which he received a Grammy.

George Martin's career has thrived on his versatility, his vision, his openness, and his tactful manner with artists. It was about all of these things that he spoke to us from his offices at AIR Studios, Ltd., in London, in 1989, just prior to his receiving his Berklee honorary degree.

 You've been involved with a wide range of different aspects of the music industry. Do you think today's record producers can have that same sort of flexibility?

I've been very lucky in that respect. I guess I've had such a varied background because I've been associated with recorded music in one form or another over a long period of time. When I first started earning money from music, technology was very primitive. Tape was in its infancy. When I went to EMI studios in 1950, they were still making records on wax, because tape had a very bad signal-to-noise ratio. Stereo was not unheard of but it was unused. And long-playing records hadn't been invented. "Synthesizer" was a word you'd never heard of. It was a different style of life altogether.

But nowadays, of course, it's so different. It's very difficult for young people to have that kind of varied background. A producer has to be well-versed in computers as well as music. He has to have at his fingertips a grasp of technology that wasn't demanded 40 years ago.

 Is it important for a producer to understand a wide range of music as well?

I think the first essentials for any producer are a curious nature and a catholic taste. If his tastes are channeled too much in one direction, then he becomes less of a successful producer because it gives him less tolerance of music. If you get a rock fanatic or a jazz fanatic or a classical fanatic, to a certain extent they'll be wearing blinders; they won't see too much on either side of them. That makes them less versatile, it makes them less tolerant, and, to be honest, I think it makes them less musicianly.

 Would you say that a producer who specializes in one area is necessarily less effective?

I don't know about that. I just think a budding record producer should keep an open mind always, examine every kind of music, and appraise the good in everything, rather than channel himself too much in one direction.

Having said all that, it's worked for me, being versatile, and being able to put my hand at different things. It may not work for other people. If you get someone who is a synthesizer expert, he may be able to produce records of a particular sort much better than someone like myself. And also, obviously, it depends upon the aptitude of the individual. It's no good my lecturing people saying what they *should* be. They're going to be what they *are*.

 You've said that tact is the *sine qua non* of a record producer. Does that mean the artist is always right?

No, it doesn't mean that by any means. It does mean that you've got to convince the artist that what you want is what he wants.

I've never been one for confrontation. I've always been one for infiltration. I get my way by trying to convince the artists that it's his way. It's a question of tact and diplomacy. You've got to know your artist. You've got to know where his strengths and weaknesses are. And you must always try and keep him in a state where he's going to give you his very best.

At the same time, I think a producer should never be so arrogant as to believe that he knows it all. I've learned a hell of a lot from people I've worked with.

 Have you ever felt that advancing technology actually got in the way of a good recording?

Yes, sometimes. I've listened to works where people have become so in love with the mechanics and the technology of what they were doing that they forgot the music. You can get a thing overloaded. In today's technology, where a lot of recordings are done on a layer-cake principle, where you start off with something and you keep adding to it, one of the problems is that a lot of people don't know when to stop adding. That is a terrible danger. Knowing when to stop is almost as important as knowing where to start.

 Have you ever found yourself in that trap?

Not really. I've always regarded technology as a tool. When I first started using automation and computers, I insisted that they should still be tools, and that the synthesizer should be an instrument. I've always liked the combination of syn-thesized sound with natural sound. That happens to be my taste. A purely synthetic sound tends to be a little bit too sterile for me.

I have used purely synthesized sounds on material I've written myself, but not for human consumption. I've only done it in order to convince people that it would sound better if I used musicians who cost a lot more money.

There also seems to be a temptation to make tracks and recordings perfect. Do you see that as a problem?

It's not a problem, really. It's merely a question of taste again. I like to have a bit of humanity in my music. These days, you can sample and reproduce everything in digital format. But a clinically accurate tempo makes me uneasy, as though I'm listening to a quartz-controlled watch. I like ebb and flow and I like dynamics. I like a bit of randomness in my music, which is what a human being is, after all. A heartbeat isn't quartz controlled; it varies with our emotions. I think music should reflect that.

 And it may be that a human mistake on a track could turn out better than you could have imagined or planned.

Exactly. Sometimes people do things that you don't expect. And sometimes they are literally mistakes. I'm not saying always, because quite often they can be pretty awful. I have known occasions where mistakes have been absolutely super and I want them, even the question of intonation. I've heard Sinatra sing out of tune and sound good. I've heard other people sing in tune and sound bad.

 Can it sometimes be the constraints of technology that lead to greater creativity, as with *Sgt. Pepper's Lonely Hearts Club Band*, recorded on a four-track?

To be honest, I don't think *Sgt. Pepper* would have changed very much if we'd had present-day technology. If I'd had 32-track digital available to me in 1967, it's quite likely that the album would have sounded not very far off from what it sounds like today. I don't think it would have sounded any better. And I doubt very much whether it would have sounded much worse.

It was a hassle doing it on four track, because you had to think in advance. You had to think where you were going to go, how much extra tape you had to put it on, and what you were going to lose in the process. It was a kind of crossword puzzle you were doing mentally. But I don't think that really made it any better. I think it just was. It might have turned out slightly different, but who's to say?

Another possible constraint on music is business. Do you think the two are necessarily at odds with each other?

Sometimes they're in conflict. Sometimes you wish that you didn't have to finish something within a limited time. Or that you have to reduce the size of your orchestra because of the money constraints. Sometimes that can be frustrating. And sometimes you have to do things because business requires it. That is also frustrating.

I think you have to compartmentalize yourself. I've always done that. When I'm a businessman, I put my business hat on; I even literally put on my business clothes. I put my armor on and I go out to war. As opposed to being an artist where I sort of supplely lie around and dream and try to translate those dreams onto a piece of score paper or in a studio. So I've become two different people. And it's necessary to do that, because you have to be cool-headed as a businessman. When you're making decisions that involve not only money but also people's livelihoods, you've got to be serious about it.

But I've been very lucky, those frustrations have been a very small percentage of my life. One of the things I had at EMI as a result of the Beatles was not a great deal of money, because I didn't earn much, but a tremendous freedom. I was able to do pretty well what I wanted. That freedom was something that I valued enormously.

 Where do you think the music business is going from here, technologically and musically?

Certainly over the past 10 years or so, music has become subjugated to vision, much more than it ever was in the early days, because "the box," the fish tank in the corner of our room, dominates everybody's life to the exclusion of almost everything else. In the world as we know it, the average man is influenced more by television or video than by any other medium. And because of that, music itself has changed. Popular music has become less profound, become much more ephemeral and much more linked to visual images. Without that link we wouldn't have Michael Jackson. Without it we wouldn't have records which are sold as videos rather than as sound.

People tend to listen with their eyes more. They don't listen too much with their ears. Because of that, I don't think music has advanced as much as I would have liked it to, which I find a matter of some regret. Whether it's going to improve or not is up to people's tastes, I think. Whether they will realize that their aural sense has got to be developed a bit more than their visual one, I don't know. But there's no hope for that at the moment. So I'm a bit depressed about where music is going right now.

 Do you think these trends will continue?

There's no reason to think they won't. Certainly young people tend to think of music in connection with visual images, much more so than they used to. Very few people just listen to a new song or performance without seeing something, or without imagining they see something.

At the same time, I'm not so conceited as to think my views are those that should be perpetuated. It's quite likely that these are the ramblings of an old man. The young people may take a quite different view and say, "Okay, so music is more visual, who cares? We're getting a great kick out of it. So why don't you shut up." That's perfectly valid.

I think the choice that is offered to young people today in music is so wide, the colors on the palette are so varied now that it's difficult to know where to go. It is a very exciting future for music. The opportunities are enormous. There is sure to be opportunity for great talent to develop in the future which will make me and the Beatles seem very old-fashioned.

George Martin Speaks to the Class of '89
Excerpts from his 1989 commencement address

I am honored and delighted to be with you today. I am particularly thrilled to share this moment with someone who has always been a hero of mine—Dizzy Gillespie.

In touring your college yesterday, I was impressed. I think that no school anywhere in the world has such vast and impressive facilities as Berklee.

But technology hasn't always been to our advantage. In Europe, there is a sinister growing dependence on visual entertainment. TV and video have become the opiate of the masses, with prerecorded and programmed sound satisfying their eternal hunger. The staple diet of millions of people is junk music. Like junk food, it may fill their bellies, but it doesn't improve their style. They are hearing with their eyes, and listening to nothing.

I think we have to do our darndest to counter this trend, and get people to realize that mimed performances are not as good as the real thing.

For music to improve it has to be created live. This may seem a paradox coming from someone who has spent his life in a recording studio. But I believe in the spontaneity of perform-ance, and the ability to move the soul of the listeners with music that happens at the time.

I love technical wizardry, and I am enormously excited at the potential that is available today. But we have to remember that technology is just a tool, nothing more. True art, true music comes from the heart and soul of the human being.

Pete Townshend said to me the other day, "George," he said, "tell the young ones how to cope with success." I knew what he meant.

Success and its hand-in-glove partner, failure, are equally difficult to handle, and everyone has to deal with both in dif-ferent quantities in their lifetimes. The despair of rejection, or failure, is easy to imagine. The perils of success are less evident. For one thing, it is a mirage, you never really get to it. There is always more to do, more to learn, and always someone better than you are. Mind you, there's always someone worse, as well!

But public approval is a heady wine, and too much can be not only intoxicating, but downright harmful. Keep a sensible opin-ion of your own worth, without the honeyed words of your *admirers. They can a eat you alive if you are not careful, and drop you like a hot brick if you dare to go out of fashion.*

Lord knows that it is hard to get to the top; but it is a darned sight harder staying there. The music business is littered with shooting stars that have burned out. So pace yourselves; it is not a sprint that you are running, it is more like a marathon. And remember you have to keep running.

Obviously, talent is required. Equally obvious is the need for plain hard work. Every first-class musician that I have known works hard at his talent. Someone like my friend Mark Knopfler seems to enjoy talent that requires no effort. But I promise you, he practices every day to keep his technique up to scratch.

I said you were running a race, a marathon. Well, on second thought that marathon is a relay race, and I am close to passing on the baton. A lot of you are going to take up the baton passed to you by those ahead of you. Music of the future is in your hands. Cherish it: It is a vital part of humanity.

Emily Remler

first impressions

In one of her last interviews, Emily Remler talks about music and the struggle of substance over image.

"I MAY LOOK LIKE A NICE JEWISH GIRL FROM NEW JERSEY," Emily Remler told *People* magazine in 1982, "but inside I'm a 50-year-old, heavyset black man with a big thumb, like Wes Montgomery." Audiences often got the wrong impression when first seeing Emily Remler. She was a woman jazz guitarist in an industry dominated by men. She first found success as a youngster among time-worn talents. In short, she didn't look like what some would expect from a major jazz talent.

At first, Remler struggled with these constrictive preconceptions. Later, she learned to let her fingers do the talking. And that usually did the trick.

Like it or not, however, Emily Remler was a nice girl from New Jersey—born in New York City on September 18, 1957, and raised in Englewood Cliffs. Although her family was "nonmusical," Remler always had a fascination with the sounds and structure of music. She taught herself to play folk guitar at age 9. Through the music of the Beatles, the Rolling Stones, Johnny Winter, and Jimi Hendrix, she was drawn into rock styles. At each step, Remler learned by absorption. She soaked in the techniques and "feel" of the musicians and music she admired, and emerged with a broader voice of her own.

In 1974, at age 16, Remler entered Berklee and her eyes were opened to jazz. The music of Paul Desmond, Pat Martino, Pat Metheny, and especially Wes Montgomery opened a new world for her. She began absorbing the styles of the jazz masters and transcribing their riffs.

"She had a lot of enthusiasm and asked a lot of questions," remembers Guitar Department Chairman Larry Baione, Remler's teacher at Berklee. "She was willing to play with anyone so she could learn."

At age 18, Remler moved to New Orleans where she had her first taste of professional life—playing gigs in clubs, venues, and music halls, and teaching 25 guitar students. Her aggressive approach to getting and keeping jobs made those early years busy ones, and helped her get her break. She met and played for Herb Ellis who was impressed enough to get her into that year's Concord Jazz Festival.

"I was working in New Orleans in 1977," Ellis told *The Independent* in London, "when this young girl, she couldn't have been 20, came and asked me for a lesson. I asked her to play something for me, and when she did, I just couldn't believe what I heard. Forget about 'girl.' She's going to be one of the greatest jazz guitar players who ever lived. She can do anything."

At 21, Remler was playing on a bill with Ellis, Cal Collins, Barney Kessel, and Tal Farlow.

In the following eleven years, Remler worked with a range of artists, including Astrud Gilberto, Eddie Gomez, Charlie Byrd, David Benoit, and Larry Coryell. She also released seven recordings, including *Firefly* in 1981, and 1988's *East to Wes*. In 1985, *Down Beat* magazine's annual International Critics Poll named her guitarist of the year.

Her astounding musical momentum was cut short in 1990, just seven months after receiving Berklee's Distinguished Alumni Award. While on tour in Sydney, Australia, she died of a heart attack at the age of 32. Although the Berklee award was intended to recognize an alumna with a solid career, a growing talent, and an extremely promising future, it served as a capstone to her astounding career.

Fortunately, the award provided the opportunity to thank Emily for sharing her musical gift, as well as the opportunity to speak with her in 1989, in what was to become one of her last interviews.

 What was your goal when you left Berklee in 1976?

My last year at Berklee, I had a dream to get a gig at a club and play standards all night long. That was it. Since then my goals have gone much higher. I reached that goal as a result of the experience I got on the stage. And the information I got at Berklee was very helpful.

 What was it that raised your sights?

First of all, I achieved that goal within the first year after leaving Berklee. Then I got a record contract, so things go up. You want to make the best record you can make. Then you want to play with this or that great musician. Recently, I've had a goal to play with McCoy Tyner. Now that dream is coming true. In February, I'm opening for McCoy with my band and we're going to play together. That's something I thought would never happen.

 Do you get the same joy from music today as you did back then, or do you take a different angle now?

I have to work very hard that it's not a different angle. It can turn into your livelihood, and your business. You can lose a lot of that innocent, pure motivation to be a great musician.

If you start writing a song, and you're writing it to please "them," whoever "they" are, it's kind of weird. I have not lost that. I'm still very much into learning and jamming. I'm working on Mick Goodrick's ['67] new book, trying to get better. I have to keep going. I don't want to stagnate.

 How do you avoid the lure of writing or playing to please other people?

I think by now, at 32, I have somewhat of a personal voice. Because I have so many years of experience, I think it sounds like me no matter what I do. I'm hoping that's the truth. If I have a funk rhythm section behind me, I'd want it to still sound like me, and I wouldn't change the way I play. Even the more mainstream stuff I'm working on right now still sounds like me.

It's just like writing. It's like the way you're going to write this article. Maybe when you first started writing you could copy someone else's style completely. But after writing a while, your writing will always have some of you in it.

 You've emulated a lot of guitarists, but the result has always sounded like you.

I think that happens naturally. I never took a Wes Montgomery solo and played it note for note. I tried to get more of his feeling.

When I was at Berklee, the thing was to sound like Pat Martino. So we all tried to sound like Pat Martino. I couldn't stand the people who were afraid of sounding too much like Pat Martino and George Benson. I said to myself, "Look, I'll get as good as Pat Martino, then I'll change my style." It just seemed ridiculous for a person who couldn't play that well to be worrying about it.

I believe that you are going to consciously imitate somebody, or you are going to unconsciously imitate somebody. Either way, you get a lot from another person. Then you take it into yourself and interpret it another way. For me, it's been happening that way since day one. Things have been done before. It's all interpretation and sound.

 When you go on stage or into a studio, are you there to please the audience or to please yourself?

It's really both. What I like to do the best is lose myself—to get my head out of the way. I try to be some kind of channel. I know this sounds esoteric. But I try to get the thinking out of the way.

You have said before that you try to "get rid of the jury in your head." What does that do for you?

Every time I can do it, which is maybe 75 percent of the time now, it's great. I have better timing, and I sound so much better.

It would be different if the condemning jury worked. If you played a few bars and the jury said, "You stink, you're terrible," and that egged you on to play better, that would be great. But it doesn't. It makes you play worse.

So if you can get those judgments out of your mind, you can be more free and play much better. And if you're going to play bebop, you don't have time for all that thinking. It's almost like driving a race car. How much can you think when you're driving?

 Does that tie into not having to prove yourself?

Yeah. I feel like that very little nowadays.

 Did you feel that way when you started out?

Tremendously so. Especially when I was at school. It's just natural that when kids are at school they're going to be competitive. Plus the fact that I was a girl. So I got this "I'm gonna show these guys" attitude—which wasn't really conducive to creative playing.

I just wanted to be accepted as a jazz guitarist. But that can drive you crazy. Because you never do get the approval—at least not completely. You can get the approval of all your peers and one guy will say you can't play and you're shattered.

So I consciously tried to put that type of feeling out of my mind. By the time I got to be about 21 years old, that feeling was gone.

 Do you connect your own personal growth with musical growth?

Absolutely. And I see it with other people, too. That's the process. That's why so many people connect being a good jazz musician with learning from life experiences. When you grow up, your music grows up too.

That part doesn't even have much to do with practicing. It's just a new attitude. You realize that on this solo you could play seven notes as opposed to 700 and still say the same thing.

 Have you ever felt your music suffered because of an attitude?

The music is going to suffer if the motivation is to compete with others, and if I'm only playing to get people's approval. It's going to suffer if I'm not that great health-wise, or if I'm worried about four million things. But if I keep myself fairly healthy and try to play with a motivation to play great and feel good, it seems to work out. That's the original motivation anyway.

 It seems like much of the music industry has turned from a self-destructive to a self-preserving attitude.

It's unbelievable. I saw it start with Pat Metheny when I was at Berklee. He was the first one that affected me by being a young, healthy jazz musician—and by having a positive attitude instead of a dark, self-destructive attitude. It seems like a lot more musicians are like that now. You go on tours and people have their vitamins and run in the morning.

That's the thing now. You don't get hired if you're all messed up on drugs or alcohol. It's much more the style to be healthy and know business and know what you're talking about and treat yourself well. Musicians are really turning into good businessmen. And it's about time.

 Are there other reasons the scene has turned around ?

I think the music has become more positive. I don't think you can say that the '50s stuff was negative and Pat Metheny stuff is positive. But you can't be dark and self-destructive and play pretty, positive music. You can't do that with bebop either—at least I can't.

 How have your own views of music and the music industry changed over the years?

In the last three or four years, I've opened myself up to look at it as a business, which is what it is, and to learn a little more about it. I still don't know very much, but I know a lot more than I used to know. I was a typical musician just wanting to play and not wanting to be bothered with the details—but then resenting things when I would get screwed or when I wasn't treated the way I thought I should be treated. I wouldn't even ask how much a gig paid and then resent it when it was too little. That's a very typical "old school" thing. I've been working on just being able to say what I think I need.

 Do you think that business can overshadow the music?

It can very much. It helps to keep in mind that they can't make the record without you. You're just as important as the managers, record promoters, and those type of people. The idea I used to have was that, "Oh, you're doing me such a big favor to allow me to play for you." But that's not the way it is. It's the other way around.

Mick Goodrick ['67] is my hero with this thing. He's self-sufficient. He's fine when he's practicing in his room. And he never entered the rat race, desperately trying to get publicity, record contracts, etc. He just kept playing and working on his music, and now he's got a great gig with Jack DeJohnette. He just kept doing what he was doing, and people would seek him out.

 Do you still have dreams of scoring for films?

I do. I'm not doing anything to reach that goal, right now. To do that, I would have to go back to school. When I was at Berklee, I took the performance route. If I could do it over again, I would take the arranging route, or composition. Since I never took any composition courses, I'm pretty moronic as far as that stuff is concerned. I think I have a good sense of composition. But I would need to go back to school if I were to do movie scores.

 What is it about film scoring that appeals to you?

I think it's the most incredible medium for expressing emotion. To make millions of people feel a certain way at a certain second is just amazing to me.

I go to movies and listen to the music, and think how ingenious it was that the composer put that chord and that voicing right there so that we would all be scared—or we would all be anticipating something, or be happy, or be some other thing he wants us to be. It's really amazing to be so in control of music that you can say, "This chord will make them happy."

 Can you get the same effect with a recording?

Yes, but coupled with a visual it's even more powerful. I think *West Side Story*, for example, was the most powerful show of music and visual. I'm still in love with *West Side Story*.

 In your opinion, what is the most important aspect of jazz?

I have to say improvisation. Jazz is the only music left that you can do any sort of improvisation on. I hope they don't want to take that away. A lot of things these days are planned and sound great and are neat. I do it myself. But I still leave big sections for improvisation because that's where I have my fun. That's the basis of jazz.

 Is improvisation losing ground in today's jazz?

As music is getting less "sloppy," there's less improvisation. We all want it to be neat. We all want it to sound perfect, with no mistakes. And there goes the improvisation, unless you're a robot.

I've just tried to play well. I play fairly "neatly" anyway. On the projects I'm doing now, I'm trying to get everything neat—as opposed to my other records, which got sloppy sometimes. I'm trying to get it nice and neat so I can live with it too, because I'm a perfectionist.

 Q. Do you have any goals for musical growth?

I've always come up to what's in front of me. That's the way I grow. I got a gig with a rhythm & blues band when I lived in New Orleans and I had to grow to that. Then I had to grow to play Broadway shows. Then I got a record contract and I had to grow up to each record.

Looking to the future, I would like to write for movies. And I would like to be able to write more 20th-century classical stuff. I would like to do what Lyle Mays does. He writes for movies; he writes incredible arrangements; he writes songs; he performs; he does everything.

And, to tell you the truth, I would really like to take time off and go back to school. I've been working pretty steadily without a break since I was 18 years old. I've earned one.

Alan Silvestri

to the abyss and back

After a bout with bad times, this film composer is at the forefront of the background business.

WITH FOUR YEARS AS COMPOSER FOR A SUCCESSFUL TELEVISION SERIES under his belt, Alan Silvestri '70 was ready for anything—anything, that is, except unemployment. When the popular police show *CHiPs* went off the air in 1983, Silvestri found himself out of work, out of options, and out of luck.

"I couldn't get an episode of anything for almost a year," he remembers. "During this time, my wife and I were expecting our first child. Plus, there was a musician's strike. It got pretty squeaky."

But, as with most of the films Silvestri has scored since then, this story has a happy ending.

After a life-saving offer to score *Romancing the Stone* in 1984, Silvestri composed the music for a string of major films including *Cat's Eye*, *Back to the Future*, *Flight of the Navigator*, *No Mercy*, *Outrageous Fortune*, *Predator*, *Who Framed Roger Rabbit?* and *The Abyss*.

He has worked with such leading directors and producers as Robert Zemeckis, Michael Douglas, Carl Reiner, Arthur Hiller, and Steven Spielberg. After that one tough year, Silvestri has become one of the busiest film composers in Hollywood.

Back in 1969, when Silvestri first arrived at Berklee from his hometown of Teaneck, NJ, he had no intention of scoring for films. All he wanted to do was play guitar.

"Berklee was really the only place in the country where someone who was a jazz player could go and be considered a legitimate music student," he recalls. "That was an amazing opportunity. It was also a very labor-intensive period for me."

Silvestri remembers the intense musical environment as the key to his learning at Berklee.

"So much of music seems to be in the doing," he says. "And there was constantly opportunity to make music. I wrote a lot of arrangements while I was in school. I played hours and hours and hours a day. I worked with all kinds of musicians of all levels of ability. All of that is directly related to the job I do now."

While Silvestri's focus at Berklee was guitar, he soon found a stronger interest upon moving to the West Coast. When he got his first opportunity to write a score for a low-budget film, *The Doberman Gang*, in 1970, he began his "long, slow slide" toward composition and away from performance. The offer to write for *CHiPs* only sped up the inevitable shift.

"When I started working on *CHiPs*, it was really the first time I had anything I could call a steady job in the film industry," he says. "That was thrilling because, for me, film scoring had always been one low-budget film a year. If it didn't cost me money I considered myself lucky."

Since then, Silvestri has considered himself very lucky. When we spoke to him in his Carmel, California home in 1990, he was just completing work on *Back to the Future II*, the highly anticipated follow-up to the 1985 Spielberg/Zemeckis smash, and beginning work on *Back to the Future III*. He was also scheduled to score *Downtown*, directed by Richard Benjamin, and he began work over Christmas on the film adaptation of *Dick Tracy*.

In 1990, Alan Silvestri was far from the abyss of unemployment of only seven years before. But despite the dramatic rise, he had yet to reach his peak.

Q. How did you finally break your streak of unemployment after *CHiPs* was canceled?

I finally begged, basically, for an episode of a different show and the producer didn't like what I did. They ended up throwing out half of my work. I started thinking, "Maybe I'm in the wrong business."

Very shortly thereafter, I got a call from a music editor I had worked with on *CHiPs* to tell me about a film he was working on. The people he was working with had listened to all kinds of tapes from all kinds of people and they still couldn't find anything that they were happy with. So he was calling to see if I was interested in doing some kind of spec demo to play for them.

This was on a Friday night. He introduced me to the director of the film on the phone that night, a man named Bob Zemeckis. Bob explained, in about five minutes, this three-minute scene having to do with this girl and this guy running through the jungle in the pouring rain, with machetes in their hands.

"They're being shot at by these bad guys," he said. "Then this guy swings across this giant gorge and comes out on the other side." After he described the scene, Bob asked if I could have something to him by lunchtime the following day.

So, of course, I said, "No problem."

I had just started to put an electronic studio together, and I didn't have much. I had a Linn drum and a Yamaha DX-7. I had a multitrack machine but no mixing console. So, I was up all night putting together this rhythm track. And I went in on the following day.

When Bob Zemeckis came down, it was probably a good omen because he walked in wearing the same sweater as me. At that point, we had a feeling that this could work out. I played him this track, and he smiled and his editor smiled, and they said they would be in touch.

That evening, I got a call from Michael Douglas, who wasn't only starring in this film, but was the producer. It was *Romancing the Stone*. On that Monday, we got a call and the deal was made within a day.

That's unheard of. There are people who work and work and work in television and never get a chance to break out of it. It's like they're two different streams. But all of a sudden, I'm standing there at the premiere with Kirk Douglas and I'm in the film business.

After that, people didn't even call me to do television anymore. It wasn't as if I wouldn't do it. I just didn't get those calls anymore.

 Are there different techniques required for film and television scoring?

The mechanics are very much the same. But there are definitely very different styles of shooting. In television, you have the constant interruptions with commercials. You very rarely have the chance to work with a sizable ensemble— usually they like to keep the numbers very low. And, for the most part, you're squeezed much more time-wise with television than you are for feature films.

When I was doing *CHiPs*, I would have about 25 minutes of music to write each week. I would see one show on a Monday morning and record the previous one on Monday afternoon. It was like that every week for 26 straight weeks.

But mechanically, it's still the same. In those days there were no video machines to do this stuff. So, we would go in and spot the film and write the entire film off of the timing notes. Now, everyone has videos. I use very exact videos with time code and all the rest of it. That's been a bit of a change.

 How else has the profession changed over the past decade?

Apart from the boom in the use of videocassettes for previewing, the marketing of films seems to have changed over the past 10 to 20 years. Markets are presold very far in advance now. Sometimes I'll be working on a film and they will have already reserved theaters a year and a half in advance.

The problem is that, in film production, things tend to slide—preproduction slides, production slides, post-production slides. Music is one of the last things to be done before the dub of the picture. All this sliding of the schedule winds up sticking you up against a wall in a number of ways. Number one, you get your hands on the film much later than you would like. And number two, because they have to preview with their backs against the wall, they're making constant changes in the picture right up against the time that you're recording.

So, for instance, when I did *The Abyss*, that film opened about one week after I had recorded the last cue. Which is unbelievable! That's a whole added difficulty that I don't recall seeing. I actually can remember getting locked film. I never see locked film anymore.

 Do you usually get a complete cut?

I always like to get a complete cut at some stage. For instance, this week I'm working on *Back to the Future II*, and I have a complete cut of the film. But on Saturday, I will get a new complete cut and just about every cue I've written for recording the following Thursday has been recut. So, I have about 30 minutes of orchestral music for a 98-piece orchestra, and every cue has been recut.

I'll have a day or so to make all of these changes in time to still proofread the scores and get them to the copyist in time for the music to be on the stands Thursday morning. That's what the business is these days.

 Have you begun to use a computer to write out your scores, or do you still write them out yourself?

I do all my orchestral scores by hand on score paper. I do use the Auricle III software on the Yamaha C1 computer to lay out all of the timing business. That has been one of the most incredible additions to the film scorer's battery of tools to come along since the Knudsen book [a listing of click-track data, tempos, and timings].

Q. What about sequencers, synthesizers, and drum machines? Do they play a role in your composition?

When I do an electronic score, I do all of the performance myself. I work with a Synclavier system along with racks of other kinds of gear. But the Synclavier and its sequencer is the heart of the system.

I did an all electronic score for *No Mercy*. And I did one for *Clan of the Cave Bear* as well as *Flight of the Navigator*.

I've done some other scores where there has either been a great deal of electronic music or a combination of electronic and acoustic. *Predator* involved a lot of scoring with electronics while working with a large orchestra. At one point, we had approximately 40 tracks of electronics running with a 90-piece orchestra live. That was pretty interesting.

 Q. Do you see the full orchestra losing ground or fading out as synthesizers become more prevalent?

I don't see the full orchestra being affected, really. What I see being lessened is the smaller ensemble used on television shows. I see more and more use of electronics for those kinds of things. But full orchestras are still what you need to get that particular effect.

 Q. Are there often creative disagreements between the director and the composer?

Sure. Very often, no matter how big they are, composers will have entire scores thrown out. It all has to do with communication. It's very easy to think you're talking about the same movie and then find out that you're not.

 Q. What do you do when your views of the film are different than the director's?

It can be a real problem. I've never thought that I was making a different film than the director. I think then you're just asking for trouble. I have found that I've not been working on the same scene as the director thought. I've not yet had the pleasure of having an entire score thrown out. I have had pieces of music thrown out and I have had to rework them.

For some reason, it seems a lot of composers don't see their piece as a work in progress. Very often, composers walk into the soundstage, into this multimillion dollar enterprise, and think that they've written their 50 minutes of music and that's it. There is nothing in the film business, or for that matter in any other creative endeavor that I know of, where that is the case. Especially in a collaborative process.

What a composer can lose sight of in the privacy of his own studio is that he is still working on a collaborative art form. Even though he's working on an aspect of it alone, it is only an aspect of a much larger whole.

That's probably where the difficulty comes. It can be very difficult without that awareness when the confrontation comes down in the recording studio.

When you play the music, it has become near and dear to your heart. But a director is not terribly concerned about all the hours spent. If you're working with a really good director, you haven't even come close to the hours he spent on the film.

Still, when the director says, "Beautiful piece of music, Al. Whose movie is it for? Because I know it's not for my movie," the composer has to muster all the perspective he or she can. Because the mission in film scoring is to enhance the director's vision. The director is the captain of this ship. And if he's not, you're in trouble.

It brings us back to communication and the awareness of what the focus and mission really is here. If you try to mutiny, it will never work. The ship cannot have two captains.

When you are working alone in your studio, it's still someone else's direction and someone else's itinerary that the ship is following. That's something that requires a great deal of emotional maturity for a composer—to be able to understand his or her place in the grand scheme of this thing called a motion picture.

One has to be a willing and able crewman. That doesn't mean not challenging the captain. If you really feel you can accomplish the director's wishes by going a certain way with the music, you have a responsibility to the music and to yourself to present that case to the director. That's what he's asking you for.

 It must also be difficult to realize that a truly successful film score is invisible, that all this work is not the focus of the art form but only an aspect of it.

It can be. But at the same time, every other member of the filmmaking entity is in the same position. It's very much like orchestral playing. The ideal is 98 pieces in a symphony orchestra playing together, not 98 soloists all vying for separate fulfillment. The music is just a voice you add to the whole. That's what the art form is all about.

The Scoring Process

"The process can be different for every film, but the preferable way is to start very early on. Bob Zemeckis will often tell me at dinner about a film he's about to do—for instance, Who Framed Roger Rabbit? And then, as soon as he has a first draft or a shooting draft of the script, he'll send me the script. I'll read that and spend some time with Bob just talking about the film—even though he hasn't started to shoot. Then, with Roger Rabbit, I went to London and spent some time on the set with him while he was shooting, just to start to get the flavor of the film.

"That's the best way. Since the film is a collaborative effort, success seems to depend upon the communication between the people involved. The more time spent with the project and between the people, the greater the possibility of the composer achieving the director's goals for the film.

"Once the film is finished, or shot at least, and they get a fairly substantial cut, we usually sit down and spot the picture. For me, that's usually done at a KEM [a 35mm film editing machine] with the director and editor. We go from reel one through the entire film and spot where music will begin and where it will come out. And the director usually talks about what he hopes the music will do for the film in these places.

"After that's done, the music editor will give me a set of spotting notes, which lists each piece of music with a brief explanation of what that scene is. Then the editor will go through each one of those sequences and provide detailed, timed notes of each scene. I usually get those notes with footages, with reel times, and with SMPTE time code. Those are the notes that I work off of along with the matching video of the scene. Then the writing begins."

Ernie Watts

the dialects of jazz

One of L.A.'s busiest session players, Ernie Watts discusses the common language of music.

ASK SAXOPHONIST ERNIE WATTS '66 HOW HE CAME TO MASTER SO MANY DIFFERENT KINDS OF MUSIC and you might not get the answer you'd expect. "There aren't any different kinds of music," he will say. Then he'll smile quietly and watch for your reaction. He's not being difficult or cryptically hip; he's expressing a belief that rests at the core of his approach to music and his approach to life. "It's all the same language," he explains. "There are just different dialects."

Whether it is a question of semantics or sage wisdom, Ernie Watts' philosophy has made him a very busy man. Musicians, producers, and music professionals have always been quick to realize that whether he is performing with the Rolling Stones, Frank Zappa, Rickie Lee Jones, Whitney Houston, Charlie Haden, or Lee Ritenour, Watts has mastered the language of the solo line. And he speaks each dialect like a native.

Ernie Watts came to Berklee in 1964 after a year of study at Westchester State Teachers College. He had already become proficient on the saxophone, clarinet, and flute family, soon adding oboe and English horn to his instrument roster. His talent was quickly recognized by faculty and others. In 1966, he began touring with Buddy Rich, gaining a reputation on both coasts as a fine musician. That tour led to a move to Los Angeles, several subbing jobs, and eventually a seat in the *Tonight Show* orchestra—a position he held for almost two decades.

As his reputation grew, Watts began doing session work with such artists as Barbra Streisand, Neil Diamond, the Jacksons, Earth, Wind and Fire, Ray Charles, Boz Scaggs, Stanley Clarke, Aretha Franklin, the Temptations, Diana Ross, and others. In the midst of this schedule, he would also find time for film and television work and club sessions with friends like Dave Grusin, Abe Laboriel ['72], Lee Ritenour, and Bob Leatherbarrow.

In 1981, Watts signed on with Qwest Records, the flagship company of fellow alumnus Quincy Jones ['51]. Since then, Watts' accomplishments have been as vast and varied as his music. He toured with the Rolling Stones in 1981, appearing in their concert film *Let's Spend the Night Together*. He has continued to play major studio, film, and television sessions, including the Grammy-winning soundtrack to *The Fabulous Baker Boys*. He also garnered two Grammys of his own for his 1981 album, *Chariots of Fire*, and 1985's *Musician*. In 1990, he was honored with a Distinguished Alumnus Award by Berklee for his continuing quest for musical excellence and for his positive role in the music industry.

Calm but intense, relaxed but driven, Ernie Watts has the spark of a creative individual voice and the honesty and humility of a team player. While those diverse aspects may only be dialects of his own personal language, they speak volumes about Watts' continuing professional and personal success.

 You've become known for your versatility in various contemporary musical forms, and yet you believe there is actually only one form. How do you mean that?

All Western music is governed by the same laws of harmony. A Dm7 chord is a Dm7 whether it's Coltrane, the Rolling Stones, Beethoven, or Bach. Western harmony solidifies the whole deal. The only thing that changes styles in music is what you do rhythmically with the notes. The difference between these dialects of rock, jazz, r&b, classical, and so on, is not so much what you play as where you play it in the bar.

A prime example of that is Miles Davis. Miles played the same stuff since 1960. He just surrounded himself with different people and he put his notes in a different place in the bar. But it was the same stuff he'd been playing since *Friday Night at the Blackhawk*. He hadn't changed his style. He just changed his rhythm section [he laughs]. But it worked. And it was good. And it was genuine.

 Is there a particular dialect that you prefer?

The music that really seems to be open to my flexibility and to what I like to do is an eclectic blend of acoustic music and fusion. With my quartet, I do acoustic tunes, straight-ahead tunes that I've written, standards, and some fusion stuff with electric bass and electric keyboards. I like the combination. I think it's important to communicate to people how all of these things are connected.

 Do you feel people are open to that idea? Musicians always seem to want something "new."

I think that people like toys. They're always looking for new diversions. But as you learn, you start to see the similarities. As you start to see the similarities, it starts to eliminate the games and it simplifies your life. You get a clearer picture of what you want to do.

Of course, when you are talking about a school environment and a younger group of musicians, all the things that you go through are normal. It's normal to feel competitive. It's normal to think that you're onto something new, until you listen to something that's 25 years old and hear the same stuff. It's normal to think all of those things when you're young. My main interest in my clinics has been to help younger people speed up the process.

I went through "being the best." I went through playing the fastest, and playing the loudest, and playing the highest. We all go through that stuff. But at some point, we say, "Okay, I've done this and this and this. Now what do I want to do? Who am I? Where do I fit?" When you get to that, you're alone. It's like you step out of the race and you are with yourself.

Music is an art form, not an athletic event. Everybody has something different to say. If two people are running 50 yards, they can be competitive about who can run 50 yards faster. But music is not a 50-yard dash. It's a totally creative thing that's related to your individual concepts. Since no two people think alike, the criteria are different. So how can you compete?

Q. So another universal in music is being genuine about what you're doing.

Right. And on the same level, that's what creates your business. That's what creates your appeal. That's what creates your success. If you look at anybody who is really successful and considered a master, he or she will be a person who is focused, who has an idea, and who does his or her thing. You can say that about Michael Brecker, David Sanborn, Miles Davis, Eric Dolphy, whoever. These are people who have made a commitment to what they believe. They've stood up for it and they've done it. That's the bottom line.

The music business is not that complicated. The first word in the music business is "music." There isn't any "business" if there isn't any music. So, as an artist, your primary concern is to create the best music you can possibly create. The business will follow. Because I always tried to be the best that I could be, and because I was focused, that created my business. People wanted me to be there because I could play. I wasn't taking contractors to dinner.

Q. Was it always that clear to you as you were growing up?

Yes, always. For some reason, a little statement came into my mind when I was young. The statement was, "A musician's security is his musicianship." That was it. That led me to do the best that I could do at all times, and to continually strive toward excellence. Some people call that focus. Some people call it obsession. It depends on where you're coming from.

Q. Can there be a conflict between being an individual and being marketable?

I went through a period of oscillation, saying, "How can I do what I want to do and make people happy, too?" You can go through all of these compromises, but in the long run you come back to what you feel anyway. So you might as well start out there and just stick with it. If you've got something in your heart, you might as well acknowledge it immediately. In a given period of time you're going to come back to that anyway.

Now I'm trying to turn that question around and make what I like to do marketable. It's just a matter of making a decision and sticking with it, rather than saying, "I think I'll do a bunch of tunes that sound like Kenny G so people will come out and listen to my band." That doesn't work. They can always go listen to Kenny G.

Of course, you can't always expect people to understand. I'll always remember my second album, *Wonderbag*, an album of Stevie Wonder tunes that I did in my own way. It was reviewed in *Down Beat*, and the reviewer spent the whole review talking about how I didn't sound like Phil Woods. He was bugged because I was a young saxophone player that wasn't trying to sound like Phil Woods! Then, when I worked with Cannonball Adderley, he respected me because I didn't try to sound like him. So what are you going to do?

 What do you remember most about your years at Berklee?

I think the thing that I remember the most was the real integrity and musical focus of the school. It was on a very professional level. As far as consistently playing really good music, good arrangements, good writing, and high level music, that was probably the best period of my life. When you get out into the world and you get involved in working, a lot of it is mediocre. You have high points of projects that are really good. Then there's a big mass of blah kind of stuff. At Berklee, every day was good music.

Of course, it was great to learn the technical aspect and the scientific approach to music, as well—tuning into chord scales and really learning the theory. Being creative is a balance of going with your heart and knowing in your head what's logically and musically right.

Do you feel you had that intuitive side when you came into Berklee?

Yeah, I had been playing with groups for a while. I started playing when I was 13, and I was playing with groups and doing dances and playing with different types of bands from the time I was 16. But I had large gaps in my playing because I learned how to improvise by ear. So I had developed my ear to quite an extent, but there were still certain harmonic patterns or turnarounds that hung me up. Getting to Berklee and learning about chords, chord patterns, and chord scales really cleared up a lot of those dead spots.

 What would you say to students studying at Berklee now?

I think the main thing is for everybody to remember that music is not an athletic event. It's not a sport. It's an art form. And everybody has their own voice. And everybody has their own place. So there's really no competition.

It's very important to go inside and see what you feel. And see what you want to play. It's part of the development process. When you're younger, you have people that you emulate. And then at a certain time, there's that period of thinking, "What do I think? What do I feel? What do I want to create? I've heard how this guy does it, I've studied him. Now how do I feel about this music?" It's really important to get to that point.

 It must be difficult to hold that attitude when you get out into the business world.

One of my points of success has been that I haven't tried to sound like anybody else. I have a unique sound. I have a different style. Because of that I have created my own place. If they want me, they call me. It's just as important to develop your own individual style and sound, because there is a place for individuality. That's what music is about.

There are a million copies of Coltrane, but Coltrane was the original. There are a million copies of Jimi Hendrix, but Hendrix was the original. If you look at the music business, the most successful people are the creators. There are 500 saxophone players that sound like David Sanborn. But David Sanborn is the original, and he's the one that's rich.

 Is there a danger of losing that drive when you are just starting out, doing jobs you might not really want to do?

When you're growing and getting established, everything you take has a positive aspect—be it a TV film or a record date or a Sunday night casual. As long as you're playing your instrument and as long as you are dealing with music on a full-time basis, you are growing.

When I first came to Los Angeles, I was playing five or six different woodwinds, doubling a lot, and playing all kinds of gigs. And whether I liked the show or not, it was valuable and positive because I was dealing with my instruments. I was growing and I was learning. That's the most important thing.

There is a positive aspect to everything. It's just a matter of being able to see it and wanting to see it.

 So what do you say to the musicians that firmly stick to one idiom?

Well, that's their choice. You choose your limitations or you choose your freedom. It's totally up to you. It's okay to say, "All I want to do is play Charlie Parker tunes." There's nothing wrong with that. It's just a matter of choice. I've chosen to have as few limitations as possible in my tastes and in my ability to perform. Because I made that choice, it has created a place for me in the business. That's why I've always been busy. If I had chosen only to play Charlie Parker music, then it would make my work situation very selective, too.

There's no right or wrong to this stuff. It's not wrong to only want to play Coltrane music your whole life. It's beautiful. And in the same breath, there's nothing wrong with wanting to play rock and roll, and r&b, and bebop, and fusion, too. It's all choice.

That's one of the complaints I have about the "Wynton Marsalis factor." He has chosen to do one thing, but he has also chosen to criticize other people who have chosen differently. I think that's very short-sighted. There are no purists. If you ever talked to Coltrane or Charlie Parker about their music, you would have seen that they were open to all kinds of music. Bird listened to everything. So did Coltrane.

The possibilities are infinite. It just depends on your mind. Whatever you can perceive and believe, you can achieve. All you have to be is undeniably good. If all you want to do is play like Charlie Parker and you play incredibly like Charlie Parker, you'll make a living.

It's not that hard to make a living. It's not us against the world. The world is on our side. We live in a friendly universe. The main thing we have to do is know what we want. When you know what you want, you focus on it, you get a clear picture, and it evolves.

It's also important to remember that music is a very gregarious thing. It's all about relationships. You can be the greatest artist that has ever lived. But if you don't know how to relate to people and how to communicate, then there you are: the greatest artist that ever lived, playing in your apartment.

If you have been given a gift, you have a responsibility to share it. I'm very interested in sharing what I have with other people.

Arif Mardin

a few minutes with arif mardin

A short break in the busy life of a Grammy-winning producer, arranger, and record executive.

ARIF MARDIN '61 LOOKS AT HIS WATCH, and then back at the control room window on the opposite wall of the studio soundstage. It has been only 15 minutes since he was in there last—mixing the tracks for a Bette Midler album—but it has been a jam-packed 15 minutes. In that quarter hour, he has eaten half an order of take-out fish and chips (the worst he has ever had, by the way), instructed the studio staff on the afternoon schedule, and discussed a lifetime of experiences and insights with a slightly dazed Berklee employee.

While his schedule is tight, Mardin never seems harried—at every step he is quiet, thoughtful, and charming. But after 15 minutes of talking about himself, he is anxious to get back to what he loves to do, and to what he does best: putting inspired musical moments on record. Like a schoolboy aching for recess, Arif Mardin is ready to get back to work.

For more than 35 years, Mardin has brought that same enthusiasm and dedication to the business he adores. Even when he first entered Berklee in 1958, fresh from his native Istanbul, he had an undeniable hunger for new ideas and an unquenchable love for music.

"I remember my arrival in Boston and the subsequent entrance to Mr. [Lawrence] Berk's office on a cold January morning," he told an audience of Berklee seniors in 1983. "It was straight out of an old Italian movie. I was wearing a wide-rimmed Borsalino hat, a clumsy long coat. I was carrying two battered suitcases that contained a mixture of manuscripts and clothing. I must have looked like a refugee who had just been released from Ellis Island."

Like a refugee, Mardin had left a lot behind him to come to America. After completing studies at the Economics and Commerce Faculty of Istanbul University, he was prepared for a steady career in business. His father was Chairman of the Board of Turkpetrol, where he was promised a respectable position.

"All went according to the master plan until Dizzy Gillespie came to Istanbul with his big band," Mardin says. "Dizzy and Quincy Jones ['51] encouraged me and helped me. The fire that had been smoldering in my heart, my desire for a career in music, was rekindled."

Quincy Jones took some of Mardin's arrangements back to New York where he recorded them for Voice of America radio with such major players as Phil Woods, Art Farmer, and Hank Jones. These tapes made their way to Berklee and won Mardin the first Quincy Jones Scholarship.

After studying and then teaching at Berklee, Mardin made the journey to New York where he found some success offering arrangements to club and touring jazz bands. In 1963, he was offered a job as a studio assistant by Atlantic Records Vice President Nesuhi Ertegun, and his auspicious career in pop music began.

Almost 40 years later, Arif Mardin is senior vice president and producer at the Atlantic Recording Corporation with an impressive list of production and arranging credits that includes recordings with Barbra Streisand, Brandy, Whitney Houston, Phil Collins, Diana Ross, and the Broadway Cast Albums of RENT and Smokey Joe's Café. He has received over ten Grammy nominations in addition to his six Grammy awards, including 1989's Record of the Year for Bette Midler's recording of "Wind Beneath My Wings." He received an honorary doctor of music degree from Berklee in 1985. That same year, his son Joe Mardin graduated from Berklee (Joe is now a producer and arranger in his own right).

We spoke to Mardin in 1990, on the heels of his award as Turkish-American Man of the Year by the Board of the Assembly of Turkish-American Associations. As an added honor, his speech from that awards event was entered into the Congressional Record as a testament to the vitality of the American dream.

Four decades have done nothing to diminish Arif Mardin's love and enthusiasm for music or the music business. Even within the span of a quarter of an hour, you sense that this collection of talent, dedication, charm, and insight was always destined to reach the peak of his profession. It was just a matter of time.

 Record producers such as yourself have played a major role in the music industry. Why do you think so little has been written about you or your profession?

At one point, what we did was considered routine. People didn't think that we were that important. I think the first producer that brought in a certain style and a personal stamp was Phil Spector—with his "wall of sound" and his very personal touch and technical imprint that people started to recognize.

Lately, I think, Michael Jackson and Quincy Jones, with their megahit *Thriller*, made it possible for producers to come to the forefront, especially in the Grammy awards. When I won my producer's award in 1974, we were pre-telecast—unimportant, not glamorous. It was like that for a long time until Quincy and Michael Jackson made it happen. When Quincy got the Producer of the Year award, it was frontline television. Now, we are on the regular program. There is also a greater awareness of producers by the record-buying public.

 Do you think you have a personal stamp?

I'm in-between. I do have a personal style. At the same time, I try to bring out the best of the artist.

I can't do the same production for different artists. First of all, singers have different ranges. Bette Midler has a wonderful mezzo range. Chaka Khan has a high range. So, when you try to provide the settings for these jewels, they all will be different. The arrangements will have different characteristics. However, in the use of reverbs and effects and certain technical aspects, I do tend to use things that I like. There, I think there is a certain personal style. But then I may change it immediately for another group.

 What was your first production project?

My first pop co-production with Tom Dowd was the Young Rascals in 1965 ("Good Lovin'"). We were house producers then, supervisors—they didn't even call us producers.

 Did you have as much control over the sound and production back then?

We had control of the sound, but not a monopoly. I hate to be a tyrant. It's not like the Svengali saying, "Liebchen, this is how it's going to be. Sing or get out." There are some people like that. I prefer a more democratic process. I love to pick brains. I love to get input from many different people. And if I hear something good discussed in the other corner of the room, I listen to it and I may apply it.

 Has that feeling helped you stay in tune with contemporary styles?

I keep up. I listen to English records, U.S. records; I have a lot of records taped for me on a periodic basis—avant garde records, r&b records. My musical growth coincided with the bebop era of Charlie Parker and Dizzy Gillespie when they were exploding. I was a youngster listening to their records. At the same time, I love modern 20th-century music from Stravinsky, Bartók, and Schoenberg to the expressionists into all the modern stuff.

At heart I'm a modernist. I may grow very old, and I still will be looking for the next new thing. I guess that keeps me alive and young.

 How much do you produce for an audience and how much for your-self or for the artist?

That is very important. I think, first of all, you have to be true to yourself and true to the artist. If I do something for Bette Midler and she is not here, I always try to second-guess the situation, saying, "Would she like this? Is this Bette?"

But then there is a danger of going too much into art and ignoring your other prime responsibility: trying to make a commercial record. So, the balancing act is making a commercial record that also will stand the test of time.

It should be something that you're proud of—you shouldn't wince when you listen to it the following year. I always like to sneak things in that are really good and will be discovered by other people.

The producer must make a competitive record. He has to make a living. But if you betray your profession by being sloppy and unmusical, that is a sin.

 Can it feel limiting to target a specific demographic?

At my age, I don't have to slave too much about it. I can pick and choose. Prestigious artists like Bette Midler or Roberta Flack don't have to compromise their reputations trying to target their audience. Because it usually backfires. If the artist or myself don't feel what we are doing and we are cynically trying to corner a certain market, it won't be commercial. People will see through that very easily.

 How has the compact disc changed the way you produce a recording?

The simplest things are different. We used to have an intermission between sides, where the listener would get up and turn the album over. Now it's a continuous 40-minute to one-hour program. Sequencing is very important. You can't let the listener get bored.

Of course, the technical aspects are great. We used to cheat when we mastered on vinyl. On loud passages, the mastering engineer used to take the levels down for two bars and then go back up, or reduce the bottom end of the record for two bars because the record skips. It's no problem with CD or cassette. That kind of mastering technique is obsolete. You just make the best sound with all the great dynamics.

 Has the CD affected anything else, like the length of a single?

The length of a single depends on what the radio stations would spare, computing the length of music versus the length of time they sell. In the '60s it was two-and-a-half minutes; three minutes was unheard of. Now it's much longer. So, who knows.

It's interesting, there is a three-minute 78 RPM record form—almost like the rondo form, the sonata form, and so on. For a lot of jazz masterpieces from the '30s or '40s, that was the time they had to work with. The frame was that two minutes and 45 seconds or three minutes and five seconds, whatever it was. And a lot of incredible Louis Armstrong or Duke Ellington masterpieces were made in the three-minute form. It was amazing how solos were allotted, how variations on a theme were done, and then how it was cut.

With LPs, that conciseness disappeared. We ended up with wallpaper music. It sounds like the same solo is playing for 10 minutes on a jazz record whereas the substance of that solo would be eight bars. But the "old-timers," in a three-minute form, had no superfluous notes. Everything was what was needed. If the man played eight bars, he put all he had in those eight bars.

 So, you can run into problems when you lose limitations.

Right. Definitely. I'm not saying that being concise is better than the long form. But definitely, mediocre musicians, or people who like to ramble a lot, are now captured. And that kind of playing is on record.

 Your first love was jazz. How did you become such a major pop producer?

I came to Berklee on the first Quincy Jones Scholarship. Then, I taught there. Then my wife and I said, "Let's move to the big city." No offense to Boston, but we moved to New York. For the first year, I gave piano lessons and wrote a few tunes. My wife was working at the United Nations; so that's how we got along.

Then, Nesuhi Ertegun, a partner at Atlantic, called me up and said, "I need an assistant at the studio." I knew it was pop music, but I said, "I'll take it. Anything to do with music, I'll take." When I went in there with my expertise from Berklee, they started to give me little projects—arranging and so on. And then, it grew.

I was a studio manager, too, so I had to learn production, test pressings, and this and that—keeping a log, tapes, libraries. At the same time, I moonlighted and wrote arrangements for Atlantic's groups—some jazz, some pop. I graduated to being a producer when the Young Rascals were signed by Atlantic. Atlantic told the group, "Look, there's a young man from Berklee who can help you with your arrangements, and this veteran engineer, Tom Dowd, who will be in charge of all the sounds." So, we became a team. Tom and I produced a lot of records together.

Then, Jerry Wexler, who was my boss, took Tom and me as his team, and the three of us produced a lot of records, including Aretha Franklin and Dusty Springfield.

I have no problem with pop because music is music. I love any kind of exciting energetic music or music that is meaningful. So now I have jazz and pop and everything in my heart.

 Do you have strong memories from coming to Berklee from Istanbul?

Oh, yes. It was amazing. It was fantastic working with people like Herb Pomeroy, who really opened up a lot of doors for me. Not only was he a friend, but he was a great teacher. He is still a great teacher. Ray Santisi was another great friend.

The school was small—one townhouse, with a few hundred students. It was like a small family atmosphere. Larry Berk's office was downstairs; the late Bob Share was across the hall; Joe Viola was down the hall, teaching saxophone. It was a really wonderful family unit. Now, they have expanded it into something much bigger. But the warmth is still there.

Are you still on the lookout for new artists?

Always. That keeps my career and my production techniques alive. For example, years ago, I had the privilege of being associated with Scritti Politti. It's great to work with creative, hip, and modern people because it rubs off on you. They may learn something from me, and I learn something from them.

My latest young artist, younger than my son, is Tommy Page. Joe and I produced a few sides on his first album. We made one song that was the most requested record in America. It was a huge success in Europe. And here we went up to 32 in the charts—which was great for a brand new artist.

 When you are putting a project together, what do you listen for in a song?

It sounds very corny to say, but it has to touch a certain honest emotion and say it in a different way. Almost everything has been written about. But it's the way you permutate and combine and recombine those elements that make it sound original. In a song, I always look for how this person said the usual stuff in a very different way.

A simple example is that you can say, "I feel so lonely," which is normal. But that song Yes recorded a few years ago, "Owner of a Lonely Heart," is a way of turning around something everybody knows and saying it a different way.

So, the title of a song or a hook line has to have something original in it, or extremely heartfelt—so simple but so wonderful. It's very difficult to find songs like that.

 In what ways do you see pop music evolving or changing?

It's still the song. However it's set, the song is very important. Technique may change. At one point, we had an unbelievable amount of machinery playing the music. Now the reaction against that has brought us to today where, again, humans are playing. I like to use synthesizers and sequencers mixed with real players.

At times, I may do a live session. But I'm not a retro person saying, "The good old days were great." The good old days were fantastic. But you have to keep moving forward and do what is best for a song. Don't record out of habit. But do what's best for a song.

Sadao Watanabe

life after 50 (albums)

With a truckload of recordings to his credit, Sadao Watanabe is Japan's elder statesman of jazz.

"BEFORE I CAME TO BERKLEE, there was nobody teaching jazz in Japan. Everything was guessing." Sadao Watanabe '65 tightens the mouthpiece on his sopranino and quickly clicks the keys. "We would buy records and copy what we heard. Like, Miles Davis would play a one and a seven-diminished, and we would copy that. Then on another recording, he would play a one-flat-three-diminished, and we would copy that. We didn't know why he did it. We thought maybe it was 'hipper,' or something. We were just guessing."

With 59 albums as a leader to his credit and a vast array of musical influences, Sadao Watanabe isn't guessing anymore. He has become a major player in the world jazz scene and a leading celebrity in his native Japan. And while his face may be associated with the many products he has endorsed in his home country—from Wrangler jeans to Coca-Cola to Bravas cologne—his name will always be synonymous with jazz.

In fact, Watanabe's successful life and career in music has paralleled in many ways the discovery, growth, and flowering of jazz in Japan. Watanabe was born in 1933 in Utsonomiya, a city 90 miles north of Tokyo. His father, an electrician, played the biwa, a Japanese counterpart to the lute. While Watanabe grew up hearing traditional and classical Japanese music, he and many other young compatriots were drawn to the vitality and expression of American jazz.

"During the Second World War, we had no chance to listen to jazz," he remembers. "I was 13 or 14, and I had never heard jazz. The day after the war was over, we could hear American Service Radio and American jazz. It was really fresh and refreshing for my generation. I remember running home from school everyday to hear 'Jazz Hour' on the radio. I was so excited by it."

Captivated by Bing Crosby in *Birth of the Blues*, Watanabe convinced his father to buy him a clarinet. He learned basic fingering from an old man in his neighborhood for three cents a lesson. Then, with a few GI music books and an armload of records, Watanabe took the rest of his early musical education upon himself.

The Dream Takes Hold

The influx of American movies, music, and styles after World War II instilled a generation of Japanese youth with hopes to make it as jazz musicians. Watanabe learned basic big band numbers from recordings—"Sentimental Journey" was an early favorite—and started to play with local jazz bands. The first few gigs were rocky ones. He remembers some patrons asking his bandleader to "please let the clarinet boy be fired." But with continued study and professional experience, the "clarinet boy" caught on fast.

Soon, he was playing clubs, hotels, and U.S. air bases, where the jobs were plentiful and the pay was low.

"If you had an instrument, you had a job," he remembers. "Even if you couldn't play, you could just hold a bass and stand onstage."

After graduating from high school, he set off for Tokyo to take his shot at the big time. Inspired by movie appearances of Les Brown and His Band of Renown, Watanabe switched over to the saxophone as his primary instrument. He began jamming after-hours with various local artists, including Toshiko Akiyoshi '57, whose Cozy Quartet he soon joined. When Akiyoshi packed off to study at Berklee, Watanabe stayed behind to lead the quartet.

Akiyoshi returned from her studies in 1962, full of the knowledge and excitement Boston and Berklee had to offer. She encouraged Watanabe to attend the school as well, and recommended him for a full scholarship. Working gigs and sessions day and night, Watanabe scraped enough money together for the plane ticket.

"Boston fit my lifestyle," he remembers. "It's like a second home to me now."

He rented a room near Berklee for $10 a week and bought a blanket and a frying pan. Those, along with his saxophone and flute, were his essential equipment for building his dream. Though gigs at first were slow in coming, he soon gained notice and some money in the local jazz scene.

"Before coming to the States," he says, "I thought I wouldn't see my family for four years. But after 10 months, I saved $1000 to bring my wife and daughter over."

The Widening of Style

Watanabe always held an interest in a vast array of musical styles. Beyond his father's traditional Japanese performances, he had discovered rhythm and blues, bebop, and classical music before coming to Berklee. In each genre, he found unique character and power. He began to incorporate his favorite aspects of each into a diverse but cohesive personal style.

In 1965, he was introduced to another musical form when a Berklee professor recommended him for a professional touring group.

"Gary McFarland called Herb Pomeroy looking for a tenor sax and flute player," he recalls. "He was doing soft samba. Herb asked me, and I went to audition in New York. It was very rare then to find a jazz player that could play flute. I had taken seven years of classical lessons before coming to Berklee. So, I got the job playing soft samba."

Watanabe was not sure that Brazilian music suited his own musical tastes.

"At first, it was dull to me," he says. "But when we went to San Francisco, Sergio Mendez and Brasil '66 was playing at the El Matadore. We were working across the street. So, at intermission, we would go to see them. That was the first time I really heard live Brazilian music played by Brazilian musicians. Then, I started to love it."

Brazilian music was to play an important role in Watanabe's musical development—both because it fit his personal style, and because it opened the door to a universe of world music influences. Later explorations included trips to Africa and Brazil, and world tours with stops in Montreux, India, Rio de Janeiro, Southeast Asia, Tanzania, and other ports of call.

Watanabe admits that the diverse mix makes it a challenge to build a cohesive album.

"When making albums, I try to focus on something," he says. "But once I start, I want to put a Brazilian flavor and an African flavor and a jazz flavor. It's okay, though, because I write everything. So, it all comes out like me."

The Homecoming

Upon his return to Japan in 1965, Watanabe was besieged by young jazz musicians aching to learn what he had learned. He found his country as he had left it: hungry for any knowledge of the vibrant form of jazz.

"When I went back, my musician friends were still guessing," he says. "So many musicians came up to me and asked what I learned at Berklee. My home was packed."

In response to the demand, he started a small jazz school to share his knowledge of theory and technique. He also formed a quartet to tour and gig in local Tokyo clubs.

Just as young musicians hungered for his knowledge, Japanese record labels clamored for his talents. Many of his 50 recordings as a leader were cut during those first few years back home. At times, it seemed he couldn't make them fast enough.

"At that time," he explains, "I would just pick up the tune and play straight ahead—some bossa nova, some samba—just playing melody. They were very easy to record. At most, I made nine albums in a year." He laughs and shakes his head. "I can't do that any more."

Success at home led to tours and recognition abroad. He played his first Newport Jazz Festival with the Billy Taylor Trio in 1968. He appeared at the Montreux Jazz Festival in 1970. He also started a jazz radio program, eventually known as "My Dear Life," that brought a wealth of world jazz to an audience of eager listeners.

Other historic performances included the first jazz concert to be performed at the Budakan, featuring Watanabe with full orchestra and an audience of 30,000. Jazz fusion performances with David Grusin and Lee Ritenour helped boost his solid reputation in the United States. His production of the Bravas Club '85, an event that brings together musicians from many countries, earned him the Japanese Ministry of Education Award in 1986. And his continuing success has placed him on the top of critics' lists and readers' polls around the world.

Watanabe has also fostered a growing love and aptitude for photography. Two books of his African photographs have been published in Japan. The most recent book was packaged with a compact disc of traditional African music.

The Future

While Watanabe has become known as the father of Japanese jazz, he sees himself more as a citizen of the world.

"I never try to be a Japanese musician," he says. "I just play what feels good to me."

Still, he is concerned about recent changes in his homeland's musical climate.

"The big problem in the Japanese jazz scene is that there is no room to jam," he says. "When I started, we could hang out at all the clubs and jam. Lately, they won't allow it. It is very difficult to get people together to jam—unless you pay money to rent a studio."

With new albums, more world tours, and annual journeys back to Africa "to clean up the mind," Watanabe continues to explore new ways to make his music better. Still, in thinking back on his most fulfilling musical memories, he remembers his years at Berklee, and he offers advice to current Berklee students.

"Around the college are the best musicians from around the world. It's like a musical town," he says. "You will never have this kind of musical experience again. It is the best time of your life. So, don't waste time."

In his 66 years, Sadao Watanabe has never wasted time. His 59th album, *Viajando*, was released in 1998.

Abe Laboriel

high style on the low end

First-call bass player Abraham Laboriel '72 gets to the bottom of it all.

"PHILOSOPHICALLY, I BELIEVE THAT MUSIC VISITS US. It doesn't stay with us all of the time," says Abraham Laboriel '72, one of the leading bass players on the Los Angeles scene. He goes on to describe this evasive visitation. "It is the moment where sound becomes music, when you can no longer recognize what is going on. It doesn't matter what song it is, or whose voice it is, or what instrument they are playing. It is wonderfully overwhelming. I have been blessed that on many of the things that I have done, music has visited for one bar or longer."

For more than 30 years, Abraham Laboriel has been coaxing music to visit. And he has always been a gracious host. The Mexican-born bassist has become a first-call musician for the likes of Quincy Jones ['51], Michael McDonald, Lee Ritenour, George Benson, Dolly Parton, Herb Alpert, Henry Mancini, Johnny Mathis, Larry Carlton, Al Jarreau, film composer Alan Silvestri ['70], and many others. His friendly, caring manner have made him a welcome visitor to studio sessions. And his heartfelt, emotional performances have ensured him a continually busy schedule.

Laboriel was born in Mexico City in 1947. His father, a musician, composer, and actor, gave him his first lessons on the classical guitar. Frustrated in his efforts by an accident that took the tip of his left-hand index finger, the young Laboriel was ready to quit at age 8. But his older brother pulled him back in.

"When I was 10," he remembers, "my brother joined the first major rock and roll band in Mexico. All of the American publishing houses were sending him songs in English to translate into Spanish. So suddenly, we were inundated with all of this music from the United States."

Laboriel studied that music on his own, listening to records and learning them on his rhythm guitar. By age 17, he was an active studio guitarist in Mexico City. One year later, his parents encouraged him to pursue a more "stable" career, and he enrolled in the Instituto Polytechnico Nacional to study aeronautical engineering. But he soon found his love for music calling him away from his studies.

At age 20, he convinced his parents to allow him one year to try a music career. Within that year, he was off to Boston, to Berklee, and to the bass. From there, as he says, "I never went back."

Throughout his career, Abraham Laboriel has accumulated a long list of valuable qualities. His unique five-finger rhythmic approach to bass playing has made him a valuable addition to any rhythm section. His collection of unique basses—among them an eight-string tuned in octaves like a mandolin, a five-string, and a hollow-body fretless—have given him a vast palette. His easygoing, supportive attitude has endeared him to his contacts and his peers.

But when you meet him, the main impression you walk away with is that this is a man who feels things deeply. Whether he is jumping like a madman during a fiery, funked-up bass solo, or speaking calmly and openly about his personal experiences, Laboriel is intimately present in the moment. And he encourages those around him to be there, too.

"Music should be about loving one another," he says in his warm, slightly accented voice. And rather than write it off as another L.A. musical platitude, you believe it. You feel it in his manner and his music. And, after a while, you feel it in yourself, as well.

We spoke to Abraham Laboriel in 1991 in Hollywood, where he had just received the Distinguished Alumni Award from Berklee's Southern California Alumni Group.

Q. Apart from talent, what is the most important attribute of a studio musician?

As a musician, and especially as a bass player, I feel that it is important to have a servant attitude. When I play for other people, I am not using their gig as an excuse to showcase my ability. I am there to say, "What can I do? How can I help you feel happy about your song? What can I give to you with my music?" I am a great advocate of relationships and dialogue. Through the years, those have proven to be the most important things for me.

Ironically, I have discovered that the main reason a lot of people hire me is because of the freedom with which I play. But I never take that for granted. I come to recording sessions and people say, "Abraham, I wrote a bass line but ignore it. Do your thing." And I say, "Well, let me first try to understand what you dreamed of as a composer and arranger and then I'll depart from that." Quickly, I learned that that kind of constant dialogue and relationship with the people you work with is really important. That way, if something that is natural for me is uncomfortable for them, there is always the possibility of adjusting it or tailoring it to their needs.

In my conversations with the top studio musicians, that has been the one thing that was constantly stressed: Don't play something that pleases you, but try very hard to play something that pleases the people you are working for. Even if what pleases you, in your mind, is better than what they want.

In the long run, I have learned that when you listen to the finished product and you have sacrificed some of your own favorite things for the sake of doing what they want, it is usually what works best. Because they have a relationship with the song that you don't. They have been living with it for a long time.

Q. What can you do when you feel strongly that a producer or artist is not taking the best approach?

If things are not happening because the song and the music is unsalvageable, then very gently we ask the artist or producer how much more material they have to choose from. If that's all they have, then we make suggestions as to how to approach the song. Or we might try some arranging on the spot. Sometimes it is possible to change their minds, and to get them to recognize that there are other alternatives that work.

The example I have of that is with Herb Alpert. The song "Rise," which has been the biggest single of his career, he recorded with three other rhythm sections after our first session. And he ended up using our version. When the record became a hit, he said, "I knew it was a hit from the moment we played it. I just didn't like your tempo." But eventually, he ended up compromising and using our tempo.

 You first started studying to be an aeronautical engineer. How did you start down that path, and how did you return to music?

All my life I was inclined toward studying. My parents felt that because I liked studying so much, it was just logical for me to get a degree, and to keep music as something that I loved. They felt I should give my first priority to something more secure. I believed that I was going to be able to do both.

Then, in my second year of engineering, I had to quit music completely, because assignments became very involved. But it really killed me to be away from music. So I begged my parents to please allow me one year to experiment with music. If it didn't work, I promised that I would return to my studies.

I started the aeronautical career when I was 18 years old. I was 20 when I asked them for that year. When I was 21, I came to Berklee. And I never went back to engineering.

 Did your inclination toward studying pay off at Berklee?

Yes. Since Berklee was the only major training to know how to deal with the music world, I took it seriously. It really shaped me. And I was blessed to run into so many teachers that had so much experience. Almost everybody that taught me had a minimum of 10 to 15 years of professional experience before coming to teach at Berklee. So they could draw on a lot of information to share with us.

Who were your musical influences during those early years?

My influences came from a tremendous amount of listening to records from the United States. I was blessed that the records that the publishing houses were sending to my brother were in all the different styles. Name a record in any style, I listened to it and learned it on my guitar. And I tried to understand all the different ways of thinking about music. So my influences are very varied.

Eventually, I remember falling in love with the music of Bill Evans and Oscar Peterson. Then at Berklee, I was introduced to Wilbur Ware, Oscar Pettiford, George Mraz ['70], and Dave Holland.

 As a guitarist, were you also influenced by John Scofield ['71] and John Abercrombie ['67]?

Scofield, Abercrombie, and I went to school at the same time. So their influence on me came from a whole different place. I would just glue my ear to the rooms where they would practice. And I could not believe that anybody could play their instrument like that. Which was one of the things that I loved most about Berklee. It gave us firsthand access to these impossible musicians.

One time Mick Goodrick ['67], George Mraz, and Peter Donald ['70] were jamming in one of the rooms, and I nearly fainted. I was ready to quit school. Mick told me the same story—that he quit school for five minutes when he heard Keith Jarrett ['64] practice. He was just too much.

 You were overwhelmed by your classmates?

I guess I shouldn't be ashamed to admit that my first two years at Berklee were spent in tears. I was very upset to not be able to function at the same level as all the other students. And I remember that a teacher very lovingly said to me, "There are many ways of making music. And Berklee's way is one of them. But the fact that you cannot fit perfectly and do everything that you think we expect of you should not discourage you." And that blessed me. Teachers kept encouraging me, and believing in me, and rooting for me.

At the end of the fourth year, fantastic things happened. Herb Pomeroy recorded my charts with the recording band. I started to record with Gary Burton ['62]. I was a featured soloist in a lot of the performances with both Ted Pease ['66] and Phil Wilson. And we had our own group with Charlie Mariano ['51]. Suddenly, a lot of the pain of the first two years started to blossom into this confidence-affirming experience.

A year after I graduated, Herb Pomeroy called to ask me to perform with the Count Basie band behind Johnny Mathis. That started my relationship with Mathis. Six months after that, Mathis called and asked me to join him on the road. Through that I met Henry Mancini and Michel Legrande. And I had already finished an album with Gary Burton and had traveled with him.

 You started at Berklee as a guitar player. When did you switch over to the bass?

I started school in 1968. In 1971, Alan Silvestri ['70] asked me to join his trio. He was doing summer engagements in New Jersey. The trio was Al on guitar, his friend on flute, and another friend on drums. Alan was getting more into the guitar and wanted to free himself up to start improvising, instead of playing accompaniment. So he asked if I would play bass.

I said, "Well, let's give it a try." His father rented a Fender bass in New York for me to play. And . . . man!

 What attracted you to the bass?

I loved the freedom to change the meaning of the chords. We were playing a lounge in New Jersey doing top-40 music. And it was great to take all this well-known music and give it a whole new meaning because of what bass line you chose to play. I had found a great new freedom. I knew beyond the shadow of a doubt I was destined to be a bass player.

By the grace of God, the Berklee faculty allowed me to switch to bass—even though officially I couldn't, because the electric bass was not recognized at that time as a primary instrument. Since I was a degree candidate, I still had to do all my juries on guitar, even though I was allowed to perform on bass.

 How many basses do you use during a session?

Most of the time, I bring three. On certain occasions I bring as many as 12. When I did the latest album with Michael McDonald, I had 15 basses there. And I tried all of them.

 Have you ever recorded on upright?

When Quincy Jones ['51] hired me to play on *The Color Purple*, he said, "Do you play upright?" I told him that I owned an upright, and that I didn't have a good pitch on it. He said, "Great, bring it, because we are trying to do music from the '30s and in those days, nobody listened to the bass. It was more like a feel." I said, "Great, if you want a feel, I've got it. But if you want pitch, please call one of the great upright players."

So I show up with my upright. And all the musicians stood staring. They wanted to see if I knew how to take it out of the case [laughs]. Then the big band started to arrive, and I wanted to die. The song was written in A-flat, which means that there were no open strings. And these guys were some of the most famous big band musicians in the world—half from Duke Ellington's band and half from Count Basie's.

I said, "Quincy, please let me use my electric bass and I promise to play with such tenderness that you won't mind." And he said, "No, no, play your upright. Don't worry, you'll be fine. All we want is the '30s sound."

So we started to record, and the engineer pushes the talk-back button and says, "Quincy, are you sure you want me to print the bass? It's really out of tune." I wanted to die.

Has modern music technology threatened the role of the bass?

The world, in general, likes to jump on the bandwagon. In the *Miami Vice* days, several bandwagons took place that did an untold amount of damage to the music business.

I heard a great description. A friend said to me, "Abraham, there is no more music business because now they are not singing melodies and there is nobody playing an instrument. They just show up with computers and they talk."

For a while that happens, and people jump on it. But those kinds of things don't last, thank God, because eventually the audience gets saturated. They get tired of the lack of genuine expression.

I should say that Jan Hammer ['69] is different. He is expressing what is genuine about himself with that music. So when you listen to it, you are not hearing somebody pretending in order to cut down on costs. He is putting his life into it.

The marriage of analog and digital—having real-time players and everything sequenced—has now become a really fine art. And it is a wonderful thing. The marriage of both concepts for the right reason is beginning to happen.

Another theory is that this new technology is forcing all of us to grow. It means that there will be not as much of a need for musicians to do things that they don't love to do, because they have a machine that can do it much better.

 What are your most challenging projects?

The high-pressure jobs are when you have to do a film where there are 80 musicians performing all at once, and the composer has written lots of unison lines between the sections. Your bass line is not free to go where you want it to go.

In those kinds of sessions, they have to get a lot of music done very quickly. So you run it once for the engineer to get his levels. Then the next time you run it is the final version. You don't have any hope of punching in because they go direct to film.

 Do you like that kind of playing?

Actually, I do. For me it is a very emotional feeling that all of those human beings at once have a power of concentration and determination not to let the composer down. And because it is film music, the composers are taking risks. They are saying things that have a lot of substance that they would not say if they were trying to have commercial success.

 What sessions are the most rewarding?

There are certain players that like to be around one another. Many times we go to a situation thinking it's going to be an average day, and it turns out to be a great surprise.

In general, I can remember several recording sessions with a certain group of people where it was almost automatic that it was going to be a great session. You see each player arrive at the studio, and right away they sit at their instruments and start trying whatever idea they have in their hearts. Then you see the other musicians joining in and everybody just having a wonderful time. You know that all of that creative energy is going to carry over. Those are the most rewarding sessions for me.

Terri Lyne Carrington

the rhythms of change

A jazz veteran since age 20, Terri Lyne Carrington is searching for a different beat.

WHEN YOU ARE JAMMING WITH THE LIKES OF CLARK TERRY, Dizzy Gillespie, and Rahsaan Roland Kirk at the age of 12, it can be a daunting task to reach still higher ground. But drummer Terri Lyne Carrington '83 has always found a way. In her 15-plus years in the music business, Carrington has constantly searched for new voices and new venues that will broaden her abilities and widen her audience.

That search for growth has led her to gigs with Wayne Shorter, Pharoah Sanders, Al Jarreau, Lalah Hathaway ['90], David Sanborn, Clark Terry, and Dianne Reeves. Her versatility earned her the house drummer position on the *Arsenio Hall Show*, a position she left to make time for other projects.

Her 1989 major-label debut, *Real Life Story*, was a testament to how far this young drummer had come, mixing burning fusion grooves with progressive jazz and even pop-oriented vocal tracks with Carrington singing lead. The album also showcased some of Carrington's roster of friends and admirers, including such guest artists as Grover Washington, Carlos Santana, Wayne Shorter, and Patrice Rushen.

In her early stages, however, Terri Lyne Carrington was almost completely focused on straight-ahead acoustic jazz. From the time she first started hitting her grandfather's drum set at age 7 up to her Berklee years, jazz had been her passion and her calling.

Much of the focus was a product of family history. Her grandfather, Matt Carrington, had played with Fats Waller, Duke Ellington, and Chu Berry. Her father, saxophonist Sonny Carrington, served as president of the Boston Jazz Society and had some impressive performance credits of his own.

At 10, Carrington was tagging along with her father to local jazz clubs, sitting in with some of the greats. At 11, she became the youngest musician to receive a scholarship to Berklee when founder and Chancellor Lawrence Berk heard her sit in with Oscar Peterson. She began studying theory, piano, and drums at Berklee, supplementing her lessons with Alan Dawson and Keith Copeland ['73].

After graduating high school, Carrington came to Berklee full time, where she met and performed with a new generation of talents including Greg Osby ['83], Kevin Eubanks ['79], and Victor Bailey ['79]. She also used the opportunity to flesh out her advanced performance chops with study of arranging, theory, and composition.

Throughout Carrington's career, the national press has been quick to pick up on the novelty of the young female drummer playing with the big boys. But the musicians who have heard her play never lost sight of the driving talent behind the publicity. That talent secured her continued success as the years went by and the novelty wore off. Today, the combination of innate ability and outstanding technical skill has made her a force to be reckoned with in contemporary music.

Terri Lyne Carrington returned to Berklee in September 1991 to serve as alumni speaker at the college's Entering Student Convocation. Continuously moving on and moving up, Carrington took a break from her summer tour with Al Jarreau and her search for a new record deal to speak with us about her current projects, her long-term goals, and her early years.

Your interests seemed to have expanded dramatically over the past few years, from straight-ahead jazz to a broad blend of music. What prompted the change?

I always listened to all kinds of music while growing up. It just so happened that I only played jazz.

When I was 18, I moved to New York and started trying to do other kinds of gigs. The first gig I got that was a little different was with Wayne Shorter. I had been doing more acoustic jazz, and his music was more fusion. Then I worked with David Sanborn, which to me is instrumental r&b. And I have been doing different things ever since. Of course, on the *Arsenio Hall Show* I played all kinds of music every night.

I have always liked playing different things. I just never had any experience doing it. The more I had experience playing contemporary music, the more I wanted to do it on my own.

 Is that broader style difficult for the music business to accept?

I worked on a second record for PolyGram. It took me over a year to finish it. And it lost focus, because different departments wanted different things from me.

I wanted to do something different. I wanted to sing more. And I felt that I wanted to move in an alternative rock direction. They wanted some rhythm and blues, which I can write. But I'm not really an r&b singer. I can sing the songs that I write. But r&b really exposes the fact that I'm not a riff singer.

To make a long story short, I had a record that had alternative music on it, and r&b, and then the jazz department wanted some instrumental music like my first record. So it had those three different elements. And the project lost focus. So when we finished, nobody really knew what to do with it.

Now, I'm looking for a new record deal where I can do what I want to do.

How is your approach different in writing instrumental and vocal music?

With vocal music, I come up with melodies and partial lyrics first in my head, and then I'll write a song from there. With instrumental music, you don't worry about making words fit to a melody.

I almost feel that if I wrote something instrumental, it couldn't be as simple as if I wrote something that had lyrics. If it was simple and instrumental, I would probably feel that it was watered down and syrupy. But with lyrics, I wouldn't feel that way. Lyrics make a big difference. They add another color or another plane.

Also, you can do so much more with a voice than you can with an instrument.

I feel now that lyrics are really important. Especially since I want to reach the average working-class person, rather than just the jazz audience. When you want reach that kind of person, it's important to say something with lyrics. Instrumental music isn't going to reach them.

Do you get any chance to sing outside your own projects?

I'm not really interested in doing any other singing. I don't consider myself a real singer. I'm more of a singer/songwriter. I sing the songs that I write. And I can't even sing all of those.

You have worked with a lot of fellow alumni—John Scofield ['73], Greg Osby ['83], Lalah Hathaway ['90], and others. Do you all talk about your Berklee connection?

Older people who have been away a long period of time don't talk about it as much, like Scofield. The next generation down, like the Osby generation and me, doesn't have to talk about it much because we were there together. We share the same experiences. If it wasn't for Berklee, we wouldn't have met. There were a lot of musicians that came out of Berklee during the time I was there who have done well for themselves. It was part of our mutual experience, so it's very important to us.

Then the next generation, like the Lalah Hathaways, talk about Berklee a lot because they recently came from there. It is still very fresh in their minds. So, where I would reminisce, they're still right there.

 What do you remember most about your Berklee years?

The best experience, for me, was just being around a lot of people that wanted to do the same thing I wanted to do. That was the first time I had been in an environment like that. You meet people that are going to be in your life for the rest of your life. And that has a big impact on you.

I cherish the people that I came into contact with. Any school setting is really a means to an end. It's normally not the actual classes that people hold onto for the rest of their lives. It's the growing experience as a human being. So that's what I tend to focus on.

Of course, Berklee did wonders for me as far as certain skills—arranging, writing, harmony, and so on. Before I went there, I didn't really have a clue about how to arrange or write. So that was great. Also, you put yourself in an environment where you have competition. So you either sink or swim.

 What was your first break out of Berklee?

I was still at Berklee, actually, when I did a few scenes in a Harry Belafonte movie called *Beat Street*. The money that I made from doing that helped me move to New York. And I started working immediately with Clark Terry. I had played with him when I was young. And he was one of the first people to let me play—he brought me to the Wichita Jazz Festival when I was 10. So we had a history.

But I didn't get that gig before I moved to New York. I called him when I got there and told him I was in town.

Have your musical and professional goals changed since then?

Most definitely. When I was at Berklee, I was more interested in getting a jazz record deal from a label that was doing straight-ahead acoustic jazz. But there you get very little money to do a record. And they are ecstatic if you sell 40,000 or 50,000 copies. That was my idea of success.

Now, that has totally changed. Now, I want to sell 500,000 records. I know what the industry is like now, and what you need to have respect in it. It's very different than what I thought then. If I'm going to do something, I want to do it to the Nth degree. I want to make a difference. So I'd like to try to go right to the source.

My ultimate goal is to have my own label, to be a major record company person. There haven't been any women, really. And there haven't been too many black people. So, my long, long, long-term goal is to be like David Geffen or like Herb Alpert.

 What would you promote with your label?

I would do things that were a little off-center but with commercial appeal. I would be the person that would sign Tracy Chapman, Sinead O'Connor, Lenny Kravitz, Joni Mitchell, or even Public Enemy. I would look for music that was a little out of the mainstream, but accessible, that could still sell a million records.

 Do you think that there is a Terri Lyne Carrington "sound"?

Probably not. A few close people that really know my playing would recognize me. But I'm not an innovator. The bottom line is that I don't want to be. I gave up on the idea of being innovative. I didn't care about being one of the greatest drummers that ever lived once I turned 18. Before that, I thought I wanted that. Now, I just want to do things that are valuable.

These days, versatility and an accommodating nature to band leaders really keeps me working. I work for some band leaders that have trouble with drummers because they are always thinking or saying, "I know what to play here. This is it and that's it." Whereas, I tend to bend over backwards to try to accommodate whoever I'm working for.

 What is the drummer's role in the band?

Somebody once said, I can't remember who, that the bass is like the heartbeat of the band and the drums are like the blood. That always stuck in my head. For the most part, drums lay the basic carpet beneath everything. They are the foundation. The band is really only as good as its drummer.

There are certain basics that you have to have together—time, dynamics, and so on. If you don't have that together, then you really aren't in business. But for the most part, the energy that you put behind the music is what moves the band. You can get away with having an adequate bass player, an adequate keyboard player, or an adequate guitar player. But you have to have a good drummer.

 Does that role change when you are the leader?

For me, it changes when you are a leader because you are concentrating on everything, not just playing drums. You are concentrating on how the musicians are playing their music, how the parts are being played, all of the business at hand, and how much money you are losing.

I have yet to master being the best leader I can be. Because you have so much on your mind that something simple like tempo can go right out the window.

 Was it a difficult transition from being a child prodigy to being an adult professional?

I don't really see it as a transition at all. It just evolved. I have always been somebody that's concerned with growth. I think when you are concerned with that, the evolution process happens naturally and quickly.

It was probably more the press that named me a child prodigy. I was always the same person. It was just a natural growth process.

 You said in an early interview that child stars can grow up and find they have nowhere to go. Are you afraid you will get to that point?

I don't think you have to get to that point. I might have been saying then that the young talents are more likely to remain stagnant. But I don't feel like anybody has to become stagnant. If you are concerned with moving on all the time, personally as well as musically, then that's going to affect you.

The greatest musicians never stop growing. I have worked with some incredible masters. They won't stop growing. They keep themselves around young energy. And they associate with up-and-coming people to keep themselves young.

You are only as old as you allow yourself to be. Most of the older people I know are more youthful than I am, because they found the key to keeping themselves young. It is to keep growing and not become stagnant, and to do music of today instead of music of yesterday. That's why somebody like Miles Davis wouldn't play straight-ahead once he moved on. Why should he?

Joe Zawinul

the sound of zawinul music

Keyboardist/composer Joe Zawinul defies definition as he defines contemporary jazz.

FOR MORE THAN 40 YEARS, Josef Zawinul has set the standard for contemporary music, even as he has evaded attempts to describe his style. His jazz has climbed the pop charts. His fusion electrified jazz. His keyboard and production skills have even hit number one in the world music world.

When pressed with these complexities, Zawinul responds with a characteristically simple answer in his charming Austrian accent.

"Somebody else puts those names on, I don't," he told a New York *Newsday* reporter. "In Copenhagen, there was this festival we played at. And everybody was classified as something: rock music, rock-fusion, jazz. Next to my group, they just called it 'Zawinul music.' That's really the best description."

Since he arrived in the United States on a Berklee scholarship in 1959, Josef Erich Zawinul has made "Zawinul music" a vibrant genre of its own. Through early work with Maynard Ferguson, Dinah Washington, and Cannonball Adderley, and groundbreaking later years with Miles Davis, Weather Report, and the Zawinul Syndicate, he forged new forms of music as he blurred the boundary between electric and acoustic instruments.

masters of music

Born in Vienna in 1932, Zawinul played accordion as a child, later studying music at the Vienna Conservatory. By the early 1950s he was playing piano for leading Austrian dance and radio orchestras, as well as for Polydor's house recording band. Friends and inspirations at that time included composer Paul Hindemith and celebrated pianist Friedrich Gulda, who gave Zawinul his first composition jobs.

In 1959, the strength of one of his recordings earned him a scholarship to Berklee, providing him with his essential bridge to the American music world.

"I actually thank my living to that scholarship program," he told a Berklee audience in 1991. "That was the only way for me to come to America."

The American jazz world was quick to pick up on Zawinul's piano talents. After touring with Maynard Ferguson, he became an accompanist to Dinah Washington, appearing on her recording of "What a Difference a Day Makes."

It was through Washington that Zawinul had his first taste of electronic instruments. At a tour stop with a particularly bad acoustic piano, Zawinul sat in on Ray Charles' 66-key Wurlitzer, and instantly loved the sound. His later playing on the electric piano, particularly with Cannonball Adderley, inspired Miles Davis, Herbie Hancock, and a legion of other jazz artists to add electronics to their bands.

During the Adderley years, Zawinul the composer began to emerge, writing several hits including "Mercy, Mercy, Mercy" and "Walk Tall." Miles Davis selected "In a Silent Way" to be the title cut of an album, signing Zawinul on to provide keyboards. He later played on three more of Davis' jazz/rock albums, including *Bitches Brew*.

In 1970, Zawinul cofounded Weather Report with Wayne Shorter, launching one of the most enduring and influential bands in jazz history. With a vibrant, organic electric sound and a unique group-improvisation approach, Weather Report dominated the jazz/rock scene for more than a decade. Instant standards such as "Birdland" and "A Remark You Made" brought the band unprecedented success and critical acclaim, and ushered the fusion sound to the forefront of contemporary music.

After Weather Report dissolved, Zawinul continued to set the jazz standard with his own band, the Zawinul Syndicate. That ever-changing band is blazing trails even in 1999, earning a Grammy nomination for "Best Contemporary Jazz Performance" for their live album, *World Tour*.

We spoke to Zawinul in 1991, when he returned to Berklee to receive his honorary doctor of music degree. It was a busy year for him, completing work on his third Syndicate album with a tight new band configuration and a vibrant world music sound, touring with the new Syndicate, and supporting the chart-topping success of *Amen*, his production/arranging/performance project with West African singer Salif Keita.

Zawinul's musical career has matched the best of his music, building in brilliant intensity as its many motifs weave together with purpose and grace. Since his music has sprouted so many followers, we began by asking about its essential root.

 Why has the bass always been so important in your music?

I need it. With my music I need drums and bass. There is an old Czech saying that goes: "If I don't hear the bass, to hell with melody." For me, there is a foundation of music, a rhythmic pulse that suggests the correct notes. Even the sound of a single note creates a rhythm. And that's how my music is built.

I have been very lucky with bass players all my life, even in Austria. The first musician I ever played with was Rudolph Hansen. He played the bass with incredible feeling, and incredible strength in beat and intonation. He taught me a lot about music.

When I came to America, I played with Gene Gerico. He was a teacher at Berklee, and he played with Frank Sinatra for 20 years or so. Gene Gerico was amazing.

Then, in New York, I played with Jimmy Rausa in Maynard Ferguson's band. Jimmy was a great, great bass player. In Cannonball's band, it was Sam Jones. And Sam was the king of all walking-bass players.

And, of course, in Weather Report we had Miroslav Vitous, then Alphonse Johnson, Jaco Pastorious, Victor Bailey ['79], and Gerald Veasley. So, in the last 20 years, I have had only four bass players.

 Beyond your bass players, you have nurtured quite a few young musicians in your bands. What attracts you to the younger player?

I don't care as much about age as about attitude. I know some really old guys that I like to play with. I have been lucky in finding players who I can groove with without any generation gap whatsoever.

 What kind of attitude do you look for?

I don't know if it is a particular thing. It's just a certain degree of humanity, of character. That is very important. I don't like people using drugs. In the older days there was a lot of that junk around. I like honesty. And I like people that take care of themselves, that dress well. They don't have to be dressed up, just clean.

It's all related to your music. Music is nothing but an extension of what you are. If you are messed up, that will come out in everything you do.

 What were your professional beginnings like in the Austrian studio circuit?

We had a great level of musicians. There were guys from the Vienna Philharmonic, the Vienna Symphony Orchestra, and the best musicians from the dance bands. So we were able to cut a tune in 20 minutes, with rehearsal. We would play the tune through so we would know all the notes and then lay it down. And these went on to be big hits. It was amazing.

That was for Polydor. And I had a nice deal with them. I didn't want to be paid by the hour, I wanted to be paid by the title. Sometimes we recorded 20 titles in a day. So I made a lot of money.

What styles of music would you record?

We played all kinds of things—opera, Gershwin, film music, really difficult classical stuff, but mostly pop. And I played a lot of instruments—vibraphone, accordion, piano, bass, trumpet. It was really an experience to learn a lot in a short amount of time.

 Did that broad experience have an effect on your later music?

It had no effect whatsoever. As a matter of fact, I tried to avoid it having any effect. It was well arranged and correctly played, but I never liked that music. I did it because I thought I could learn something from it. I did learn how to sightread really well. And, besides, it was fun. It was a good gig.

I couldn't do today what I did then. I could read so well. It's like in sports; what you don't use, you lose. And I have been playing my own music for so long.

As recently as a couple years ago I played classical music in Europe in major performances. But it had been a while. You lose your connection. When you haven't driven an automobile for a while, it takes you a few days to get the speed back in your eyes. With music it is exactly the same.

 And yet you are still doing new things, like the album you produced with West African singer Salif Keita.

That is a killer album. But it took a lot of my time, because I recorded everybody individually. First, I thought I would produce the album and play on it. Then, all of a sudden, everything was in my lap—the entire thing, the budget, everything. It was a severe project.

When they first contacted me, I had never heard of him. So they sent me a tape, and I liked it. Then I never listened to that music again. I only wanted to listen to him sing, and think about what I would do with it. I improvised all of that accompaniment. I wanted to show that nothing is being taken away from his culture.

But, on the other hand, the reason they hired me was because they wanted to have some of that soul.

 Why do you think your approach worked so well with that "world beat"?

I am a peasant. I come from a peasant family. I always respected classical music, but I never appreciated it that much. Whenever my family would get together, it was always folklore. That was the music from my heart. Not that I ever took a song out of folklore, but the rhythms and little variations are in my heart and in my belly.

I have always loved that feeling of the earth, of working in the fields, which I did plenty. I guess that is why my music blended so well with the African peasant music.

 So, where does jazz fit in?

Jazz, to me, is another kind of folklore. But in the later years, it got too hybrid, too aloof, too miscellaneous. With so much of jazz, you hear melodies that are already improvised lines, more or less, instead of tunes. Then, on top of that, you hear a tenor solo and a trumpet solo that never give you a clue of the meat of the melody. That, to me, is miscellaneous. A lot of jazz in the later years is like that.

I enjoy more organized music—when you have a nice melody and some serious rhythm underneath. Then you have a motif, and a variation to a motif. That is what I like, not just noodling. The true masters I love in jazz are all very organized mentally—like Duke Ellington, Louis Armstrong, Miles Davis, Dizzy Gillespie, Bird, Sonny Rollins, and Wayne Shorter.

 How do you write your music in order to get that sound?

I hardly ever write anything down first. First comes the improvisation. I have a drum machine and I just fool around. I fiddle with my sounds, and if I like something, I put the tape recorder on and improvise. Then, I write it down and I work on it.

I would say that about 90 percent of the time I don't change anything from the original improvisation, because that's the way it came to me, or through me. It's not all as serious as it sounds. It's easy for me. That's the lucky part of it.

 Is that improvisational approach what has always given your electronic performances such life?

That is something that a lot of people who play electronic instruments don't allow themselves to do, to really play from the heart. To me, those things are nothing but tools. A trumpet is nothing. An acoustic piano is nothing. It is a tool. The player is the one who is going to either do something with it or not. The moment you let these novelties take over, you're gone.

A lot of people just translate what they do on acoustic piano to synthesizer, and it doesn't work. It's a tool, and let's keep it like that. It's the individual who is going to get something out of it.

 Now you have a new album coming out. How is it different from your past recordings?

I think it's much better. It's much stronger. I took more time. I have been working on it for a couple of years. And there are some really good tunes. We do a lot of overdubbed improvisations, but we still kept a freedom in the band. It sounds like a band is playing. I think people are going to like it.

 What are a few of your favorite tracks?

One is called "South Africa," which celebrates the day when Apartheid is stricken from the law. On the day they announce that Apartheid is finally over, I think there is going to be a worldwide celebration. This song is talking about it. [Percussionist] Bobby Thomas originally brought the lyrics in. And we worked a lot on them. We had some translated into Zulu.

Another song is called "Patriots." The main theme is the blues, underneath a very fast beat. It was inspired by this black kid I saw on CNN with an alto saxophone, sitting out in the desert by himself during Desert Storm. He was just sitting there playing alone with the alto in the desert. He was not a great saxophone player, but in his tone and the expression of his music there was so much feeling, so much wanting to come home, and yet so much resolve. There is this Arab overtone to the music. Then underneath is the slow blues against the fast tempo. It has a very powerful rhythm track.

I have always believed in the military. I always thought that anybody that went into the military gained something from it. And I admired that so many kids go into the army because the life out here doesn't give them much. That's why I called the song "Patriots."

 What is new about this configuration of your Syndicate?

This band is probably the best I have had. The bass player is phenomenal. And the emergence of [guitarist] Randy Bernsen is really remarkable. He followed Scott Henderson and it immediately made a big difference in the band, because he is a real band player. Scott was more of a "hey check me out" player on everything. He was more or less out for himself, which is understandable. But when Randy came in, the band immediately started to become a band.

At the beginning, Randy lost some confidence, because I was on him quite a bit. I didn't want the same thing happening to him that happened with Scott. But then, all of a sudden, he became a solid, solid player, in every respect. He is going to be one of the guys to be reckoned with. I think he's got it.

I know when you are young, you can lose a little confidence sometimes. You just have to overcome that, let the smoke clear, and be there.

 Are you touring a lot with the new band?

Oh, yes. It has been amazing. We played in Umea, an amazing little town 350 kilometers from the last lines of the North Pole. The average age in that city is 35

years, so I felt like I was Methuselah—nothing but kids. So, we played there that night. We had to take the bus after the concert, drive nine hours to Stockholm and then take an airplane to Brussels in Belgium. There, we were picked up by the bus and driven to Maastricht in Holland, which was about three hours away. There we had a few hours to rest before we played a midnight concert. Then, we had to leave at 5:30 in the morning back to Brussels to catch an early morning flight to Copenhagen. In Copenhagen, our bus picked us up to go on the ferry and drive back to Göteborg, Sweden. It seemed like the whole tour was like that. It was tough. But it was great, too.

 And you have been doing that for 30 years?

You only realize this when you get old, but everything in life is just a couple of months ago. It seems like I was always the youngest guy in the band until recently. I talked to Ahmad Jamaal a few weeks ago, and he said the same thing. He said, "Joe, man, these last 30 years were like a flash." The last time I saw Miles, we talked about the same thing.

When I met Miles, I was 26 years old and he was 31. And I remember that as if it were this morning. Life goes very quickly. If you are really busy and have many things to do, it goes in no time.

John Scofield

welcome to the scofield zone

Electric guitar master John Scofield '73 on the weird wonder of the jazz vocabulary.

PICTURE IF YOU WILL: a church talent show featuring four preteen pre-musicians. The music is "House of the Rising Sun" and the Ventures' classic "Pipeline." The roster: one drummer, one guitarist, and two accordion players. It is an odd mix, to say the least—one that could only exist in the Scofield Zone.

While this first band experience may not have forged the future of guitar great John Scofield '73, it most definitely set the tone. Scofield's style and career have always mixed an eclectic batch of elements into a dynamic, cohesive whole. In his compositions and his arching solos, the strange companions of bebop, blues, folk, r&b, funk, and rock have found a common voice. The two-accordion rock band may not have had a future. John Scofield certainly did.

Scofield came to Berklee in 1970 with a background full of rhythm and blues but a future filled with jazz. His bread and butter were Miles Davis and John Coltrane. And Berklee was his key to learning their secrets.

"Berklee was the only place that had done some serious thinking about how to teach that kind of music," he explains.

Still, his rock and rhythm and blues upbringing served him well. After his seven-night-a-week student gig in Kenmore Square playing "stupid top-40 stuff" with a killer band—featuring Jeff Berlin ['74]—he would wander to the Jazz Workshop to finish the night in style.

His versatility also proved invaluable to his early professional career. Out of Berklee, he earned a touring job with Gerry Mulligan and Chet Baker—playing in their famed Carnegie Hall reunion. He then replaced fellow alumnus John Abercrombie ['67] in Billy Cobham's band, which led to work with Charles Mingus, Gary Burton ['62], Lee Konitz, and Dave Liebman.

In 1982, Scofield began his highest-profile project—a several-year, multi-album gig with Miles Davis. His term as the jazz legend's sideman, soloist, and writing partner placed him among the leading guitarists of his generation. His solo albums for Gramavision—including *Still Warm* and *Loud Jazz*—set that status in stone.

In recent years, Scofield has returned to a more acoustic sound, with a Blue Note contract and a tight, insightful quartet. But still, his music runs the gamut from bebop to blues and beyond.

We spoke to Scofield in 1992, on the heels of the release of *Grace Under Pressure* featuring fellow alumnus Bill Frisell ['77]. From the astounding normalcy of his manner, it was clear that the Scofield Zone is not such a strange place after all. Like Scofield's music, it makes brilliantly perfect sense.

 What first attracted you to the guitar?

When I was 11, I got my first guitar. And, believe it or not, I was influenced by the rock music on the radio and the folk music that was becoming popular then. I wasn't a folkie—by the time I was 13, I was into the urban blues. But my initial influence was really folk music, which I think gave me a nice background in the folk and Appalachian harmonies.

Then I got heavily into the blues. When I was about 13, I fell in love with B.B. King, Howlin' Wolf, and Muddy Waters, and that whole Chicago blues sound. By the time I was 16, that led me to jazz.

So, you started on an acoustic guitar?

It was the typical thing. My parents didn't want to buy me an electric guitar, so we rented an acoustic.

After six months, I convinced them that I was serious about it, so they plunked down for a Hagstrom electric guitar and a little Univox amp. The whole package probably cost 100 dollars, which seemed like an unbelievable amount in 1963 or 1964.

 What was it that kept you playing?

Once I had bought it, I couldn't afford anything else. Plus, the guitar was the cool instrument. You could play chords and sing along. And it was the instrument that folk and rock musicians played. When I was 11 or 12, it seemed like the only instrument there was.

Later, when I went to Berklee, I had a period when the guitar didn't seem to be as much of a jazz instrument as piano, horns, bass, and drums. I was listening to the so-called "classic" jazz—Miles Davis, John Coltrane, Charlie Parker, and Bill Evans. And there wasn't any guitar on those records.

So, I bought an old Kay upright bass and played for six months. But soon I gave that up and went back to guitar.

 It must have been a relief to see the electric guitar coming into jazz.

It was something that happened simultaneously with me coming on the jazz scene. The fusion boom brought the guitar into the forefront in the early '70s. And I was part of this generation that came to Berklee and schools like it, sort of the rock generation, which got serious and tried to play jazz on the electric guitar.

 And yet your style wasn't strictly jazz-based.

I never tried to be eclectic. When you're young, you just listen to what's on the radio. And even though I had dedicated myself to learning about improvisation and jazz since I was 16, my roots really were in the rock, folk, and blues I grew up with.

And whose roots wouldn't be? If you were a guitar player, there was no other way around it. You couldn't avoid rock and roll. It was just too seductive. So, even though people say that I have "melded different music together," I never tried to do that. It just all seemed obvious.

 At the same time, you didn't partition your playing into separate styles.

I never really liked that. I admire studio musicians who can do it. But I fell for the whole jazz image—and I still believe in it—of telling a story with your instrument. That's the beautiful thing of what jazz musicians do. Their style and their message is their personality. So even though I play some things that sound bluesy and others that sound like jazz, it is all supposed to be me.

 Is that what makes you a "stylist"?

Yes. I always wanted to be a stylist. Because I really loved jazz and listening to Charlie Parker, or Bill Evans, or Joe Zawinul ['59], or any of these players that had their unique style.

The studio players aren't called on to tell a story or say something when they blow. They're called on to be incredibly proficient and have incredible rhythm and accuracy and intonation—but all within 32 seconds. If you do get a solo, it's on a little break between the verses on a song. That's an incredible craft, but it's different.

 How do music theory and chord scales fit in?

Music theory is there from the first time you start to play. When you learn a chord on the guitar, there is a theoretical aspect to it. People tend to divide music into emotional music and theoretical music. I don't see that division in the same way. Learning to play a rock-and-roll tune, you apply theoretical knowledge. Even going from a one to a four chord, you are realizing that there is a relationship there.

It's the same thing with any of the scales or chords you learn at Berklee, or at another school, or on your own, or from a book. To take this theoretical knowledge and to incorporate it into your style is essential. People do it who don't even know what the scales are called. Any sophisticated or serious musician does music theory all the time.

I get interviews where people ask what I think of jazz education now, as if there wasn't jazz education before. There was. A jazz musician has to be educated. Whether they educate themselves or whether they get it from a formal program, in a way, it makes no difference. I was glad I was able to go to a school where the ideas were coming at me, and I didn't have to dig for them myself. The previous generation, when there were no jazz schools, had to get that education from other musicians, and from listening to records, and studying privately.

I think the innovators of jazz knew exactly what they were doing. They might not have used a name for it. Names and labels and definitions come after the fact. But the great musicians weren't playing by chance. The technical and emotional live together. The technical aspect becomes a part of you, becomes ingrained in you, and then you use it in a musical way.

 It is like building your vocabulary.

That's right. It's completely a vocabulary. And the scale or the chord or the technique, in itself, is nothing until you internalize it and throw it back in a musical way. By that point, you have forgotten where you got it. You are using it in a sentence or a word or a conversation.

You can tell when people are throwing in words that they just got out of a thesaurus. You can hear that. But after they get used to using the word, they can use it in a more craftsmanly way.

Q. Is the long-solo format important in learning and exploring that language?

In 1944, nobody played long solos. It just wasn't done. Now the music has progressed to a point where it is almost expected that you will stretch out and take a long solo to make room for some experimentation—which is really a dangerous thing. Because any band that's playing like that, my band included, runs the risk of going over the limit and being excessive.

I think you have to run that risk if you are going to get creative results as a band. The jazz curse is playing too many notes and not saying anything. But that's the risk we run.

Q. Do you also consider your audience when you're out there experimenting?

It's a fine line. I have heard people say, "I know what I would do to make jazz more listenable to the public. I would cut the solos down and make them shorter to fit the attention span of most people." But, unfortunately, when you do that, you lose the creative room that it takes to wander around in a solo. You need that in order to get to the high peaks that make jazz music incredible. If you try to condense it too much, you run the risk of losing that.

So, if you play down to your audience too much, you lose the essence of the music. If you are unaware of your audience, you lose them.

Q. Do you think about that in the studio, where a "perfect reality" is often the goal?

I've stopped trying to make perfect realities. Just by being in the studio, everything gets condensed by itself. Usually, a studio take never reaches the fantastic climax that a second set on a good night will reach. But the sound is really good in the studio. And there are not outside stimuli such as a waitress dropping her drinks in front of you or the weird lights or somebody talking or somebody blowing smoke in your face. Those things don't happen, so you are able to concentrate on the music.

But if I try to make a perfect album, I'm afraid that I will lose some of the spontaneity that can happen. So, all of my records have imperfect moments all over the place. Every good album or good piece that I have done has had fluffs in it. But if you go back to fix it, the solo is not as good or the feel is not as good.

 Still, that "perfect" sound seems to be an essential quality for jazz radio airplay.

I can't think about airplay. If I thought about airplay I would be playing a different kind of music. I think about making records that are concise and listenable to me.

Of course, I'm thinking about my audience all the time—about what we do on the gigs, and what goes over, and what seems to have appeal. Maybe I'm not looking for hooks, but I watch for things that I like that other people like, as well. Radio airplay is another thing completely. On my last album, *Grace Under Pressure*, there were two tunes that sounded like they could be played on those pop/jazz stations. But when I went to the radio expert at Capitol Records, she said, "John, those are jazz tunes."

I'm lucky enough to have a career established where I can do this music. It's not incredibly profitable, although I'm doing really well. It's nothing compared to pop music. But I work all the time with my own band. I have a record contract with a major label. And I play my own music. My fingers are crossed. I hope it keeps going.

 Do you also like the luxury of a fairly consistent band roster?

Record companies would prefer that every record be completely different. Those records are a lot easier to sell. But, for the kind of records I'm making, it's necessary for my band to play a couple of records together and play for a couple of years. We need to be able to get to certain rhythms or feels without talking about it.

Too many players today are either jazz soloists in front of an anonymous rhythm section or studio craftsmen without enough gig time to develop their ideas. I love the fact that this quartet with Joe Lovano ['72], Bill Stewart, and Dennis Irwin has put in a lot of playing time together.

What about fronting the band as opposed to being in the band?

I'm fronting the band, but I'm in the band, as well. We are musical equals. It's my tune, I call the shots, but once we start to play, these players are all as strong as me. That's the way I want it. I have played in bands where I was a lot stronger than the rhythm section. It doesn't feel good to me. I like to have that strength around me. I'm addicted to it.

So, sure, it's the John Scofield Group and the album has a big picture of me. But the honest-to-God truth is that once you count off the tune and everybody is playing, we are all in there together.

 What do you remember most about your years at Berklee?

The most important thing about Berklee for me was the people—the other musicians and the teachers. It was amazing coming from a small town in Connecticut into an atmosphere of music, 24 hours a day. Also, the curriculum was great for me, because I didn't know how to read that well. I had some idea of chord construction, but not much. And I couldn't write out music. I had a good feel. But the theoretical aspect was not happening.

Still, I think what got me were the people, and the different ways that people played and taught and studied music. We were all trying to get into music, the faculty too. It was really a beautiful, pure thing. It helped me set my sights.

I often think about where I would be if I hadn't gone to school. I know I would have gotten to the same place. But, I think I got here quicker because of that big dose of music theory.

 You have been a leader in the evolution of fusion and jazz/rock. What do you see as the style's next step?

When I played with Miles, we were playing electric stuff. And I was really influenced by that. Before that, I had played more in the bag that I'm using now. Now,

I've gone back to using acoustic bass and a jazz drum kit—although I don't think of it as "going back." It's a reevaluation of the importance of jazz rhythm. If you lose that, you lose a lot.

I think people are going back to acoustic rhythm sections because there is so much room for flexibility there. That's what I like about it. I think from that, another small step in the evolution will be made.

There are so many shades of rhythms that you can use. And jazz allows that. When you get a drum machine going with the perfect groove for a Janet Jackson record, that's great. But that's all it is. There's not enough room for other rhythms. The flexibility of the jazz feel can get lost in the funk.

At my gig last night we played blues. And the drummer was playing a triplet feel while I was playing a sixteenth-note feel. And we kept it going for a long time. We were both aware of what we were doing. And it became this fantastic overlapping thing. That's really important. And that doesn't happen in other kinds of music.

 How would you describe your style now?

If I try to look at it too much, I start to define myself. And if you define yourself, then you're limiting yourself. I see myself as existing in a time period. I'm a reflection of the music that has gone on around me. I play what I play because of what I have heard and because of who I am. That's how I see it.

 So, listening is important.

Listening is number one. I think it's as important as playing. If somebody has to be told to listen, maybe they should try another line. To me, the music was there, and it was incredible. And for whatever reason, I decided to be a guitar player.

Hearing those classic jazz records completely changed me and made me believe in magic. It sounds naive here in 1992, but it's not. There is a spirituality that comes through in that music. And I believe in it now more than ever.

Branford Marsalis

jazz messenger

Saxophonist Branford Marsalis '81 brings jazz to a new generation.

AMONG THE "YOUNG LIONS" OF JAZZ who have captivated the jazz public for the past decade, none has had a more diversified or highly charged career than their "elder statesman," Branford Marsalis '81. At 31, he had already logged in 12 years on the road with his own group and with such luminaries as Art Blakey, Lionel Hampton, Herbie Hancock, Wynton Marsalis, Sting, and others.

Branford's career has continuously spiraled upward over the past decade, so it's premature to predict that he's at the summit. His past endeavors include testing his mettle as a soloist with everyone from Sonny Rollins and Chick Corea to Public Enemy and the Grateful Dead. For four years he was a member of Sting's post-Police band. That stint included world tours and appearances at such high-profile events as the 1988 Freedomfest, and the Amnesty International tour, and the recording of two chart-topping Sting albums. His affable clowning in the Sting documentary, *Bring on the Night*, netted him cameo roles in *Throw Momma from the Train*, and *School Daze*. Branford himself is the star of a recent 60-minute jazz documentary, *The Music Tells You*, directed by D. A. Pennebaker. His compositions and sax work are featured on several movie soundtracks, including those of two fall releases—*Sneakers*, starring Robert Redford, and Spike Lee's *Malcolm X*.

At the time of this article, Branford had just released his Grammy-winning eighth album for CBS, *I Heard You Twice the First Time*. The much-anticipated blues project features compelling performances turned in by such artists as B.B. King, John Lee Hooker, Linda Hopkins, Joe Louis Walker, and Wynton Marsalis. Branford and the disc's collaborators spin diverse tales borne from the legacy of the blues, melding influences from the field holler, gospel music, Delta blues, and Dixieland traditions with those of contemporary urban jazz.

 What inspired you to make a blues album this time around?

The blues was the inspiration. I've always had an affinity for the blues, particularly after meeting Willie Dixon at a concert at the Montreal Jazz Festival in 1982.

 The record is a real chronicle of blues styles.

Well, most of the guys in my idiom have a tendency to concentrate more on the blues in the swing style, or the Duke-style shuffle blues. I've always been touched by the folk blues tradition, and the impact that it had on what we do. I wanted to make a record that would reflect that.

 What was your involvement on the a cappella slave song "Berta, Berta"?

I sang on it. The other guys who sing on that song were from the original cast of the August Wilson play, The Piano Lesson. I was touched by that song when I heard it, so I called up their management to see if they could perform for my record. The lyrics are a reminiscence about being a slave on a parchment farm in Mississippi. Without the play's dialog it was a bit ineffective, so we made it into a chain gang song by adding sound effects.

 Many jazz albums these days feature the leader playing 90% of the solos, but you are very generous in sharing the solo space.

I do that on almost all of my records, I don't really take a lot of the solos. On my early records I took more solo space because the players weren't part of my regular group. But I've played with the guys on the new record before, and I had them in to play because I respect their abilities and I gave them room to say their thing.

On songs like "Stretto from the Ghetto" and several other cuts, there are some odd times and complex layers of polyrhythms. In your opinion, is that the most fruitful direction for jazz players to explore?

It always has been. Charlie Parker knew that, Art Blakey definitely knew that. The two most essential elements of any music in the world are melody and rhythm. They are also the most difficult elements to get to. It is easy to memorize licks and recite them on cue. That is not really responding to what you hear or to what the group is doing and trying to invent new melodies, or play them differently.

 What about harmony? Is there room in jazz for more exploration of chord structures that cannot be labeled in a traditional way?

We haven't played traditional chord structures since 1982. In Wynton's band we picked up on that Miles Phrygian thing. With Kenny Kirkland playing, Phrygian takes on a whole new meaning. Our tunes take very unusual twists compared to traditional bebop songs with predictable chord sequences. We've also been working with polytonality for a long time. Almost all of my songs are written with googobs of polytonality. But I'm very aware that there is nothing that we can play that hasn't been played already.

Monk wasn't the first person to play unusual chords, but he was the first to play them the way that he did. The legacy of jazz is the ability to bring about a different musical perspective. A G7 is a G7 chord, but how each musician plays it is what makes it different and special. There are only 12 notes; we can't invent new ones. It is all in the way we string the notes together and manipulate them in different ways. My group has been doing that for a long time and it's finally starting to make sense to me.

 Today's classical audiences favor music from earlier style periods over new works by contemporary composers. Do you see a similar situation in jazz with the reverence paid to the early work of Miles and Coltrane?

The reverence it has now it didn't have then—maybe Miles had it. You can hear live bootleg tapes of Coltrane playing and three people are clapping. They didn't get what he was doing. Wynton and I get a lot of attention from the press, but we have never been deluded into thinking it is because people appreciate or understand what we play.

 Do you feel that formal music education is important for upcoming players?

If a student is strong enough personally to go in and get what he wants from a school, it can be an asset. Most students walk in saying, okay, I'm in school, now teach me. The Eurocentric approach to music education, teaching musical rules, is great in a lot of respects, but jazz is one of those things that cannot be acade- mized in the conventional ways. When you really think about it, classical music can't either. I would love to teach at a school. I would teach students how to lis- ten and how to react.

I had a listening and analysis class at Berklee with Billy Pierce and that was cool. You need the right teachers and they are hard to come by. A teacher has a lot of power. Depending on a student's personal constitution, the influence of the wrong teacher can make a person feel like quitting music.

 It is well known that you came up in a home with a lot of music. Do you feel that gave you a head start before you went on to higher education in music?

Yes, but I can think of a lot of major musicians with children and none of their kids are major players. There is more to it than just growing up with music in the home. I was lucky that I had a mother who was adamant about making sure we knew what we wanted out of life.

 What do you tell the young players you meet who are hoping to make a career in music?

My advice is to pray, work hard, and know why you are going into music. There is a big difference between striving to be a good musician and striving only to be a successful one. You have to decide what kind of musician you want to be. Sometimes you get lucky and you can be both.

Since the time of this article, Branford has released several critically acclaimed albums, including *Bloomington* (1993), *Buckshot LeFonque* (1994), *The Dark Keys* (1996), *Music Evolution* (1997), and *Requiem* (1999).

Branford now teaches jazz studies at Michigan State University. He also serves as a creative consultant to Columbia Records' Jazz Department, where he signs new talent and provides creative input to the development of some of Columbia's artists. In this capacity, he produced saxophonist David Sanchez's *Obsesión*, which was nominated for Grammy in Best Latin Jazz Performance.

In the months ahead, Branford will be back on the road, playing his music across the country and throughout the world. In reflecting on his life to date, Branford recently noted, "In retrospect, my life has been relatively pain-free. The things that affected me have affected me deeply. But when I think about the good fortune I've had, the great family I have, I know I'm a very lucky man."

Toshiko Akiyoshi

toshiko's odyssey

A pathfinder for women in jazz, Toshiko Akiyoshi '57 is still on the move.

IT'S BEEN A LONG, EVENTFUL JOURNEY from Manchuria to Manhattan for jazz composer/pianist/band leader Toshiko Akiyoshi '57. For nearly three decades, Toshiko has been the most celebrated female composer/instrumentalist in American jazz. At various ports of call during her musical odyssey, Toshiko performed with such greats as Charles Mingus, Sonny Stitt, Clifford Brown, and dozens more. Her most acclaimed work, however, has been as composer and leader of the Toshiko Akiyoshi-Lew Tabackin Big Band, and the Toshiko Akiyoshi Jazz Orchestra. In her career she has released more than 50 albums, garnered 11 Grammy nominations, and topped countless magazine music polls in numerous categories.

Jazz journalist Nat Hentoff places Toshiko "among that relatively small company of truly original jazz composers—Jelly Roll Morton, Duke Ellington, Thelonious Monk, George Russell, Gil Evans, and Charles Mingus." Jazz critic Leonard Feather declared that no other woman in jazz has received the kind of acclaim that Toshiko has.

Her odyssey began in Dairen, Manchuria, where Toshiko was born the youngest daughter of a Japanese textile and steel industries magnate. She began studying classical piano in Manchuria while seven years old. Following the Japanese defeat in World War II, Toshiko, then 15, and her family were forced to flee Manchuria as the Chinese Communist revolution rolled over the country, and return to Japan with only what possessions they could carry. The family traveled hundreds of miles in cargo trains and endured weeks of stopovers at makeshift camps before completing the last leg of their trip on a ship that delivered them to Japanese soil.

Not long after reaching Japan, Toshiko found work as the pianist in a band at a military dance hall. There she became acquainted with the many American jazz musicians who were passing through Tokyo on U.S.O. tours. By 1951 she was leading her own quartet, which featured the youthful, rising saxophone star Sadao Watanabe ['65]. Toshiko established a formidable reputation as a performer and band leader, and became one of Japan's highest-paid studio musicians and arrangers. Oscar Peterson introduced Toshiko to jazz record producer Norman Granz, who launched her recording career in 1953 with the release of *Norman Granz Presents Toshiko*, the first record on which she appears as leader.

In a quest for musical knowledge, Toshiko wrote to Berklee founder Lawrence Berk, who, based upon the recommendations of Granz and Peterson, offered her an airline ticket to America and a full Berklee scholarship.

After arriving in Boston, Toshiko was hired to play four nights a week at jazz impresario George Wein's legendary Storyville club. As pianist in the house band, she was invited to sit in with countless jazz giants, including Miles Davis, John Coltrane, and Duke Ellington, who were booked at the club on weekends.

In 1963, Toshiko and her first husband, saxophonist Charlie Mariano ['51], had a daughter, Michiru, who is well known in Japan as film star and vocalist "Monday Michiru." Toshiko married her current husband, saxophonist Lew Tabackin, in 1969. The two founded Akiyoshi's most renowned ensemble, the Toshiko Akiyoshi-Lew Tabackin Big Band, in Los Angeles in 1973. With Lew as soloist and the band as her vehicle, Toshiko gained critical acclaim as a jazz composer. *Jazz Is My Native Language*, an insightful documentary by film maker Renée Cho, chronicles Toshiko's life and times. The film focuses on Toshiko's decision to continue her odyssey—to leave Los Angeles in 1983 and reform her group in New York.

With New York as her locus, Toshiko performs with both her trio and the Toshiko Akiyoshi Jazz Orchestra. In the autumn of 1992, Evidence Records issued a recording of Toshiko in a small group setting, and Columbia Records released the

Toshiko Akiyoshi Jazz Orchestra Featuring Lew Tabackin Carnegie Hall Concert. The Columbia disc showcases eight compositions, which display Toshiko's singular ability to take her oriental influences and western jazz sensibilities and weave them together in an innovative jazz orchestra fabric.

These discs chart the latest course in the four-decades-long musical odyssey of a uniquely international jazz artist.

 There is a great story about how you began playing jazz piano.

The year after I returned to Japan with my parents after the war, I saw a sign outside of a dance hall saying they needed a pianist. Because it was occupation time, there were many dance halls for the military people. A violin player who was an ex-Navy band conductor was the musical leader. I played Beethoven's "Piano Sonata no. 3" and some fugues by Bach at my audition. I got the job immediately, even after I told him I had never seen chord symbols before. He told me to start that night and to just play whatever I could. He told me he would teach me about chord symbols the next day.

The band consisted of accordion, alto saxophone, violin, drums, and piano. I really didn't like the music, but I could practice on the piano at the club during the day. This was great since my parents had to leave our piano behind in Manchuria. Musicians also got paid very well at that time too.

One night, a Japanese man came into the club and told me he thought that if I studied a bit I could become the number one jazz pianist on Kyushu Island [laughs]. He was a record collector, and played me Teddy Wilson's "Sweet Lorraine." That was it—I wanted to play like that! I also listened to Willie Smith, the lead alto player with the Harry James band. I transcribed one of his short solos and played it a lot. I worked hard at music.

 Was American music popular in Japan then?

Yes, there was a great appreciation for American things; the people wanted to have a Parker pen, taste Coca-Cola, and hear American music.

How did you end up coming to America?

Jazz producer Norman Granz was booking American groups for U.S.O. tours of Japan in the early '50s. Oscar Peterson had come over to play and my friends introduced me to him. He invited me to his hotel the next day to meet Norman Granz. Norman ended up producing a record for me and writing stories about me for *Metronome* and *Down Beat* magazines.

At that time I knew there was a lot I had to learn, but the information wasn't available. There wasn't even a good tune book to learn from. I would pick things up from the professional musicians who were passing through. I really wanted to go to the U.S. and play with American musicians.

Tony Teixiera, a musician from Boston who later taught at Berklee, heard my group in Japan and encouraged me to write a letter to Lawrence Berk. Mr. Berk ended up sending me a plane ticket to bring me to Boston to attend Berklee on a scholarship.

 There were probably very few women at Berklee in the early '50s.

There were two others in school with me. I used to spend time with them, but they left after a few semesters and put an all-girl band together. There was another lady who came the next year. She was also a pianist and eventually married Lennie Tristano.

 Did you encounter skepticism when you began your career?

Sometimes I'd hear this thing about authenticity. People would say, "She is Japanese, how authentic can the music she writes and plays be?" Some people resented that. In Japan there is a saying: "Nails sticking out will be beaten." I think anybody who might be considered a pioneer finds resistance.

I've done all right when I compare myself to someone like Béla Bartók who died of malnutrition. Some people don't have their artistry recognized until after they are dead, so I feel very fortunate.

Q. You faced the dual hardships of raising your daughter Michiru while supporting yourself and establishing a career as a jazz musician.

People figure I had a very hard time back in the '50s. I don't remember feeling then that I was having a hard time. But when I look back, I wonder if I could do it now—I don't think that I could.

It was hard to be a single mother supporting myself as a jazz musician in the early '60s. I always felt so bad about leaving my daughter at night to go to gigs. In Japanese culture, the mother's first responsibility is to her children, and I kept feeling I wasn't being a good mother because I had to leave her to work gigs at night.

I think sometimes that my daughter quit music after seeing how hard Lew and I worked at being musicians. Lew is very diligent about practicing. Michiru used to get up in the morning and see that I had been up all night copying parts. She probably got the impression it was too hard.

 Q. Do you think sitting-in to get yourself heard by great players is a thing of the past?

I think so. But when I sat in, it wasn't to get recognized, it was to learn how to play or how not to play. When sitting in with top players, you get a better feeling. I got to really learn what swing was all about. Young players today have very little chance to do this anymore.

 Q. Today, many jazz groups play their original music, so it is not as easy to sit in as it was when everyone was playing standards.

That's true. These days it is different because the music and the music business have changed. Even the original tunes back then were not that complicated. You could pretty much follow after listening for a while. That was true until Wayne Shorter came along.

I was playing with Mingus and Coltrane at the Town Hall and Art Blakey's band was playing around the corner at the Showboat. Saxophonist Charlie McPherson and I went over to listen. Cedar Walton was playing piano and Blakey invited me to sit in. They were playing Wayne's tunes, which are not simple. Cedar was calling out the changes to me and I was struggling through. Thinking they were trying to make me look bad, Charlie McPherson got steaming mad and said to them, "Now you come over and play with us!" I felt a certain camaraderie, he was being protective. Actually, since Art Blakey was the drummer, he probably had no idea how difficult Wayne's tunes were for a pianist.

I always enjoyed sitting in back then. My husband Lew asks if I want to do that now and I say no. It is great to do while you are young, you can learn a lot. If you have too much ego and are worried about looking bad, then you won't learn anything.

 Why did you disband the successful Toshiko Akiyoshi-Lew Tabackin Big Band in Los Angeles and move to New York in 1983?

Lew wanted to move back to New York to further his career. He quit the *Tonight Show* band when our band got too busy. But after he quit the *Tonight Show* there was no reason for him to stay in L.A. Historically, in all the best large jazz bands there was always a great soloist. As a writer, I have been lucky to have Lew in the band as my main soloist, but for him, he was always playing my music, and he wanted to play his own too. Now the band is called the Toshiko Akiyoshi Jazz Orchestra, and I add "featuring Lew Tabackin" to the title when he plays with us.

 How has the business of jazz changed over the course of your career?

In the '40s and '50s, there were more minor labels here. Today, there are more jazz labels starting up in Europe than in America. In Japan you need to have a name to get recorded. In Europe it is like it was here a long time ago; if you are an up-and-coming player and they like you, they will record you.

American record companies today seem more like movie studios—always looking for blockbusters. I haven't seen one blockbuster in straight-ahead jazz. Most classical records don't sell a lot either, but companies will record an orchestra playing Beethoven's Ninth Symphony because they see it as culture. Jazz hasn't fully attained that status yet; it will someday.

Do you have any personal observations from your years as a band leader?

When I formed my band 20 or 21 years ago, I learned how sensitive musicians are. Women tend to take everything so personally, and I was no exception. By having a band I learned not to do that.

I've known female players in bands who could not take suggestions from fellow musicians. You can learn quite a bit from the older guys in the band. I would tell women musicians not to take everything personally, learn to take advice.

People have said that as a writer I have been able to bring something new and recognizable to jazz. My strength is in writing. In the past 20 years I have tried to bring something new to the music without being entirely new. Basically, I dislike big band music. I like to think that my music is different, something new breathed into the tradition. I utilize what was done before by the great jazz masters and add something that hasn't been done.

 What would you tell people entering the jazz area of the business today?

Ideally, people should be in the business as a result of their accomplishments. You are a professional performer when you reach the point where the audience wants to hear you so badly that they will pay. You achieve that because you love what you do. If you love music you will put in a lot of time learning it.

I don't think you should be a career-oriented from the beginning, just hoping to be in the business. Some young players aim for the business instead of the music.

 You once said that to be a successful in music, an artist must have a certain naiveté.

I think it is true. You need you need to be optimistic even when you have more reasons to be pessimistic. Without that optimism, I don't really think you can keep going year after year. And if you are not naive, you won't keep chasing after rainbows.

Jan Hammer

beyond the mind's ear

Master synthesizer colorist and composer Jan Hammer '69 speaks about
the virtues of Miami Vice, Mahavishnu, and technology.

JAN HAMMER CROSSES THE GRAVEL DRIVEWAY of his rural upstate New York
home, pauses, and then extends his right hand to greet me while hushing his
watchdog Sasha with his left. "Let's talk in the studio," he says nodding towards
the barn a few yards away. Ascending the stairs we enter Jan's world, a spacious
control room outfitted with dozens of keyboards, racks of outboard gear, and a
large mixing console. The monitors of several computers add their soft blue glow
to the ambience of the room.

This studio is Jan's instrument these days. The compleat musician in more than
the traditional sense of the expression, Jan composes and plays all drum, keyboard, bass, and guitar parts on his music here. Most times he plays all parts on
synthesizer with enough idiomatic flair to fool the most discerning listener.

Music was a family tradition in the Hammer household back in Prague,
Czechoslovakia. Jan's father, a renowned cardiologist, was also a popular Czech
musician. He sang, played vibes and bass, and composed a few hit songs while
working his way through medical school. In April 1993, Jan's mother Vlasta
Pruchova, still an active professional singer, won the lifetime achievement award
from the Czechoslovakian Committee on the Arts.

masters of music

It was anticipated that Jan would become a doctor, as had generations of men in his family, but soon it became apparent that music was his calling. He began playing piano at four, and later took up drums. Jan studied classical music at the Prague Academy of Muse Arts (the school where Dvořák taught) in his high school years, but played jazz with bassist Miroslav Vitous and drummer Alan Vitous by night.

In 1968, Jan came to Berklee to learn more about jazz. In response to the communist crackdown taking place in his homeland, he applied for and received asylum in America. A few years later he was on the road as pianist and musical director for Sarah Vaughan. The following year, living in Manhattan, Jan began working with Elvin Jones and Jeremy Steig. In 1971, he joined the original line-up of guitarist John McLaughlin's Mahavishnu Orchestra. Together with drummer Billy Cobham, bassist Rick Laird, and violinist Jerry Goodman, they defined the sound of jazz-fusion by integrating a hefty dose of rock and roll, European classical, and Indian music elements into the genre. The seminal group recorded three albums, which sold more than two million copies, and played 530 shows before their farewell concert on New Year's Eve, 1973.

During the remainder of the '70s, Jan released six solo albums and contributed compositions as well as keyboard and drum tracks to 14 other albums with such artists as Stanley Clarke, Tony Williams, Al Di Meola, Billy Cobham, Tommy Bolin, Glen Moore, Jeff Beck, and John Abercrombie. *Wired*, one of his four collaborations with Jeff Beck, went platinum. The '80s found Jan recording with Mick Jagger, Clarence Clemons, and Neal Schon, and composing TV and movie soundtracks.

To date, Jan has provided music for eight feature-length films, four TV movies, three TV pilots, and 20 episodes of the British TV drama *Chancer*. His groundbreaking work on 90 episodes of *Miami Vice* earned him two Emmy nominations. His *Miami Vice* theme, which hit the number one spot on Billboard's Hot 100 Singles chart and was a top five hit around the world, earned him two Grammy Awards. The first of four *Miami Vice* soundtrack albums ultimately sold more than four million copies in the United States alone. All told, Jan's performances and compositions have graced 40 albums with combined sales in excess of 25 million copies.

Jan's latest effort is the original score for *Beyond the Mind's Eye*, a series of computer-animated vignettes. Pulling out all the stops for this sonic tour de force, Jan taps influences ranging from hip-hop grooves to the aural landscapes of Aaron Copland. His trademark searing guitar-like solos and power chords soar over funky bass lines that recall James Jamerson, and are juxtaposed by plaintive synthesized oboe melodies and crisp, rhythmic acoustic piano breaks. The video resided on Billboard's Top Video Sales charts for six months, and the companion Miramar album received airplay nationwide.

The impact of Jan's music on American popular culture is felt on several fronts. Years from now, historians may speculate on how different the music of the '70s, '80s, and '90s might have been if the Russians had rolled into Prague in the winter rather than the summer of '68.

 You came to Berklee just after the Soviets took control of your homeland in 1968. Did you have any trouble leaving?

I was lucky to be out of the country in Munich at the time, playing at the Domicile club. Out of the blue, the Russians invaded the country. I was planning on attending Berklee on a scholarship that fall, so I stayed in Germany and then came directly to Boston. My family was stuck in Prague for a little while. There was no communication or hard news coming out of there at first, and I didn't know if there had been mass deaths or what. They managed to get to Vienna, and then called me. My father, who was a doctor, was planning to do research work at the Veterans Administration Hospital in Washington, D.C. on a science exchange. Their papers were in order, so with help from the American consulate they got away too.

 What kind of music were you playing in Munich back then?

Absolutely 100 percent jazz. I guess that was when jazz was at its best. After that, in my opinion, it sort of ended. Today, there is kind of a restoration of the jazz of an earlier time rather than continued evolution into something new. I think that this is wonderful, but it is similar to classical musicians who concentrate on a particular style period. Certainly, it is needed and it's good, but let's not fool ourselves.

Q. It is interesting to hear you say that. In a sense, you and the Mahavishnu Orchestra totally changed the course of jazz.

Maybe we killed it [laughs]. The excesses that were created by groups that copied us make it very hard for me to listen to the music that developed afterwards. What we did worked somehow because it was the first time. It was sort of like bungee jumping off a bridge, and then coming back up and saying, that was nice—but enough of that. The groups that followed insisted on doing it over and over, and the sense of wonder was not there any more.

 Q. There was much in the Mahavishnu music that was innovative—the odd-time signatures, unique harmonic and melodic language, and the group's intensity.

Yeah, it just clicked. What made it all so special was that everyone in the group had truly absorbed the Indian musical influences. Other groups got stuck in a loop and kept recycling old ideas.

 Q. I'm sure you've been asked this before—will there be a Mahavishnu reunion?

I could hear that question coming a mile away [laughs]. I am not interested in doing it. I may be the spoilsport, but I can't go back there, I don't have the passion for it. Ultimately, I don't believe in it any more, and I would feel like an impostor doing it.

 Q. What made the deepest impression on you during your Berklee years?

I really enjoyed the freeform workshops they used to have downstairs in the Boylston Street building. I remember being just over from Europe, and Junior Cook, who I'd listened to on record, was there, and I got to play with him. The hands-on playing situations at the school were great. I would play with Ray Santisi in his studio with two pianos; that was a wonderful way to work things out. Herb Pomeroy's classes were great too.

More than any other keyboardist, you've developed a unique ability for playing rock guitar-like solos.

I had been really drawn to rock since I was a kid. Even though I loved jazz, there was something really exciting about rock. When I heard Hendrix, it really shook me up. I wondered, why can't I express myself like this on keyboard? I felt that the pianistic melodic approach was limited. Hammond organ players used to turn the power off to get some bending on the notes. When the Fender Rhodes came out, I used a ring modulator to do something to the pitch. It wasn't until the Mini Moog synthesizer that I could start realizing my ideas.

How did you get involved with the *Miami Vice* TV series?

A friend got me together with the producer Michael Mann. We talked about styles of music for the show, and he wanted to go off the deep end. He wanted something that sounded very different from the TV music of that time. I played Mann and the director, Thomas Carter, a cassette of some things I'd been working on before the show even came up. One selection ended up becoming the *Miami Vice* theme.

I understand that you got more freedom to create those soundtracks than most TV composers get.

It was a very unusual situation. I did the pilot in the traditional way with the director and producer sitting in the screening room looking at film and deciding where the music would go and how it should sound. After the pilot was finished, NBC and everyone else was crazy about it. Michael took me aside and told me that when it went to series I could just run with it and do what I wanted musically. Ultimately, they sent me film, and I sent back the music with notes telling where it should go. It was an amazing situation. The majority of people in movie making and TV will never go this far. Michael is such a brave guy.

When the TV series came up, you got to work at home and curtailed your touring.

Keep in mind that I had been touring for 18 years by then, and for 10 of those years I was playing with rock bands doing one-nighters year-round—not playing weeklong engagements at jazz clubs. Touring is fun for the first 10 years, then it gets old. You really age. We started a family at the same time, so it was perfect. I got to work here at home and see my kids grow.

 How do you approach writing music for film and video?

Some things look like they already have a beat; there may be a distinct rhythm to the visuals. I don't just start with a drum beat and put things on top of it. Sometimes I'll find a snippet of a melody that fits and I work back from there to find the beat. There is no method, just madness. I think of the writing process as a slowed down improvisation.

 How did the *Beyond the Mind's Eye* project come about?

Miramar, a video and record company making video concept albums, had success with their first video, *The Mind's Eye*, and wanted the sequel to have a hard-hitting pop score, so they called me. I was overdue for my next album on MCA, so the record company worked with Miramar so that I could release an album from the material in the video.

I got to work the way I like and write a soundtrack that was instrumental pop with classical and jazz undertones. We sent film and music back and forth. Sometimes they recut the pictures to fit the music. It wasn't all scoring to picture. That would be hard to do with a dance-oriented soundtrack. You can't arbitrarily lose a couple of seconds here or there to fit the needs of the picture.

 On the cut "Magic Theater," there is a very convincing Miles-like muted trumpet solo. You have a great way of emulating acoustic instruments on synthesizer.

I just go by what sounds right. If a part doesn't sound like that instrument would play it, I automatically stop myself. It is unconscious, I don't think about phrasing or figure out that some notes wouldn't go this or that way. Sometimes when I am doing guitar-like parts, I enjoy breaking the mold to play something a guitar could never play. So I will try to use something familiar but totally different at the same time.

 You prefer to play all musical parts yourself or on synthesizer, and rarely hire outside musicians to record in your studio.

Maybe if I lived in L.A. or New York City I might write a part and have someone in to play it, but I don't write things out anymore. I play them in on the sequencer. I know just how I want to phrase it, and if I am telling a player all of this, I might kill his inspiration. I hear it a certain way, so it is easier for me to just play it.

After having worked with some of the world's best drummers, like Billy Cobham, Elvin Jones, and Tony Williams, it is hard to play with someone else, try to explain how the part goes, and then take days miking the drums properly. I play the drum parts in on a sophisticated sequencer like Studio Vision where I can do complex rhythmic things.

 Would you ever put aside the synthesizers to work with acoustic instruments?

I wouldn't be interested in doing a purely acoustic project. My mind is very removed from that world. I am so used to going in to edit things that I couldn't face the fact that I couldn't go in and pull a note out or change its level. I cannot live without this ability anymore; I'm too accustomed to working that way.

 Your new record reflects all sorts of musical styles. What bin do they put your discs in at record stores?

I have done so many different things that I can be found in rock, jazz, new age, and pop bins. It hurts me because I haven't made a big dent in any one field. To make headway you have to stay in one field all the time. I bore very easily and have to do different things, preferably on the same album. But once it gets past the gatekeepers—those guardians of good taste—the people like it.

What will you be working on next?

I am at a plateau where I am looking around, taking a step back to see what is out there. I want to get Jeff Beck over here to work out some ideas in the studio. We've been talking about it for years. He is an amazing musician. Of the guitar triumvirate of the '60s [Clapton, Page, and Beck] he is ultimately the most interesting, in my opinion. Right now, I am going around doing screenings for the video. I am also getting reconnected with some people in Europe to do film and TV work over there.

I'm presently a bit discouraged with the way radio has gotten lately. Al Di Meola said it perfectly in his article in *Berklee Today*. [See "Music or Wallpaper?" page 32, Spring 1993 issue.] It's almost to the point where radio is dictating what chord changes and instrumentation you can have in your songs. My tune, "Seeds of Life," is one that everybody thinks would do well on radio, but since it has some rock-and-roll rhythm guitar on it, it doesn't fit adult contemporary and smooth jazz formats. I just had to go back to remix it and replace that crunch guitar with polite guitar so that they would play it.

 After all of your experiences in the music business, do you have anything to tell those coming up through the ranks?

You'd better love music a lot, because inevitably, you will get hurt along the way—not once, but many times. But you may get a moment that is great. I'm in it because I love it so much that I have to do it. It is like an unconditional kind of love. Sometimes you will be totally in love, and other times you go on a trial separation and don't do anything for a while. But you come back; it is a constant in life.

To sustain a career you have to be versatile. Unless you're the Rolling Stones, you can't do the same thing for 30 to 40 years. Don't learn to do just one thing and expect it to last your whole life. I have been playing professionally for 30 years in jazz, rock, pop, Indian hybrid music, new age, and all of these combined. There will always be something new.

Steve Vai

rock guitar's top gun

For guitar hero Steve Vai '79, music has to come from the heart and mind . . . with an edge.

STEVE VAI '79, IN HIS OWN WORDS, IS A WALKING DICHOTOMY. As a former key member of Frank Zappa's band and top-drawing arena acts Whitesnake and the David Lee Roth band, Vai earned his stripes before stadium audiences across the globe in the '80s, coaxing hyper-speed solos and bizarre sound effects out of his guitar while engaging in flamboyant rock-and-roll stage antics.

What might appear (to some) to contradict that history is Vai's sometimes intellectual approach to his own music. For example, for "Down Deep into the Pain" from his 1993 album *Sex & Religion*, Vai worked with a scale he created which divides the octave into 16 equal divisions instead of the 12 divisions of the equal temperament, to evoke a "divine dissonance" in the tune's final section. With unbridled creative license in his own studio, Vai has consistently produced thoughtful and technically astonishing music on his solo albums.

Vai's dual nature shows up in his personal as well as musical life. He eschews the stereotypical excesses viewed by many as the spoils of rock-and-roll stardom. Today, he is a devoted family man with a wife and two sons, and is quite outspoken about his aversion to drug and alcohol use.

Raised in an Italian-American household in Carle Place, New York, Steve started out playing the accordion, and later played tuba in his high school band. But after the first hearing of his sister's Led Zeppelin albums, Steve was inseparable from the guitar. Even in his teen years, Vai's energy for music went beyond playing cover tunes in Long Island's pubs by night with his garage band. At the same time he composed his first score, "Sweet Wind from Orange County," for his school orchestra.

Vai's thirst for musical knowledge brought him to Berklee in the fall of 1978. His roommate at Berklee got him interested in transcribing music from records—a vitally important development for Vai's future. With his typical intensity, he set about meticulously transcribing some of Frank Zappa's most challenging music. After weeks of work on "The Black Page," Vai sent a copy to Zappa, who wrote back offering him a job as his transcriber. By the time he was 20, Steve was playing in Zappa's band, frequently being introduced by Frank as his "little Italian virtuoso."

Vai's playing and transcribing prowess caught the attention of the editors of *Guitar Player* magazine, who made Steve's fusion rave-up "The Attitude Song" their premiere soundpage insert and featured his transcription work in a monthly column. Doors began opening, and his first album, *Flex-able* sold 250,000 copies. His unforgettable guitar duel scene as "Jack Butler," the devil's top guitarist in the blues-fantasy film *Crossroads*, gave Vai even greater visibility.

Notable stints as David Lee Roth's post-Eddie Van Halen lead player, and as the replacement for guitar-slingers Yngwie Malmsteen in Alcatrazz and Adrian Vandenberg in Whitesnake, boosted ticket and album sales for each act. In 1990, Vai released *Passion & Warfare*, a fiery instrumental disc that sold over 800,000 copies and shored up his position at the summit of the rock guitar heap—a spot he has maintained for nearly a decade.

In the years since the *Passion & Warfare* album, Steve released *Sex & Religion*, and toured as one third of a hugely successful guitar triumvirate featuring Eric Johnson and Joe Satriani. A live CD from the tour was released in 1998. Steve has since gone back into the studio to polish up some outtakes from his *Flex-able* sessions for a much anticipated CD.

This interview was conducted back in 1993 as Steve sat on the sun-drenched deck of his Lake Tahoe home thinking about where he's been and where he's headed.

Do you ever play with any of the people you met when you were at Berklee?

As a matter of fact, on August 6, my band was featured playing with Branford Marsalis and the *Tonight Show* band at the end of the program. I wrote an arrangement of a song from my album so our bands could play together. Branford and his guitarist Kevin Eubanks went to Berklee at the same time I did. They are really fine musicians.

 What are your thoughts on musical literacy for rock musicians?

A lot of people like to knock music schools, but I really enjoyed my time at Berklee and got a whole lot out of it. That is one of the few environments where you can go knock on someone's door, whether they are a sax player, flute player, or heavy metal guitarist, and ask them if they'd like to jam.

If a person has the right attitude, a music school like Berklee is a good place to learn. I saw that those with a good attitude got more out of the school than those with a bad attitude.

 A lot of rock musicians would rather not learn to read music or know theory.

I would not say knowing theory or not knowing it is good or bad. For me, I like to know the music because it helps my expression. I can sit with manuscript paper and compose music that I couldn't do if I didn't know music. The big mistake some people make is thinking that if you know music you can't play from the heart, but it is all up to the individual. Those statements usually come from someone who has not taken the time or had the discipline to sit and learn. If they did, they would realize that there is a whole other world of expression.

It would be wrong to say that because he understood music, Mozart couldn't write or play from the heart. Those great classical composers' only choice was to write their music down. You can't dismiss what they've done because they knew how to write down the little black dots. Sometimes you find trained musicians who can't really express themselves very well, but can resort to the little technicalities or mathematics. It is easy for some with a very analytical mind to write melodies and counterpoint without breaking the rules. But the bottom line is how it sounds.

 You originally came to Berklee to learn arranging and film scoring. Were you hopeful then of making a name as a rock guitarist?

Today I am pretty much what I was back then. My guitar technique has changed, but I was always interested in arranging and playing challenging music. What I did on my *Passion & Warfare* and *Sex & Religion* albums is very similar to what I did back then. Actually, my song "Sleep" from the *Flex-Able* album was written while I was at Berklee. I wrote it for a harmony class that Mike Metheny taught.

 Was he an influential teacher for you during your Berklee years?

I had some really great teachers. Mike Metheny was one. Wes Hensel was also a fabulous teacher. Mike Palermo was my ear-training teacher, and he was really into Frank Zappa. He told our class that in order to play with Zappa, first of all you had to be good, and second, there was a two-year waiting list.

 What are your thoughts on Zappa's band being a proving ground for rock musicians as the Miles Davis band was for jazz players?

Drummers like Terry Bozzio and Vinnie Colaiuta ['75] had innate abilities that go way beyond those of the average drummer, but they may not have gotten the exposure they got if there wasn't a field like Frank's to play in.

Going to work for Frank was an education, but he was really not concerned with educating people. He was interested in having his music played properly by people who are proficient. He really knew how to identify a person's talent. He always found something extreme that he can pull out of a player. In my case, I had the ability to understand and perform difficult rhythms and to make weird sounds on the guitar. He really dragged that out of me in the best possible way. That was his genius.

Do you think there will ever be a musicological value to the rock guitar transcriptions now proliferating in books and magazines, or are they mostly of immediate value?

It is good to have a document representing the music so that someone who hasn't heard it can learn it. The first piece of music I learned how to read was "Since I've Been Lovin' You" by Led Zeppelin. I couldn't figure out the guitar riffs, but I got the songbook and learned it note-for-note from the transcription.

 But some of those transcriptions are so rhythmically complex that even the best musicians could never read them without having the record as a guide.

Well, some of the music I transcribed for Frank Zappa's guitar book, I did almost as an art-type project. I didn't expect that something like that would be thrown in front of somebody for sight-reading. That work was like a meditational journey for me. I had never seen anything as complex as that stuff. It was fun for me to notate it and decorate the page with the proper articulations.

 With so many musically literate musicians playing popular music, do you think that someday it might be considered more a serious art form than a popular one?

It is hard to say. It is up to the individuals. Some people don't want to have to think about it or work so hard at it. They just want to grab a microphone and do a rap and say, "This is my art." Then, some want to learn enough about music that they could have 120 instruments play their ideas.

I am writing a piece for a 30-piece orchestra and a rock band with me playing lead guitar. It is with a group called Orchestra of Our Time from New York. We hope to do a concert in the spring of 1994. I am in the midst of orchestrating a lot of my past and present compositions. After that I will do a series of concerts in Germany with the Orchestre Moderne. They worked with Frank Zappa on his *Yellow Shark* album. I visited Zappa at Warner Bros. Studios where he and

Orchestre Moderne were recording some music by Edgar Varèse. Frank told me to get an amp and play with the orchestra. It was a blast.

 How did you end up playing the role of Jack Butler in the movie *Crossroads*?

Slide guitarist Ry Cooder was doing the soundtrack, and he called *Guitar Player* magazine to get the name of a hot rock guitarist for some sections. They recommended me. Ry called me, and I went down to work on the musical duel section with him. I had to discuss certain aspects of the scene with the film director, and he asked me if I wanted to act out the part. It was simpler than teaching an actor to mimic what I was playing. I guess I also had the perfect "Jack Butler" eyebrow.

 Did the film bring you to the attention of David Lee Roth?

No, we met before the film was released. In fact, he went with me to the premiere of the movie. I was bubbling under back then. After *Guitar Player* used my "Attitude Song" for their soundpage, and then my *Flex-Able* album came out with a few cool guitar things on it, things began to happen. Dave had heard the record I did with Alcatrazz and liked that too.

 There was a lot of media attention focused on Roth's split from Van Halen. Did you feel a lot of pressure as the one who had to fill the spot Eddie Van Halen had carved out?

How do you compete with Eddie Van Halen? I loved his playing and knew I would be compared to him; I was honored to be in the position. I didn't know what would happen at the concerts—whether the audience would accept or ignore me. By the middle of the tour they were chanting my name before I got on stage. It was a thrill. I enjoyed the whole thing.

 Was it a big adjustment to shift gears from the complex instrumental material you'd been doing to playing in an arena rock band?

I had always hoped to be able to play in big places. I am sort of a walking dichotomy. I do like playing rock and roll with acts like Roth and Whitesnake, but I also like to expand my horizons. The ultimate would be to go out with a huge band and play hardcore rock with horns and an orchestra in arenas. I don't know if it will ever happen, but it would be great.

 Q. Is the new album a synthesis of both the instrumental and mainstream rock music you've been playing over the course of your career?

The album's single, "Down Deep Into the Pain," is a lot more hardcore than anything I did with the other bands I've been in. It is musical, there is tender melody, and bone-crunching thrash. I like high-energy music—whether it is a Stravinsky melody or a 21-year-old kid screaming into the mike—it's got to have that intensity. I like music with an edge.

 Q. Will you tour with the band that played on your new album *Sex & Religion*?

I'm working on it. I don't know if I can get Terry Bozzio, he's got a lot of commitments. He is one of my favorite drummers. [Ed. note: Abraham Laboriel Jr. '93 played drums for the tour.] The singer, Devin Townsend, is a wild man and really musical. He is also an incredible guitar player. He will be playing a lot of guitar in the shows. With him I can really do some great dual guitar stuff. Between him, [bassist] T.M. Stevens, and myself, there are a lot of possibilities for some cool pyro playing.

 Q. Do you think we are seeing the end of the pyrotechnical guitar hero era?

The music scene is groping for an identity right now. You are always going to have people interested in being virtuosos who are really proficient on their instruments. But I love the thrash thing, and some of grunge stuff, if it is inspired. There are kids reacting to the albums with polished guitar playing and production by saying, "I can't do that." So they go into their garage with a beat up guitar and amp and they start slashing away on these grungy sounding chords. The next thing you know, there are some really inspired kids making good music. I can appreciate that, but I like to be able to play fast and proficiently. So if some guitar magazines are saying that shred is dead, and the trend is toward grunge, it gives me incentive to go and shred even more. I try to stay as far out of trends as possible.

 Your song "Still My Bleeding Heart" was inspired by your encounter with a young person in a hospital with terminal cancer. How did that all come about?

As an artist, I get requests from places like the Starlight Foundation. I received a request to give this boy a call in the hospital because he was terminally ill. I've done this a number of times, sometimes the kids pull through, but that was not the case this time. He requested me because he was a fan.

It was funny, when I called he didn't believe it was really me. I had to answer a series of questions to convince him. He was a really sweet kid, and I was taken by his bravery—I felt kind of dwarfed by it. He would just lay in bed playing his guitar. I got a letter from his parents a few months later telling me that the phone call helped him in his last months, but that he'd lost his battle with cancer. It was very moving for me. That is why artists write songs—because of significant events in their lives.

 As someone in the rock-and-roll spotlight, is it a challenge to balance your professional and family life?

Not at all. A lot of rock-and-roll musicians have families, but it is what they do in their mind or in their spare time when they are away from home that has the most effect on their mental health and family life. I've been exposed to a lot, having come up in the bands I've been with. I have had any kind of vice you can imagine made available to me. I didn't overindulge. I never did any drugs, and at this point I don't drink anymore.

Q. Is there anything else you want to say?

Yeah. I want to tell the Berklee students that when I was at Berklee, I didn't realize how good it was until I left. When you get out into the professional world is when the real education begins. Going to Berklee is a great opportunity to hone your chops, make new friends, and to explore a completely musical environment. You don't have to worry about the daily business affairs that come into a musician's life once he or she has to make a living. So sit back, study hard, and enjoy your time there—it's probably the only time you are going to have to do something like that.

Joe Lovano

out of the tradition

For Joe Lovano '72, the history of the jazz idiom is just as important as its future.

NOBEL PRIZE WINNER TONI MORRISON ONCE STATED, "We have to know the past so that we can understand now." Jazz star Joe Lovano '72 would undoubtedly concur. It is no coincidence that a growing audience hears his music as the "now" in jazz, and that Lovano possesses a commanding knowledge of the personalities and stylistic evolution of the idiom's past. Ultimately, Lovano plays and writes music that is rich with invention yet mindful of convention.

In his hard-blowing live sets, you won't hear Joe running licks. You will hear him stretching melody, harmony, and rhythm to their limits, and blending the history of jazz with his own perspective at that moment. For Joe, the music is at its best when true improvisation is occurring, and interaction among the players is high.

"Jazz is a very social music," says the gregarious Lovano. Since his arrival in New York around 1976, Joe has "socialized" live and on record with the brightest lights of the jazz world. Great ideas, lots of chops and energy, and a muscular yet warm tone have contributed to his stature as one of the most sought-after tenor men among jazz modernists of the '80s and '90s. Joe has played with numerous artists and been a charter member of John Scofield's quartet, the Woody Herman band, Paul Motian's trio, Charlie Haden's Liberation Jazz Orchestra, Carla Bley's band, and others before deciding it was time to don the band leader's mantle himself.

Joe grew up in Cleveland with the sounds of jazz in his ears and a saxophone in his hands. His father, Tony "Big T" Lovano, was a prominent tenor player on the Cleveland jazz scene from the '50s to the '70s. He nurtured Joe's love for the jazz legacy. In conversation, Joe gives the impression that his father was probably his most important musical influence. The elder Lovano helped his son develop not only a sound on the horn, but also confidence in his abilities. Joe came to Berklee in 1971 to polish his craft and expand his horizons. At the college he met players with whom he continues to play and record two decades later.

Joe's career is in full swing—he has released seven records as leader and appears on more than 75 others as sideman. At the time of this interview, his 1993 outing, *Universal Language*, was being lauded by critics as his most ambitious album to date. The writing showcases some unusual instrumentation—two basses, and Joe's wife Judi Silvano's wordless soprano vocals interwoven with sax and trumpet for concerted sections of tune heads. In February 1994, Joe and fellow sax star Joshua Redman released *Tenor Legacy*, a session featuring five Lovano originals and five standards. Later that year, Joe joined forces with composer Gunther Schuller for a recording with orchestra. Over lunch, Joe gave his perspective on the jazz continuum and his place in it.

 You have often mentioned the influence your father had on you musically. Do you think the musical influences from a person's youth are the strongest ones?

They have been for me. Hearing my father practice around the house had great impact. He was also a barber, but he played five or six nights a week. Hearing him practice and the sound he got from his horn made me want to create a sound too. When he came home from work, I'd want him to hear me practicing. We also played together—just two saxophones. He would get me into playing throughout the range of my horn, and playing pianissimo. He also started taking me around to sit in with his groups and at jam sessions. I learned from the other musicians what records to check out. Now I realize how important that was.

Cleveland was an important town in the bebop school. Tadd Dameron was from Cleveland and was a friend of my dad's. Albert Ailer and some of the free jazz players were also from there. My dad and his group would open in clubs for artists like Stan Getz and Flip Phillips when they came through town. He frequently talked about these experiences around the house.

 That must have nurtured your feelings for the music.

It really hipped me to the history of jazz; I really studied it as a kid. Knowing who came out of Cleveland made me want to learn who came out of Detroit and Pittsburgh, and to know who the important players were and how they influenced each other.

 Did you listen to all kinds of music or were you mostly focused on jazz?

Of course I grew up in the Beatles era so I heard all that music too. I thought jazz was the more advanced music, but I played in bands at high school dances and weddings. I earned my tuition money to come to Berklee from these gigs around Cleveland.

 Did you know from the outset that you wanted to be a jazz musician?

When I was young, I knew who I wanted to play with and what kind of music I wanted to play; I set goals for myself. When I was at Berklee, I wanted to play with Paul Motian, in the Mel Lewis band, or with Lee Konitz, which I have done.

As I was coming up, I worked on getting my doubles together so I could play in a saxophone section and play clarinet or flute parts. I've played behind Tony Bennett, Sarah Vaughan, and Billy Eckstine. There I was called upon to play flute or clarinet. Making a living as a musician is one of the first things you have to concentrate on. My dad always told me that you have to develop your sound and your soloing, but you have to be able to do the gig when your phone rings. Because of my dad and his scene, I grew up playing with people of his generation. I have always been comfortable sitting in with a lot of people.

 Did you know John Scofield during your Berklee years?

Yeah, I met Scofield, Bill Frisell, Billy Pierce, and George Garzone at Berklee. A lot of great players were there who have become friends I play with a lot. I also met [saxophonists] Billy Drews, Steve Slagel, [trombonist] Keith O'Quinn, [pianists] Kenny Werner, and Ted Lo. There were a lot of us who moved to New York together around '75 or '76.

Q. What were your first impressions when you came to the college?

By the time I came to Berklee, I had already been playing a lot of gigs. Sonny Stitt and Sonny Rollins were my idols, and that whole bebop thing is what I was into. I was placed in Gary Burton's ensemble with rhythm players who were in their final semester. It was great. We were playing Chick Corea's music, and tunes by Keith Jarrett and Wayne Shorter. Playing tunes with these harmonic sounds and different forms really opened me up to explore and discover different ways to play through harmony.

I also had an improvisation class with John LaPorta where he taught how to look at chords and pick available notes and then make your own shapes with them. It was inspiring to be around him because I had heard him playing with Charlie Parker on some albums in my dad's record collection.

Q. How did you decide on having two bass players, Steve Swallow and Charlie Haden, on several of the cuts on *Universal Language?*

I first played with Steve Swallow in Carla Bley's band in 1983. He has these beautiful chordal, single-line, and bass approaches on electric bass. We did a tour with French bassist Henri Texier, and Aldo Romano on drums, a two-bass band in '86 to '87. We recorded two records as the Transatlantic Quartet, and one with John Abercrombie added on guitar. That was the first time I'd worked with an electric and an acoustic bass together. The sounds are really different from each other, so I wrote specifically for Steve to play with the horns, to comp chords, and sometimes to play a bass role. I really wanted to put him together with Charlie Haden on that record. The combination of those two and Jack DeJohnette on drums was really magic.

Some music journalists have made a big deal of you finally going out as a leader at 40.

I never rushed to get my own record contract and be a leader because I've been involved in some great bands where I have really been able to contribute.

Actually, I did my first record as a leader in 1985 for Soul Note records with Mel Lewis on drums, Kenny Werner on piano, and Dennis Irwin on bass. I have been working as a leader on the East coast and in Europe throughout much of the '80s.

I wouldn't have been able to make a record like *Universal Language* when I was 20 or 25. I would have made a record of the music I was studying then. When you get a record contract at 20, you make a record of the music you are listening to and playing then. At that point, you are so influenced by what you are hearing that all you can do is copy it. I feel I'm making records at the right time. They reflect my experiences as a player with some great bands.

 The music you were playing in your set last night was very abstract rhythmically.

Each tune is built differently. Some tunes have parts for the players to feed off that create a multilayered rhythmic concept. By feeding off a polyrhythmic idea played by someone else, the soloist is free to play inside, or go into a different tempo. We are exploring rhythm and finding a groove, but not always playing the same beat. We want to really feel the polyrhythmic interplay.

 Your playing and writing reflect influences from Ornette Coleman, Monk, and Coltrane as well as international influences.

The more music you play and experience, the more your repertoire and vocabulary grow. The music of Ellington, Mingus, Miles, and Monk covers a lot of the history and tradition of jazz; there is so much there. If you think of what improvising really is, you have to incorporate everything.

masters of music

It is a small world in terms of traveling these days. I've played in the Middle East, Africa, and the Orient, and it all influences my music. Many people don't realize that jazz ties a lot of the world's music together.

 Have you found that there is an audience for jazz in the Middle East?

Yeah, it's opening up. I did a tour of the Middle East with French bassist Henri Texier that was sponsored by the French Cultural Ministry. We played three concerts in Turkey, four in Israel, and two in Greece. We were at universities and played for diplomats. I played with John Scofield's band in Istanbul at an annual arts festival. We were featured in the jazz portion, and it was incredible. The people there are starting to tune into jazz.

All over Europe audiences were built up by people like Sidney Bechet, Don Byas, Kenny Clark, Ben Webster, and others who went over there in the 1960s and earlier. They created a scene that is thriving today. Coltrane only went to Europe twice as a leader. Now there are a lot of records coming out, but basically, they are all from radio broadcasts taped during those tours. These days, jazz musicians go to Europe three times a year.

 Dizzy Gillespie once said that jazz was born in America, but the Europeans discovered it first.

Dizzy really brought music to many different parts of the planet. He played with musicians from everywhere, and let the influences come through in his music. Ellington had a lot to do with that growth too. Some of his works, like the "Far East Suite," were inspired by his travels.

 Travel is really a major component in your life as a jazz musician.

It is hard to travel all the time, but if you keep yourself together and let it come through in your playing, you'll find a lot of flavors that you can incorporate in your music.

What are the bottom-line realities of touring with a jazz group?

I toured in the States with Scofield, but with Carla Bley, Mel Lewis, Paul Motian, the Charlie Haden Liberation Orchestra, and Elvin Jones, we only toured in Europe. We played occasional concerts here, but no full-blown American tours.

The States is a different market. Most towns are weekend towns—you can play Friday and Saturday and sometimes a Thursday or Sunday, and that's it. You can't tour. You will have to fly into someplace like St. Louis on a Friday and you'll have a packed house. Unless you were able to get something in Kansas City for Saturday, you have to go back home until the next weekend. Not many bands can sustain the expense of travel and all for an American tour.

East Coast towns like Boston and New York are different. You can play Tuesday through Sunday and people will come out, but in most cities, the early week-nights are dark. In Europe, you could tour for three weeks and play 18 nights. Most of the venues are theaters, the shows are earlier, and the whole thing isn't about eating or drinking—it's about listening.

 Do you practice much on the road?

It is hard to practice in a hotel room. I don't want to bug anybody, so I may play really pianissimo. Mainly I do a lot of writing on the road. I also love to walk around and explore a lot of the places I go. In Europe, I check out the cathedrals. They are very peaceful, and you really get a feeling for the history of humanity. My piece "Worship" on *Universal Language* was inspired by a cathedral I visited in France. I went in at the middle of a mass, and they were doing a call-and-response thing—a prayer with triplets and eighth notes. I let it just carry me, and I left there with all these ideas. I worked out the piece back at my hotel.

 What do you feel is the quality that people like Miles, Coltrane, Bill Evans, Bird, and others had in their music that enabled them to leave a permanent mark on jazz?

It comes from inspiration and inner confidence, and letting the music develop around the musicians you are playing with. Those people all had their own personality, but their music came through the people they played with. Everyone around them had their influence. You can't try to be there either; you just have to search and play.

If you really understand what improvising is, you try to focus on the material you are playing and not just play what you know about chords and scales. How many times are you going to play on an F7 in your life? There are many cats who are wizards on their instruments, but they basically play the same solo on every tune. The greats dig beyond their instrument and influence players of all instruments. Dizzy could have played "I Can't Get Started" a million times in his life and still discovered pretty notes.

 Because you play so many different horns, your solo albums and live work feature a wide range of sounds.

I have studied a lot of horns—you know, clarinets and flutes. Alto was my first horn as a kid. I got a tenor sax when I was 12, and tenor became my main love because that's what my dad played. I've doubled in the big bands I've played with, but in groups like Paul Motian's, and Scofield's, I only played tenor. In my own bands, I incorporate all of the other instruments, and it gives my records a different identity from the other ones where I was a sideman. Now I may play the head and a solo on tenor, and then pick up a different horn and play again with that sound.

 What would you tell a young player who is determined to be a career jazz musician?

No matter what instrument you play, you have to have a deep dedication to your horn. It's got to be a very heavy relationship. If you want to play bass the way Dave Holland does, you gotta love that horn, man; otherwise it is just technique.

When you practice and play alone, getting yourself together, those are some intimate moments. It can be a struggle, or it can be very beautiful. When it gets beautiful is when you start playing with a tone that's yours, not a copy of someone else's. You have to develop beyond your dreams, and then open up your mind and let the music be creative so that it is not just technique.

 Do you feel that the complete jazz player should have a knowledge of the history of jazz?

I think so. As a young player, I just embraced it all without being told I should do it. My dad's record collection helped a lot with that. My father had a style that came out of Illinois Jacquet, Lester Young, Gene Ammons, and Dexter Gordon—a real "walk the bar" tenor style. For a long time I sounded more like my dad than anyone else. When I came to Berklee I realized that, and I dug deeper.

 Where do you think acoustic, free jazz music is headed?

I think the future is about the combinations of sounds as well as the personalities of the players. The whole acoustic approach is in the tradition. You can play from triple piano to triple forte and explore many areas.

On the other hand, Bill Frisell plays electric guitar but has an acoustic approach. The instrument in your hands is almost secondary after a while. Bill uses all kinds of effects on his instrument, but he played clarinet in marching bands in high school, and breathes in the music. All of these things add up to why he plays like that.

 Do you think that the large numbers of musicians recording today makes it harder for an up-and-coming player to find a voice?

I think it takes imagination. The combination of many influences makes a style of your own. We have a lot to draw from. I think it is silly to copy one period and even more silly to copy one kind of a player. I have a lot of students who are so trapped into copying Mike Brecker's style, or copying players who copied Mike—which is even worse. The key is to find your own way in this music.

John Robinson

a place in time

Studio mainstay John "J.R." Robinson '75: a rock-steady presence in an ever-changing industry.

AFTER MORE NEARLY 20 YEARS IN L.A., where many musical careers flash then fade within months, John Robinson '75 (alias "J.R.") continues to be one of the most sought-after drummers in the business. J.R.'s soulful, razor-sharp timekeeping has been the heartbeat for a good portion of the soundtrack to contemporary American life heard via radio, TV, and movies since 1978. Some of his studio colleagues refer to him as the "Hit Man" because he holds the record for playing on more hit singles than any other drummer in the recording world—including studio veteran Hal Blaine.

The roster of superstars whose gold and platinum discs feature J.R.'s stickwork is extensive and includes Rufus, Eric Clapton, Madonna, Steve Winwood, Diana Ross, Earth, Wind, and Fire, Michael Jackson, Stevie Nicks, Rod Stewart, Whitney Houston, Vince Gill, Elton John, Michael Bolton, Quincy Jones ['51], Peter Cetera, Natalie Cole, and dozens more.

Raised in Creston, Iowa, J.R. was in the garage with his first band at 10. Attending summer band camps in Missouri and Illinois during his junior high school years solidified his desire to become a professional musician. After graduating high school in 1973, J.R. left the heartland for Berklee where he studied for six consecutive semesters. He began working with various jazz groups around Boston, and ultimately went on the road with a show band called Shelter.

A providential gig the band played in Cleveland in 1978 catapulted J.R. from the nightclub circuit to the concert stage and studios. One night, Rufus and Chaka Khan stopped in at Cleveland's Rare Cherry club and liked what they heard from the drums. Things happened fast, and within 24 hours J.R. was asked to join Rufus, finish their world tour, and then record their *Numbers* album.

Quincy Jones produced *Masterjam* for Rufus the following year and liked J.R.'s drumming (Quincy also started calling him "J.R."). Quincy invited him to play on Michael Jackson's blockbuster album *Off the Wall*. When that record soared to multiplatinum status, J.R.'s stock as a session player rose with it. Hundreds of sessions with the top artists, producers, and film composers in the business followed. In 1983, J.R. and Rufus won a Grammy for their hit "Ain't Nobody." In 1987 alone, J.R.'s drumming was heard on eight Grammy-winning songs. By now he has played on more than 25 Grammy-winning efforts.

In the weeks before we met (in January 1994), J.R. had spent six days recording with Stephen Curtis Chapman, completed a live taping of "Comic Relief" and a few episodes of *Murder, She Wrote*, and played with an all-star lineup at the 40th Anniversary of the Playboy Jazz Festival. He also signed on for Barbra Streisand's international tour, which opened in London April 17.

With the big gigs comes big pressure. In talking with him, it is apparent that J.R. has always thrived under pressure. This fact combined with his unique abilities and charismatic personality keep him on the short list of the producers, artists, and contractors who are spinning out gold and platinum records in southern California's studios.

 Your initial encounter with Rufus and Chaka Khan is one of the classic, fairy tale "discovery stories." Do you think that kind of thing happens much today?

I pray it does, but I think discoveries happen more by recommendation today. I remember being in Boston playing clubs, and if a famous musician walked in to listen, I would find myself over-playing. When I would pack up my drums that night I would feel really bad about over-playing because I knew the cat would not call me.

I was playing with an eight-piece soul/show band in Cleveland, just after leaving Berklee. We were at a huge, 3,000-seat club that had one of those lightboards that flashes messages. I looked up and it read, "Welcome Rufus and Chaka Khan," and my heart started beating faster. When they sat in the front row, I got even more paranoid, but I remembered not to over-play. They asked us if their whole band, except their drummer, could sit in to play with me. We did a bunch of Rufus tunes, and I thought I was in heaven. They asked me to come to their soundcheck at Cleveland's Front Row Theater the next night to play some more.

We played again and it was burning. I could see their drummer fading behind the speaker cabinets. He was their second drummer and had only been with them a short time. Incidentally, he and I are still friends to this day. After we played, they told me I was in, and we figured out the logistics of getting me moved to L.A. to rehearse and then join the tour.

 What do you think attracted Quincy Jones to your playing?

When Quincy produced Rufus and Chaka Khan, he had the option of using a studio drummer, but he wanted to use me. I think he liked the fact that I listened to him, I had song sense, my playing was understated, and my time was strong. I also think he was attracted because I am a Berklee alumnus as he is. He'd been using Ernie Watts ['65], Neil Stubenhaus ['74], Abe Laboriel ['72], and a lot of other alumni.

 What did you pick up from working with him so closely on several hit albums?

I learned about producing and about the business. Quincy says that a producer is like a casting director. You cast the right people around you to make the record successful. For instance, on "We Are the World," he cast Greg Philinganes on piano, Louis Johnson on bass, and me on drums. That was the rhythm section that cut the tune—after we kicked 50 cameramen out of the studio so we could work.

Did you know Neil Stubenhaus when you were both students at Berklee?

Yeah, we played the same show-band circuit in Boston with different groups, and did some jamming together as did most of the young players from Berklee. Now 21 years later, we are close friends. When I get calls for sessions and I'm asked who I would like on bass, Neil is my first choice. I work with bassist Abe Laboriel a lot, too, probably once a month. Abe and I have a lot in common—spiritual things as well as ideas about the industry.

 What Berklee faculty members had an impact on your musical development?

I was a performance major with drums as my principal instrument. I couldn't choose piano as my secondary instrument, so I took vibes with Dave Samuels. He got me into Gary Burton's four-mallet technique, but I found it was giving me blisters, which interfered with my drum playing. Dave and I became good friends and have since worked on gigs together.

I studied drums with Alan Dawson at Berklee. He was a legend and an incredible player. I wasn't from an urban area with a jazz scene as he was; I used to love to go into my lessons just to hear him talk. During my lessons, he would play vibes and I would play drums. He got me singing rhythms out of a syncopation book and working on single strokes with a metronome. He was very influential.

 What was the most useful experience you had at the college?

Learning to play with the click in the studio. I went into one of Berklee's first studios in the Mass. Ave. building with fellow student Doug Getschal ['75] who was working as Joe Hostetter's engineering assistant. The engineers asked me if I knew what a click was. I said no, and they played it for me and asked if I thought I could read a chart and play to it. I said no problem, and nailed the track on the first take.

They had been having trouble finding a drummer who could play in time with the click while maintaining a human feel, and read a chart at the same time. Consequently, I started working a lot in that studio. I ended up playing drums on all of the instrumental performance tapes of 1974, replacing the drum tracks by other drummers—which is something I am frequently called upon to do today.

 To what do you attribute your longevity in the studios?

Style is one factor, and being able to adapt and change that style is very important. I can think of a lot of drummers in L.A. who had a style that was in for a while but found that their work dried up when their style went out.

When I came into the studios in 1978 and began working with Quincy, the four-to-the-floor style on the bass drum was really in. On some of the albums I did, like George Benson's *Give Me the Night*, the Brothers Johnson's *Stomp*, and a bunch of others, I played that, but on top of the drum kit I would add other syncopations to make the groove sound different. From the *Off the Wall* album by Michael Jackson through the '80s to Steve Winwood's "Higher Love," I've been able to add to the current drum style, as well as adapt.

I've gotten a reputation for being a human clock. With the influx of machines and everything being locked to SMPTE code now, drummers really have to be as precise as possible without sacrificing style, musicality, feel, or dynamics. A lot of drummers freak out trying to handle all of those aspects. They start feeling a train wreck approaching and drag the tempo or miss something in the track. Then they have to go back and do it over again or, worse, they get axed from the session.

 You have been in heavy demand in the studios even through a time when drum machines have been used extensively.

To deal with that, you need to master the drum machine as well. I have always been electronically inclined. My dad's hobby was electronics. He made a Heathkit television set once, and I helped by passing him the resistors, capacitors, and diodes. It was a natural for me to learn programming. Drum machines did cut into the work for a lot of drummers, and I saw many leave town or get a totally electronic drum set up to imitate that sound. I've always been pro acoustic, and I've played acoustic drums on all the records.

Rufus did a reunion album called *Stompin' at the Savoy* in 1983; we won a Grammy for "Ain't Nobody" off that album. That tune has a very syncopated groove, it is precise like a machine, but feels human. After hearing it, Mike Baird [studio drummer] came up to me and complimented me for what he thought was a great Linn drum program on the tune. I told him that I had played everything, it wasn't a programmed part. He didn't believe me—a lot of people still think it was a drum program.

 Do you get studio calls for one particular style or because you can cover many styles?

Originally I was a typecast because I was a member of Rufus, and they were known for mixing funk and rock. The band was regarded as a black band even though three of the members were white. A lot of people heard that John Robinson played in Rufus and assumed I was black. I personally don't think race or color has any bearing on musicianship.

I worked with a guy, Jim Stuart, who was one of the owners of Stax Records in the old days. He flew me down to Memphis to work with some musicians in their studio. We had never met, and he came to pick me up at the airport. After everyone had filtered off the plane and out of the airport, I was standing there with my bags. I saw this guy looking all around and I knew what was happening. Finally he came up to me and said "John? John Robinson?" I said, "Hi, Jim." He knew my playing, and that I came out of Rufus, and told me he was expecting to meet a tall black guy. I told him I considered that a compliment.

 What are producers expecting when they hire you for their sessions?

Sometimes I get called in to help repair a track. For Rod Stewart's "Rhythm of Your Heart," Trevor Horn called me because they couldn't get what they wanted from three drummers they tried in New York. I did all kinds of overdubs—full kit, timpani, and rudimental snare drum—which gave the song a very Scottish feel.

I get calls to come in and add something to a track. It might just be a high-hat which will give a human feel to a track that is too machine-like. Sometimes you can just punch in a little part that adds some beauty. Something that simple can make a hit record.

I got called to work on George Benson's version of "Beyond the Sea." Russ Titelman, the producer, came out from New York to have Joe Sample and me play on the tracks he'd cut with a big band. It was a great band, but the acoustic bass player and the drummer were not together, the time was all over the place. I wrote a chart and made notes of every little idiosyncrasy in the time, and Joe did the same. I had to really bend to get with the horns. It was a challenge, but that tune ended up being the big one off the record.

 Beyond talent, what attributes make someone successful in the studio?

Personality, promptness, and reading ability. Wes Hensel used to tell his Berklee classes that to be a professional musician you have to be a good reader and be on time. You never want to be late. I always show up early.

As for personality, if you come off cold, hard, or uncaring, chances are the producer won't call you again even if you did well on his session. You have to remember that you are building a 360-degree circle of people you work for. You don't want things to end after you have been around the circle once, you want to work with those people again. That happened in the early '80s for me—I started around the circle again.

Since a lot of drummers are not great readers, they can't do movie dates, which are very lucrative. They pay double scale like records, but have extra incentives like residuals from films that sell well and then go to cable.

 Are you doing a lot of TV and movies?

I do TV primarily when I am in-between other projects. It really keeps you on your toes—there is a lot of reading and the pace is quick. I have been doing a lot of motion pictures recently. I did *My Cousin Vinny, Dennis the Menace, Wayne's*

World II, Diggstown, Grand Canyon, Intersection, and a lot of others. I hope to get into composing for films.

 Q. What's next in your career?

I have been writing for years and would like to eventually spend more time producing than playing, although my playing will always continue—God willing. I have a full studio in my new home, so I could do most of the production on my own projects there.

I originally had a goal of spending 15 years in Los Angeles. I'm past that now. I figure I'll just rock this thing out and see what happens.

When Multi-Grammy Winning Producer Russ Titelman Needs a Drummer...

"I call John Robinson for sessions because he is one of the best drummers on earth. He's musical and plays any style from big band to funk. He gets the concept fast, spots any problems in a track right away, and his time is impeccable.

"The Rufus tune 'Ain't Nobody' from the Stompin' at the Savoy *album started with a drum machine program that Hawk [the keyboardist] wrote. John basically copied the machine part, but added this power that you will never get from a machine. We put his drum track down in pieces. First he played the high hat, then he played kick and snare. I think we put in the tom fills— those explosions—a few days later. It is hard on drummers when you make them play in a way they are unaccustomed to, but as I recall, John got each part on the first take.*

"If you give a great musician like John an idea, he'll play it better than you imagined it. On Steve Winwood's song 'Back in the High Life Again,' I asked him to try a press roll in the section following the chorus. When he did it, I just said, yeah, that's it! He always gets what I want."

Mike Stern

taking the lead

After backing Miles, Jaco, Brecker, and more, Tele-master Mike Stern '75 now commands center stage.

IT IS QUITE APPARENT IN WATCHING MIKE STERN PERFORM that he was born to play the guitar. Innate coordination between his hands gives him a technical command over the instrument that places him in a league with few peers, though there be many comers. Jazz is Stern's native tongue, yet his musical speech is heavily inflected with gritty artifacts from the rock and blues dialects he absorbed in his formative years. Stern's uniquely aggressive "bop and roll" linearity initially sent shock waves through the international jazz community in the early '80s. His fresh style offered tutelage for both jazz and rock guitarists. For jazzers: it is possible to swing hard on a Tele or a Strat. Rockers: possessing a deeper knowledge of theory and other musical traditions is not deleterious to one's rock-and-roll sensibilities.

Boston's jazz insiders used to crowd the small, smoky clubs lying within Berklee's penumbra in the late '70s whenever Mike shared the bandstand with local headliners (saxophonist) Jerry Bergonzi ['68], (trumpeters) Tiger Okoshi ['75] and Mike Metheny, or fellow guitarists Mick Goodrick ['69], Bill Frisell ['77], and Randy Roos ['78]. Stern was bubbling under then; you could feel it at those gigs.

A strong buzz among respected players positioned Stern as a sought-after sideman. His tenure with Blood Sweat and Tears around 1975 placed him in a lineup that included Jaco Pastorius. A subsequent recording session with BS&T singer David Clayton Thomas introduced Stern's fretwork to the Brecker Brothers and

David Sanborn. It came as little surprise when word spread that he'd left town with former Mahavishnu Orchestra drummer Billy Cobham's touring band, only to be hired away by Miles Davis for his historic 1981 comeback recordings and tours. In his post-Miles days, Stern would work extensively with the Brecker Brothers Band, Steps Ahead, Jaco, and David Sanborn.

One of the many things Mike learned from the 1981 Miles comeback tour was the truism that even bad press is good press. Music critics turned out in droves with the false hope that the man with the horn would uncork some of his vintage jazz. Some reviewers complained bitterly that Miles had hired a brash rock guitarist. Stern's name was trumpeted abroad—for better or worse—in every review. Eventually their acrimony turned to approbation as Stern's musical depth came clearly into focus, earning him a loyal following. He was recently named an "Artist Deserving Wider Recognition" by *Down Beat*. He took honors as "Best Jazz Guitarist" and his *Standards* album was named "Best Jazz Album" in the 1993 *Guitar Player* readers' poll.

As a sideman, Stern's incendiary soloing heated up dozens of albums and concert halls worldwide with a variety of major jazz acts. Now, his own music is the focus. He has made seven records as leader, all but the first for the Atlantic Jazz label. Now a seasoned veteran with career in full swing, Stern lives in Manhattan with his wife Leni (Magdalena Thora) Stern ['80], who is a respected guitarist and recording artist in her own right. I caught up with Mike at his East Side apartment shortly after his return from touring Europe with his trio, just before he left for further concerts on two other continents.

 It seems word-of-mouth was a major factor in the initial launch of your career.

That is kind of what happened, I lucked into some gigs. I really consider myself very fortunate to have gotten play with these people. It started with Blood Sweat and Tears. At Berklee, I studied guitar with Pat Metheny. He was telling me that I should be playing out more. He had heard that Blood Sweat and Tears was looking for a guitar player and told me to go for it. I auditioned and got the gig. Next came the gig with Billy Cobham and then Miles. One led to the next.

Where did Miles hear you?

I had played with Bill Evans (sax player) at Michael's Pub in Boston, and he told me he had been recording with Miles. When the guitarist Miles had been using didn't work out, Bill recommended me. Miles came down to the Bottom Line where I was playing with Billy Cobham. He liked it, and I got the call for the gig. I am thrilled that I got a chance to record and play with Miles Davis.

 What do you think he heard in your playing that made him hire you full-time?

He told me he liked my time feel. He liked the fact that I played bebop lines and that I could rock. Victor Bailey ['79] (bassist) used to describe what I do as "bop and roll." I grew up listening to Hendrix, Beck, Clapton, and a lot of blues. I fell in love with jazz a few years later and started listening to Jim Hall and Wes Montgomery.

 Was your solo on "Fat Time" from *Man With The Horn* from a live or an overdub session?

It was all live. The band played a couple of takes and I wanted to redo my solo. But Miles told me in that raspy voice, "That's it . . . when you're at a party, you gotta know when to leave!" He called the tune "Fat Time" because he liked my time feel and I was a little overweight back then.

 That was a very influential guitar solo. Did you feel it was good when you heard it back?

I never feel that way. I always feel like I could improve on a take. I'm generally too self-critical. Some of that is good, but sometimes it is excessive. It is hard for me to listen back until later. I can sometimes hear my own playing from outside of myself, but it is hard to get perspective.

Your work with Miles—the sound of your guitar and the intensity—seemed to set a new standard among the "fusion" guitarists of the '80s. You had more raw, rock-and-roll energy while everyone else was playing jazz lines with smooth distortion—without an edge.

That may be so, but for me, it was just a natural combination of my influences. I like the sense of fun in rock and the energy. In general, I listen for the energy and soul in music. A sense of fun is very important too. I prefer a grittier approach like you hear in rock and blues, where you can hear the pick on the string when a player is digging in.

The critics were rough on you during Miles' comeback, saying you were an unsophisticated rocker.

That was the least of it! Miles just said, "Who cares, don't listen to the critics, the only critic you need to listen to is me… and you're playing your ass off." It wasn't easy being thrust into a situation where there was more press about Miles coming back than there was for any other musical act—in jazz or otherwise. What he wanted for his music is what I had to do. He told me to turn it up or turn it off. He wanted me to play like Hendrix.

It was hard for me to read the reviews, but some of those critics started turning around and finding more there than they first thought. They all wanted Miles to play straight-ahead music, which he did not want to do at that time. Now I think that the critics are a necessary part of the process. You just do the best you can and they can say what they want. I am getting much more positive press now, and I appreciate that. The bottom line is, you have to be true to yourself as much as possible, and that's not an easy thing to do. You have to do what you do and know that it is honest. Some will dig it, some won't.

In the extreme, a musician caring only about what he or she does can appear aloof from the audience.

You know, Miles was always very aware of the audience. He would turn his back to them, but do not be fooled, he was always looking around. That cat knew exactly who was sitting out there. He learned to include people in his music. He found that balance in doing what he wanted, even if he turned some people off temporarily. They wanted him to play *Kind of Blue*, and he'd be going left. But he would end up including them in his music. As corny as it sounds, music is a language and it is for communicating with people.

 Have you noticed that winning polls as you have in *Guitar Player* magazine translates into a larger audience?

Sure, you get some gigs after a thing like that. It was really an honor to be voted best jazz guitarist for 1993 and to have the *Standards* album be voted best jazz album. That was a fun record to make, with Al Foster playing drums—I worked with him with Miles. He is such a swinging player.

I may do a live album next—I mean really live, most of my records are kind of live in the studio, on some the music is more arranged. But I would like to try a live album with an audience, not in the studio.

 What do you think audiences in Europe and Japan are hearing in the music of artists like yourself and others that makes those areas more fertile territory for American jazz musicians?

I think there is the same interest here, but I don't think there is enough support because things aren't set up the same way here. A lot of it is the funding. In Europe, there is more emphasis on the arts and supporting them. Over there, you find city councils which actually help the jazz clubs. They subsidize these jazz festivals so that they can bring musicians over. The people hear the music, they like the surroundings of the festival, and they get into it. Then they buy the records and the audience grows.

I did gigs in different formats in Europe this summer. I went over there with Jeff Andrews (bass) and Dave Weckl (drums). We played at big places with lots of people. I am used to playing smaller venues like clubs; some of these halls seated 8,000 people. They have festivals all over and we try to make as many as possible, so the travel is nuts.

How much time do you spend abroad in a year?

I spend about four months each year playing out of the country. I haven't been doing all of that with my own group though. Not too long ago I toured with the Brecker Brothers, and I co-led a band with Bob Berg. I've been going out with my own band now for a few years, and lately I've been giving that more priority. After playing with Miles, Jaco Pastorius, the Brecker Brothers, and others, the next challenge was to go out on my own. I still like to work with others. I did some gigs with Joe Henderson last year and it was great. But it is a natural progression for me to be doing my own group.

 You must be very comfortable with life on the road by now.

Sometimes it drives me crazy if it is too much. This summer we came back to the U.S. from Japan, spent six hours in the airport and then went right to Brazil. But this is what I do. If you want to go out and play in front of people—which I love— touring is the name of the game. I am trying to balance it so that I'm here a little bit more. My wife, Leni, goes on the road for her own gigs, so we will try to go out at the same time, and sometimes she will come along with me.

 Music is a driving force in both of your lives.

It is really inspiring for me to see Leni's energy for music and how she tries different things. She has some great recordings out on Lipstick Records. I recorded her tune "Sandbox" on my *Odds or Evens* album. Except for standards, I rarely play other people's tunes.

 Did you two meet at Berklee?

No, but we met in Boston. She was friends with Bill Frisell and he introduced us. I had just come back from playing with Blood Sweat and Tears and was playing with Jerry Bergonzi and Tiger Okoshi when I met her.

Do you still play with musicians you met at Berklee?

Sure, I play with saxophonist Steve Slagel ['74], and guitarists Wayne Krantz ['76] and Jay Azolina ['76]. Jay is a great player; he and I come from a similar background in a lot of ways. I think he is really exceptional; people don't know about him. Jeff Andrews ['74] plays bass in my trio. I also just played on four cuts with Tiger Okoshi on his new record *Two Sides to Every Story*, with Jack DeJohnette, Dave Holland, and Gil Goldstein. Not long ago I sat in with Branford Marsalis ['79] and Kevin Eubanks ['79] on the *Tonight Show*.

 What are your recollections of your years at Berklee ?

For me the situation at Berklee was terrific—just what I needed. It is what you make of it. Some people say you sound too much like everybody else if you go to a music school. But I never felt that. There is this atmosphere there where everyone is trying to develop their musical potential. For me it was a way to enhance my vocabulary and give me more musical options.

Gary Burton was a great teacher. I had him for some ensembles and classes and he was always so clear and really to the point. I like where he is coming from musically, he seems very open-minded. In guitar, I learned a lot studying with Larry Senibaldi. We covered Bill Leavitt's books, which are very clear on the fundamentals. I came to Berklee mainly as a rock player; I needed to learn the neck of the guitar and become a better reader. John LaPorta was also a phenomenal teacher. He taught some of the basic material like improvising with pentatonic scales with added blues notes. But, after he taught it, you just wanted to go and check it out in every possible way. He had so much energy for music. Another guy was Mick Goodrick. He was a great teacher.

After Berklee, I studied with Charlie Banacos who has been very influential. I still do correspondence lessons with him.

Do you have a daily routine and still search out ways to improve as a player?

It is the same as it has always been; I'm just trying to develop my potential. Sometimes I try to examine too much stuff and just don't have the time to do it all. For instance, I will learn classical guitar pieces, but I never get them to the point where I could perform them. I can't devote that much time to doing that. My priority is to try and sound like a horn player as much as possible. I love the phrasing and lines that you hear on either on piano or horn. I don't listen to that much guitar music at this point. For about 10 years I've tried to zero in on other instruments, transcribe the music, and try to play it on guitar. You come up with different ideas that way.

 After you learn a line or a concept in that way, how hard is it to bring it out in your playing on the gig?

It takes a while, and you have to know when to stop practicing, if it is not coming out, and play the gig. But you have to try new things on your gig. Someone told me to try and play just one new line or concept in the course of a gig. I try not to memorize any solo that I've transcribed. I read through them and hope to get something by osmosis and make it my own. It is most important to have your own voice, even if it is a combination of different things you have heard other players do. Combining things is one way to find your voice.

Q. Do you think finding your voice is a key to longevity as a jazz musician?

I think it is a very important part—for any kind of musician. It is also the kind of thing you can't force. You should find your own voice, even if it is a combination of different things you have heard other players do. Combining is one way to discover it. You wouldn't transcribe and learn only Wes Montgomery solos because you would sound like him, and he already did that pretty well himself. But, you might want to learn some things by Wes or Jimi Hendrix because what they did has become part of the tradition and vocabulary of music. It is so important to listen and play.

If you were to choose one album as your best, which would it be?

I like the way this last one, Is *What It Is*, came out. Maybe it's because the last one is the one I feel closest to, it is very hard for me to judge my own work. I put in a lot of effort into all the records—writing, getting good players, and then playing. I have been lucky to get great players and people to help me with them.

 The material you play with your trio includes tunes from your recordings, but the format is more open.

Yeah, it's wide open. I include some standards, which I always like to do in a trio setting. The challenge of playing in a trio is great. I have to reach for a lot of stuff; it is not like having a lot of arranged material where you take a solo or two each night. It is really lean, there is not a lot to fall back on.

 Does that burning desire that propels young musicians to face the long odds needed to succeed still burn as brightly in you as it did when you were playing for $15 a night at Michael's Pub on Gainsborough Street?

Even more. I've exceeded my expectations. I would have been happy just teaching and playing at small places—I still do both by the way. I was hopeful that I might make a record or two, but I didn't think I'd work with Miles or some of the other great musicians. Much to my own amazement, I still really just love to play. It doesn't take much; I really enjoy just sitting in a room with my guitar and listening to or reading some music I can learn from. It's very natural for me to put a lot of effort into that.

Even if they are not into a particular kind of music, people respect the effort and the heart that a serious musician has invested. It is important to work hard; you will have more fun with music, but you really develop your passion from putting more into it. You become disciplined and practice everyday, even though there is nobody saying you have to do it. You can't guarantee that you will get to play with the Rolling Stones or Sonny Rollins, so much of that is up to chance. What you can guarantee is that by working hard, you will enjoy music more.

Would you ever entertain thoughts of playing with a rock group again?

In a way I think it would be a lot of fun, but it might be a tough adjustment because I've gotten so used to playing in a jazz context with lots of room to solo. I spoke with Mike Brecker, he did the Paul Simon tour. Mike had it written into his contract that he got to play one of his own tunes each night and really stretch out. Playing rock is great, but it doesn't give the kind of freedom you have on a jazz gig. I might find it restrictive. [After a pause] But now if Sting was to call...

Quincy Jones

the best is yet to come

A music industry visionary for nearly five decades, Quincy Jones '51 stays focused on what lies ahead.

THERE ARE MANY IMPOSING FIGURES in the annals of American popular music history and culture, but one would be hard-pressed to find any individual who has had a greater or more enduring impact than Quincy Jones. He is an impresario in the broadest, most creative sense of the word. Through five decades he has alternately worn the hats of composer, performer, arranger, and conductor; of record, TV, and film producer; of record executive; and now, of multimedia entrepreneur.

Always looking forward, Quincy has never been content to rest on past achievements, no matter how celebrated. He is most comfortable conquering uncharted territory. As vice president of Mercury Records in 1961, Quincy was the first high-level black executive at a major label. With the release of *The Pawnbroker* in 1963, Quincy became the first African-American composer to score a major Hollywood movie. (He would ultimately score 33 before turning his attention to other pursuits.) Michael Jackson's *Thriller* album, produced by Quincy in 1982, sold in excess of 40 million copies—the best selling record in history. The list of gold and platinum records Quincy has worked on seems endless and includes titles from the 32 albums he has released as leader. A quick inventory of his awards reveals 27 Grammys, the Grammy Legend award, an Emmy, seven honorary doctorates, five NAACP Image awards, arts prizes from three foreign governments, and much more.

masters of music

Born Quincy Delight Jones Jr. in Chicago in 1933 and raised around Seattle, Quincy was smitten by the muse as a child. By the time he was 14 years old, he was studying trumpet and playing locally with parturient r&b artists Bumps Blackwell and a then-16-year-old singer named Ray Charles. The "Q" absorbed all he could playing in Seattle pickup orchestras behind touring artists like Billie Holiday and Billy Eckstine, and studying their big-band charts over the shoulders of their arrangers.

He came to Lawrence Berk's Schillinger House [now Berklee] in an effort to slake his thirst for musical knowledge. (Today he is a member of Berklee's board of overseers.) An offer to become trumpeter and arranger for Lionel Hampton followed within a year, luring Quincy to New York where he met every jazz legend of the day. During his three-year tenure with Hamp, Quincy traversed Europe and made his first recordings. He left to freelance as arranger, producer, and trumpeter for jazz luminaries James Moody, Clifford Brown, Dinah Washington, Duke Ellington, Cannonball Adderley, Dizzy Gillespie, and Sonny Stitt.

In 1957, he relocated to Paris to arrange and conduct recording sessions for Barclay Disques. At the same time, he studied composition with famed classical pedagogue Nadia Boulanger, whose pupils included Igor Stravinsky, Aaron Copland, and Heitor Villa Lobos.

The '60s found Quincy back in New York and then relocating to Los Angeles while spinning gold with Leslie Gore ("It's My Party"), Frank Sinatra and Count Basie, Sammy Davis Jr., and Ringo Starr; and scoring for the TV show *Ironside* and top films. The '70s unfolded with Quincy receiving a Grammy for his own *Smackwater Jack* album, producing chart-bound recordings for Donny Hathaway, Aretha Franklin, the Brothers Johnson, Michael Jackson, Ashford and Simpson, Rufus and Chaka Khan, and film and TV scores, including the soundtrack to *Roots*—the most watched series in television history.

Quincy dominated the '80s as the preeminent pop producer of a pair of multi-platinum albums for Michael Jackson, one for Donna Summer, and the mega-hit "We Are the World." He launched his own Qwest Records and released hit-laden discs by George Benson, James Ingram, Frank Sinatra, Patty Austin, and his own

1989 multi-Grammy winner *Back on the Block*. He also coproduced his first film, *The Color Purple*, directed by Steven Spielberg, starring Quincy's discovery, Oprah Winfrey. His adventures for the '90s include founding *Vibe* magazine, a journal of black urban culture (now a weekly TV show), and Qwest Broadcasting, which is acquiring television properties across America.

Now in his mid-60s, Quincy shows no sign of slowing his incredible pace. His new multimedia coventure with Time Warner, Quincy Jones-David Salzman Entertainment, will produce movies, TV shows, stage plays, recordings, and more. Q calls it his most momentous undertaking yet, one which will eclipse his past achievements. A tall order, but if he said it, odds are he'll deliver.

 What made you decide to leave Seattle and come to Schillinger House in 1951?

When I was a kid, well before MTV, we could only hear about our idols through the grapevine. We'd hear what Charlie Parker, Miles, and Dizzy were doing. In Seattle I never had any close contact with them. I wanted to get closer to New York, the mecca. I also wanted to go to the school very badly. In Boston, I figured I could go to school and I'd be close to New York. I'd heard a lot about the Schillinger House being a place where you could really study jazz orchestration, technique, and soloing. It was one of the most unique schools in the country at that time.

 Do you remember any significant musical developments you experienced during your time at the school?

As a student, you are at a very embryonic and impressionable stage—everything touches you. Your mouth is open about everything you're going through. It is a great experience developing as a musician. I took 10 subjects a day, from ear training to arranging, to orchestra laboratory. Herb Pomeroy and Charlie Mariano were students then too. In order to afford tuition, I had to play at a place called Izzy Ort's, which was a real dive down in Boston's "combat zone." It was funky down there. I worked with Preston Sandiford, a pianist and arranger, and an alto player named Bunny Campbell. They were very good musicians and were influential in my musical development.

Q. Did you continue your affiliations with the people you met at the school?

Alan Dawson was the drummer in Lionel Hampton's band. We used to call him The Senator—a very dignified guy. Trombonist Lenny Johnson was in my band in Europe. [Johnson and Dawson later joined the Berklee faculty.]

Q. You toured Europe with Lionel Hampton after leaving the school and participated in some covert recording sessions there because Hamp didn't want his band taking offers to record.

Yeah. We had to write the material on trains and planes coming from Oslo. Gigi Gryce told us we had these recording sessions in Stockholm. We wanted to record for two reasons. Monk Montgomery [Hampton's bassist] had been given one of the first electric basses by Leo Fender just before we went on tour. We liked the instrument a lot because its sound was so pronounced. It turned out to be one of the godfathers of rock and roll, but we used it in a jazz context. We were also excited about recording the players in the band—Art Farmer, Clifford Brown, Gigi Gryce, Annie Ross, and Jimmy Cleveland. We were warned not to record solo projects, but were determined to do these sessions. We figured if we left the hotel at 2:00 a.m. it would be dark enough that no one would see us. But when we climbed out on the fire escape, it was as bright as noon because of the midnight sun and anyone could have seen us.

Q. In Europe, you studied with Nadia Boulanger, were friends with Messiaen, and later visited Villa Lobos at his home in Rio during a South American tour with Dizzy. Do you feel contact with leading classical composers had much influence on your music at that early stage?

I was just friends with people like Messiaen and Boulez. My primary association was with Nadia Boulanger at her home in Paris. That was an experience of a lifetime. She had a big influence on me and still does to this day.

Q. What do you feel Boulanger brought out of you musically?

She said that Americans came to her in Paris trying to learn how to write the great American symphony. She told me, "Your own culture has the richest music in the world, and that is the mine that needs to be ored and explored." That was some great advice. I had already been doing that, but she confirmed for me that I was going in the right direction.

Q. Do you still feel as you did in the 1950s that the natural resources of jazz are so vast and deep that there is no likelihood of their being exhausted?

I still feel that way. Nobody is within 30 light-years of what Charlie Parker and the 52nd Street musicians laid down in terms of breakthroughs. Do you know a soloist who has the dynamic vitality of Charlie Parker? I can't think of one. We've got a lot of brilliant soloists today, but there are no Charlie Parkers around. Think of what Dizzy, Miles, and Parker contributed, then add saxophonists like Coltrane and Lester Young. It doesn't get any better than that.

Q. What is your view of the vitality of jazz since the revolutionary mood of the bebop era has long passed and many other influences have become part of the genre.

Everybody keeps getting hung up with categories. There are a lot of contradictions in Black music because of categories. Black music feels like a music that is a voice of the whole people, so it will jump around to different sources at various times—from rhythm and blues to delta blues, or jazz. There is always something fermenting somewhere even if it is in the rap and hip hop community. It is always going to be very vital to what is going on.

It has not been considered an "art music" even though a lot of it is art music. Its creators didn't think of it that way until the Billy Eckstine band and the movement growing out of the Charlie Parker and Jay McShann bands. The Billy Eckstine band was the real spawning ground—it had great people in it: Dexter Gordon, Gene Ammons, Bird, Miles, Dizzy, Art Blakey, Sarah Vaughan. At that time, the musicians decided they didn't want to be entertainers anymore, they wanted to be pure musicians. The consequences were grave. The alienation and rejection that followed caused a lot of musicians to get deeper into drugs.

Coming from bebop, was it a big shift for you to get into producing commercial sessions for Barclay Disques in Paris and other companies in New York around 1957?

It was an expansion. I didn't shift gears, I just went into another territory. When I was 14, back in Seattle, working with musicians like Ernestine Anderson and Ray Charles, we had to play everything. We'd start at 7:00 p.m. at the Seattle Tennis Club wearing cardigans and bow ties playing dinner music and we'd try to sneak some bebop in. At 10:00 p.m., we'd change clothes and go play at the Black clubs like the Rocking Chair and the Booker T. Washington Educational Social Club doing r&b, comedy shows, strip music, and funk. At 3:00 in the morning the musicians—even the touring musicians passing through town—would go to the Elks Club, where we'd play bebop until 7:00 a.m. That was the ritual.

We played a lot of different styles of music—including schottisches or "Claire de Lune." At one point we tried to make everything sound hip because we were such beboppers. Then Ray Charles said we should just play each style with its own soul. That was a good lesson; it all had its own vitality when we let it stay pure.

 Have you identified any universal qualities among the successful musicians with whom you have worked through the years?

Yeah. A unique, God-given talent given to a person who understands that he or she has an obligation to develop, nurture, and build it. The most communicable characteristic would be sincerity—believing in what they are doing. That is what is going to communicate. That is why I am not hung up on musical categories and thinking this is going to work, or people will like this. The charts today are so diverse. You will find *Lion King* on one hand and *Forrest Gump* on the other, rap stuff, or monks singing Gregorian chant. It's pretty diversified.

 In recent years, you have produced big events like the Clinton inaugural concert. What do you think people are expecting when they hire Quincy Jones for a production?

I don't know. I hope they expect a good show that is interesting and has some integrity. The inaugural was to show everyone coming together in America—the melting pot. So we dealt with a very multicultural platform and had artists representing all kinds of American music. It was a very exciting night; it all came together in very little time, but man, it was cold out there at the Lincoln Memorial.

 Of all the offers coming into your office these days, what projects are you most likely to sign on for?

Well, I pass on 99 percent of them because so much comes in. Now that we're a multimedia company, we get hundreds of cassettes, videotapes, scripts, and any idea anyone has for a magazine, TV special, mini-series, a Broadway show, a film, a video game—we get all of it. Most of what comes off the street doesn't work, but we get an equal amount from very reputable people. Actor Larry Fishburne, who was in *The Color Purple*, wrote a script, which I'm getting ready to read now. When you get things from people like that with a real commitment, it makes you want to support them.

 Are you committing to produce any albums?

No. That's one thing I can't be promiscuous about. It takes a lot of time. Even for Michael Jackson I don't have the time. In the '80s I had it, but in the '90s it's just not there. I could do my own album. I've been trying to turn my projects into multimedia ones that will have more of a life than a record will. I'm writing a street musical now for a record.

 Will your new company try to find a TV or film use for all your new ventures?

Yes, when it makes a good organic fit. It is easier to do a project if it has more applications than one. Maybe it could be a stage play, a film, a record, and an interactive CD-ROM. But if we like something that is good for just one application, we may go ahead and do it. Our logo describes us having one foot in the 20th century and one in the 21st. I'm enjoying it very much. We have done a lot of homework on the converging technologies and about how new communications systems are going to work. We are in one of the significant technological revolutions that civilization has seen since the invention of the printing press.

 So you will want to see four applications for any given project you undertake now?

It doesn't have to have all of them, as long as it is multifaceted. It is nice when we can see that it will work for two or three applications. But if we like something that is good for just one application, we go ahead and do it. We are not governed by that, we can make our own decisions.

 Is there any project you have underway that you could discuss?

We have a lot of movies right now, but they are hard to talk about until you get all the people signed. Actually, until the cameras are rolling, you can't be sure that everything is going to happen the way it is planned. Be assured that we have some very exciting things going on. One of the films we have discussed is *A Star Is Born* with Whitney Houston and Denzel Washington.

 How many people do you have on staff?

For the record company I have 50 to 60. We have 46 people in New York working on *Vibe* magazine. We have gotten a lot of interest in doing a TV show called the *Vibe Tribe*, so it is likely we will be doing that soon.

 Do you still compose just for the sake of writing—with no project in the wings?

I do it all the time. I have always got a few music projects that are my own thing. I have a basket of my ideas on snippets of music paper.

Is it possible for a young musician to have a career as all-encompassing as yours, or has the industry expanded and changed too much since your early days to permit that?

I think it is possible, maybe more so. A lot of the mining, so to speak, has been done. There was a tribute to Benny Carter recently, and in my speech I mentioned that not only did Benny lead us, and show us the light, but he would lift us on his back and take us into the light. That is the spirit that I think should be prevalent today—taking the young ones in to really see what it is about and bringing along all the history of the past with them.

There are some really beautiful things that have happened in the past that should be brought forward. We shouldn't deal as if we have a disposable culture.

 Is there one accomplishment from your five decades in the music business that stands out above the rest?

The ones we are going to do in the next four years will stand out above everything. It is astounding, that's the way I feel. I have been fortunate to have been involved in a lot of very exciting things in the past. But what's to come is even more exciting. This is an exciting time to be alive. I wouldn't trade the time that I got on earth for anything—it was just right. I've felt and experienced a lot of different attitudes and eras. I thank God for it.

Herb Pomeroy

herb pomeroy looks back

After a 40-year career, Berklee's top jazz composition teacher has a different perspective on life and music.

THOUGH HIS NAME IS NOT A HOUSEHOLD WORD, Herb Pomeroy's musical influence as an educator has been felt around the world. A busy professional trumpeter and band leader as well, Pomeroy has shared the stage with many jazz greats—including Charlie Parker at some of Bird's Boston appearances.

Herb began teaching at Berklee over four decades ago, and helped to nurture the talents of many in his jazz composition and arranging courses. He also directed the college's premier jazz ensemble, the Berklee Recording Orchestra.

During his 111 semesters at Berklee, some of the music industry's most prominent composers, arrangers, and instrumentalists came under the influence of his tutelage. The short list includes TV and film composers Alan Silvestri, Alf Clausen, and Rob Mounsey; Columbia recording artist and composer Toshiko Akiyoshi; saxophonist Ernie Watts; and Atlantic Studios Senior Vice President Arif Mardin.

Herb was raised in a home that fostered his musical development. His mother Alice Pomeroy, a pianist trained at the New England Conservatory, worked professionally as a 1920s-style jazz player. When he was 11, after he and his mother saw a movie starring Louis Armstrong, Herb decided that he had to take up the trumpet. He immersed himself in Dixieland jazz and the early swing efforts of Armstrong and Benny Goodman. By the time he was in his freshman year of high school, he was playing professionally with dance bands around his home-town of Gloucester, Massachusetts.

A turning point in his musical direction came when a friend loaned him some early bebop recordings by Dizzy Gillespie and Charlie Parker. At first, Herb could not accept the new music, but after a few more listenings, he perceived that this was the direction jazz was going, and became deeply engrossed in bebop.

At Williston Academy, a prep school in Easthampton, Massachusetts, Herb met other students interested in music. He set his sights on becoming a jazz musician despite the fact that his father and grandfather, both dentists, were prodding Herb to follow in their footsteps. While home during the summer of 1948, Herb took private lessons at Schillinger House (now Berklee). He studied piano with Berklee founder Lawrence Berk's partner Harry Smith, trumpet with Fred Berman, and arranging with Dick Hogan. Most of his fellow students were returned ser-vicemen. The 18-year-old Herb found the atmosphere among so many mature musicians to be exhilarating.

After the summer, Herb went back to Williston for his senior year. He graduated second in his class, with prizes in math and trigonometry. That fall, Herb enrolled at Harvard in a pre-dental program. By the middle of the year, Herb felt like a fish out of water at the Ivy League college. After graduating second in his class at Williston, by contrast, Herb now found himself on academic probation at Harvard. Music beckoned him more than German, philosophy, or the other sub-jects he was studying. He left Harvard for Schillinger House and a career in music.

After completing five semesters by 1952, Herb performed around New England with a number of acts before hitting the road with the Lionel Hampton and Stan Kenton bands and the Serge Chaloff sextet. Berklee founder Lawrence Berk asked Herb to join the Berklee faculty in the fall of 1955. Over the course of his 40-year tenure, Herb developed three highly specialized courses: Line Writing, Jazz Composition, and Arranging in the Style of Duke Ellington, which have drawn students from around the world to his classes.

Herb continued an active performing career leading the 16-piece Herb Pomeroy Orchestra throughout the Northeast. The group released four critically acclaimed albums for the Roulette, United Artists, and Shiah record labels. Their first, *Life Is a Many Splendored Gig*, stayed in the top 10 on the *Down Beat jazz* charts for nearly five months in 1957.

In the late '60's, Herb was commissioned to create two scores for the Boston Ballet. "The Road of the Phoebe Snow" and "Wilderness of Mirrors" are based on the music of Ellington and Mingus respectively. His original score to "Jolly Chocolate" was commissioned by the National Jazz Ensemble, and premiered at New York's Alice Tully Hall at Lincoln Center in 1974. Widely noted as a specialist in big band jazz, Herb was sent by the U.S. State Department in 1962 to Malaysia as a music consultant to the Malaya Radio Orchestra. A similar assignment from the State Department in 1968 sent him on a cultural exchange to Finland to direct an orchestra at a Finnish government-sponsored arts festival. Over the past decade, Herb has been in demand internationally to conduct concerts with the New Music Orchestra of Finland, the Stockholm Jazz Orchestra, North German Radio Orchestra, the New Music Orchestra of Copenhagen, and the H.E.D. Music Center Orchestra in Tel Aviv.

Entering retirement, Herb doesn't plan to slow his pace. He looks forward to practicing his trumpet again, and continuing to travel internationally to play, conduct, and present seminars.

It was fitting closure to Herb's educational career that he received Berklee's honorary doctorate at the May 7, 1995 commencement for his achievements. He went into retirement feeling that he excelled in the career he desired and that he carried on the Pomeroy family tradition to finally become a "doctor."

 What was the musical atmosphere like at Berklee when you were a student?

A few soloists around the school were bebop oriented but most everyone else was writing dance band and big band arrangements. There were not many faculty members who were primarily jazz musicians at that time. That changed over the next decade as the school evolved. I was in classes with people who were jazz oriented—like [pianists] Ray Santisi ['54] and Bob Winter ['54], [saxophonist] Charlie Mariano ['52], and [bassist] Ray Oliveri ['53].

 What are some recollections of your gigs with Charlie Parker?

When I speak of working with Charlie Parker, I do it with a sense of humility. I was 23 years old and I really had no right being on the bandstand with him. The reason I was fortunate enough to work with him was because his career was on the way down. This was after he had worked with Miles, Kenny Durham, and Red Rodney. Bird would come to town and play with a pickup rhythm section and trumpet player. He usually called trumpeter Joe Gordon when he came to Boston, but I got the call that time.

Ironically, in 1953, the week I was on stage at the Hi-Hat Club with Bird, the class I would have graduated with at Harvard was on stage with caps and gowns on. I felt there was some just-due going on there. I remember walking into the club with my knees shaking, but Bird was great to me. Here was this man who had virtually been a god to me for eight or nine years whispering in my ear "Herbert, you're wailing." I knew I wasn't wailing though.

He was always a gentleman to the musicians on the stand. If he called a tune and the piano player said he knew it, and then scuffled a bit, Bird wouldn't pitch a fit. I have worked with lesser name artists who would do a big ego number when that happened. Bird would just go stand next to the piano player and call out the changes to him. I greatly respected him for that. He counted off the "52nd Street Theme" so fast that the drummer had to use two hands just to play time on the ride cymbal. Bird played four or five choruses and then went back into the head. The piano player and I were very grateful he didn't have us solo. He was very considerate that way.

 Shortly thereafter, you went on the road with Lionel Hampton. What was road work like back then?

In 1953, I might have earned as much as $80 a week playing in Boston. But if I made $40 to $50, we got by. I lived with my family in a cold-water flat in Charlestown with no heat; rent was $21 a month. Times were hard, so when I auditioned for Hampton and he said I'd earn $150 a week, it sounded great.

I quit my local gigs and went to New York to rehearse with the band. Lionel's wife, Gladys, came in and told us we'd be getting paid pro rata, $21 each night. So if we worked seven nights, we would get about $150. Frequently we only worked four nights. After taxes, and $35 a week for food and rooming expenses, I would send what was left home.

Lionel mostly played one-nighters. Sometimes we would not check into a hotel for four nights while we traveled 700 miles to the next city. We would finish a gig, and travel night and day to the next one. Often we didn't check into our hotel until after we played. The band was fun, but it wasn't easy working with Hamp. When I quit in the spring of 1954, I was pretty disillusioned. I started thinking about college again and took out my books from Harvard.

 How did you join the Berklee faculty?

After leaving Hampton, I went on the road again with the Kenton band and then with [baritone saxophonist] Serge Chaloff's sextet. In the summer of '55, at Joe Viola's recommendation, Larry Berk called and asked if I would like to start teaching that fall. I had a wife and two children at the time and I'd had enough of the road by then. Even though it was a hot sextet, I left Serge and came to the school. It was not too difficult for me to say "yes" to Larry Berk.

I often thanked Larry for providing me the opportunity to do my thing in an academic environment unaffected by any aspects of the commercial world. I was able to write the music I felt was honest, and to be in a school where so many great students from around the world come to study.

Over the years, many of the members of my band were Berklee faculty members. I could not have had a band of that caliber without Berklee existing. The school has made it possible for a number of musicians to have a great teaching experience and keep their playing career alive without having to go on the road. I worked with faculty members like Ray Santisi [piano] and John Neves [bass], trumpeters Greg Hopkins and Lennie Johnson. Also, without the school, perhaps musicians like Arif Mardin ['61] or Mike Gibbs ['63] might have stayed back in Istanbul and Southern Rhodesia.

 Is there any truth to the rumor that you are not really a fan of big band jazz?

I tell my classes, tongue-in-cheek, that I hate big bands [laughs]. Of course I say this after they have taken my three arranging classes, in the last week of the semester. Those who have come to know me know I'm sort of jiving, but the others will be taken aback.

I always loved playing in a small group. I reacted as a young person to the physical excitement of a big band—the rich harmonies, intricate sax solos, and high trumpets. But I enjoy the interaction of a small group better.

 How did the Line Writing course develop?

During the first few years I taught, I knew in my heart that I was a poor teacher. My thoughts weren't organized for presenting the material in the classroom. Some of my students knew more than I did. I began by putting examples on the board that I knew worked, and excerpts from various artists' scores. I began to note principles for why certain things worked in these arrangements.

As a trumpet player, I knew well that the second, third, and fourth voices in a section were usually unmusical. They were just harmony notes from a vertical structure under the melody, strung together with little concern for their melodic content. Playing those would turn me off. The melody would be soaring while the second trumpet part would have a bunch of repeated notes, or would have wide interval leaps while the melody was smooth. I started to look at ways to make the under parts musical and have melodic shape.

After working leading bands from scores for thousands of hours, I have developed a good eye-ear relationship. Unless it is something very unusual, I can see music on paper and know how it will sound. This eye-ear relationship was very important in developing the course materials.

 Q. Can you mention any students who really grabbed the concepts you were teaching and ran with them?

There have been so many, and I don't like to take a lot of credit for what they have gone on to do. Alf Clausen ['66] was one. He was also the first to play French horn in the Recording Band. Alan Broadbent ['69] was another. He took a number of courses with me, played piano in the recording band, and wrote a lot of music for the group. In the '60s and '70s we had the Richard Levy Memorial concerts for composers, and one year Broadbent was chosen to present an entire concert of his music. [Levy '66 was Berklee student and trumpet player when he died in a car accident. Levy's parents funded an annual concert in his memory.]

Jaxon Stock ['71] became a great jazz composer; he is one of my all-time favorite former students. He is a gloriously talented musician, and a very down-to-earth person. He also put on a Levy concert. His mother and father, who were Dixieland players, came out from San Francisco to play a few tunes in his concert. It was one of those events that had everything—the warmth of the family and the best of Berklee. Jaxon came here with a great understanding of older jazz styles and was able to lay contemporary styles onto that foundation. I had a great visit with them all two years ago in Monterey.

Hal Crook ['71] was another great student, a wonderful writer and now, a faculty member. Mike Gibbs ['63] also studied with me. He has influences from outside the college too. While he was a student here, he was going to New York once a week to study with Gunther Schuller. He has broadened his horizons beautifully.

Teaching was a two way street—these people really enriched my life. It was fulfilling to have students who came here without ever having written for band, and in a few years they are writing great charts.

Q. Do you have any anecdotes about the students you have taught who later became greats?

I remember the first day I met Arif Mardin ['61]. He is a classy human being. I remember seeing him at the corner of Gloucester and Newbury with a hat on. He didn't look like the typical Berklee student. He came here without having any of the scores he'd written or played. The first arrangement he brought for my orchestra was top professional-level writing. He left Boston to work at Atlantic Records, first as a studio assistant, and now he is a senior vice president.

Q. Have there been people in your classes whose talent developed and surprised you?

The first year I taught, Larry Berk wanted the school to be involved with the local community. He started a high school ensemble, which I directed. A young fellow came in to audition for the piano spot, and I didn't choose him for the group. He let me know how disappointed he was. That was Roger Kellaway.

I hated to audition people for the recording band, but when we didn't have someone to fill a certain chair, we would hold auditions. Someone who I didn't choose was the great drummer Steve Smith. In hindsight, that was probably a mistake, seeing how he has developed.

Q. Can you speak about the two years you were the host of a TV show on jazz?

It was for WGBH in Boston from '65 to '67. I would interview major jazz artists like Earl Hines, Jimmy Witherspoon, Stan Getz, and Lee Konitz live on the air. Live TV is risky—sometimes it was great, sometimes you would bomb. Sonny Rollins came on wearing a New York Yankees baseball cap. No matter what I asked him, he would steer the conversation back to the Yankees. Some of the shows were wonderful though.

Q. You often state your feeling that people are more important than music. How did you come to feel this way?

It is easy for me to espouse that philosophy, but it is not so easy for me to go back and say what brought me to it. After the death of my second wife in 1982, I looked at a lot of things in my life.

I had been working really hard to provide a decent life for my family. I was teaching five days at Berklee and two at MIT, leading my own band in 45 to 50 dates a year, contracting the Boston Garden and the Wilbur Theater, and working at the Colonial Theater as a trumpeter 20 to 30 weeks a year. It was ludicrous. I would look at my book and tell my wife that I wouldn't have a day off for the next 42 days. After she died, I did some soul searching.

In other musicians, I would see the drive they brought to their music, and I would see an imbalance there. It is healthy for a person from their teen years into their 20s to do that, but there is so much more in life. I didn't start coming out of that until I was in my 40s. Don't misunderstand me, I still love music. I am very fortunate to have found a new wife at age 60 who is a glorious woman. Being in her presence is a richer experience than music ever was.

I have made many musical acquaintances. I've played gigs with them, we've sat in the band room at intermission, and driven to and from gigs together. Faculty member Greg Hopkins has played trumpet in my band for 20 years. I keep telling him we have to find time to get together at my house and sit and talk a bit. Coming to feel these things has made me realize how important people are.

Next to the love I have for my family is the love I feel for the musician I'm standing next to on the bandstand. To be giving as openly as you do in jazz is very special. I want to know more about those people. But we were all so involved in our work that for many years those relationships stayed on the surface. In my early years, I had put music on a pedestal—to me, music was the most important thing. It felt good to love music for all those years, but I came to realize that I was wrong.... It is people that are most important.

Harvie Swartz

the bottom of his heart

Ace bassist Harvie Swartz '70 is at the top of his form handling the low-end chores.

HARVIE SWARTZ '70, ONE OF NEW YORK'S HARDEST-WORKING JAZZMEN, has always resisted the temptation to play the music that was in vogue if it wasn't what was in his heart. Though he came of age musically during the British rock invasion of the '60s, the alluring sounds from Liverpool and the Mersey Beat had little impact on his direction. Since he was 15, Harvey has stayed his course with jazz as the lodestar.

Growing up in Marblehead, Massachusetts, Harvie began his musical odyssey as a pianist before discovering the bass. There was little sustenance in his surroundings to nourish his growing hunger for jazz. His high school band director disliked America's only indigenous art form, as did all but a few of his friends. Nonetheless, while still a teen, Harvie became a fixture on Sunday afternoons at Boston's [now defunct] Jazz Workshop. Frequently making the trip alone with only enough money for bus fare, admission, and one Coke, Harvie would stay until the last note faded from sets by Coltrane, Mingus, Monk, Miles, and other greats.

Ignoring the advice of a high school guidance counselor to pursue trade school, Harvie opted to study composition and arranging at Berklee. Even though his keyboard work was strong enough to earn him the pianist's chair in Phil Wilson's Dues Band, he switched to bass after a few semesters and immersed himself in mastering that instrument. After graduation, he spent a summer roaming across

Europe and got a glimpse of the player's life backing several renowned American jazz expatriates at festivals and clubs in Denmark.

Returning to the U.S. in the dead of winter 1971, Harvie found the jazz scene in Boston as bleak as the weather. A promise of gigs in New York soon lured him to Manhattan and he never left. Bass in hand, he has traveled throughout the world as a jazz emissary. The number of albums featuring his bass work tops 100. The long and varied roster of musicians he has worked with includes Stan Getz, Phil Woods, Pacquito D'Rivera, Al Di Meola, Jim Hall, Michael Brecker, Jimmy Heath, Chet Baker, Toots Thielmans, James Brown, Jean Pierre Rampal, Ben Verdery, David Sanborn, Jane Ira Bloom, and many more. He has recorded 50 of his own compositions and released seven albums under his own name.

A packed schedule kept him touring for seven months last year. His days in New York were divided between recording sessions, club work, and his teaching position at Manhattan School of Music. We spoke during some of his rare downtime at his home in Westchester County, a peaceful outpost along the Hudson north of Manhattan.

 You became interested in jazz at 15 when most kids your age were listening to the Beatles. What attracted you to jazz instead?

I liked what I heard on the radio, but I was drawn to other kinds of music. I liked the Motown artists. I found out later that James Jamerson was the bassist on that stuff. He was a great innovator on the instrument. The blues hooked me though—the blues feel was it. When I was 15, I heard "Bag's Groove," and immediately loved the jazz style of blues.

 How did you end up coming to Berklee?

Quite truthfully, Berklee was about the only place to study jazz at that time. I entered as a pianist and studied with Dean Earl. I was not really serious when I was younger; to me it was just fun to play. Maybe if I had stayed with piano I might not have gone anywhere. It is a rhetorical question, but what if Miles played drums, would he have reached the heights he did?

When I was in high school I picked up the *Waltz for Debbie* album by Bill Evans with Scott LaFaro on bass. I had a terrible stereo, and I could never hear bass on other recordings, but on this one Paul Motian and Bill Evans played very gently so Scott could be heard. On that record the bass came out beautifully—I still think it is one of the best recordings of a bass. After I heard what the bass could do, it stuck in my mind. He had wonderful time, a nice sound, great notes. I was drawn to the bass after that.

 Were there any courses or instructors at Berklee that had an impact on your direction?

I have to mention Herb Pomeroy—it was amazing to work under him. John Bavicchi was another. When I started his composition course I was working hard at it, and he would compliment me on what I wrote. To get a compliment from John was a big deal. John LaPorta was also great.

 The summer after graduation from Berklee, you went to Europe and connected with some major jazz expatriates like Dexter Gordon and Johnny Griffin. How did that happen?

By the time I was finishing at Berklee, I was the bass player in the recording band for a year—George Mraz had already left. Herb Pomeroy asked me to go to Europe and play at the Montreux Festival with the MIT band, which he directed at the time. Their bass player said he couldn't go. I had no work, so I said yes. Herb called back to say that now their bass player said he could play the gig, and Herb really had to use him. He told me he'd get me a ticket anyway, and I went.

After the festival, I hung around Switzerland and went into a music store and started playing a bass. The store owner came running up saying "maestro, maestro!" The next thing I knew, I'd bought the bass. I ended up in Denmark and began playing with Jimmy Heath and Dexter Gordon. I began getting recommended for other gigs. My biggest thrill over there was playing with Art Taylor, Kenny Drew, Dexter Gordon, Johnny Griffin, and Drew Moore.

Q. What was your next move?

As it got to be winter, I was running out of money so I got a ticket home. I came back to Boston, and jazz was dead there—this was 1971. I got a gig in a rock band playing electric bass. For about a year I didn't play any acoustic. I started getting calls to play acoustic bass at clubs like Lennie's on the Turnpike, backing up [saxophonists] Zoot Sims, Al Cohn, [trumpeter] Charlie Shavers, [pianist] Mose Allison, and others. I met Mike Abene, pianist for singer Chris Connors, and he invited me to New York for some gigs. I was petrified. The thought of going to New York was something I'd never dreamed of doing. But things were so slow around Boston that I started doing gigs in New York. I had to be pushed though. I'm the kind of guy who thinks he can't swim, but when I get pushed into the pool, I swim.

Q. What made you pursue acoustic bass at a time when electric bass was more popular?

Early on I had gotten some very good offers to play electric bass for some big name groups. I turned them down because I just didn't want to go into it full time. Don't get me wrong, I think electric bass is a phenomenal instrument and is as demanding to play as acoustic bass. I just really wanted to play acoustic.

Q. Was it discouraging then when acoustic bass amplification systems were not great and leading artists like Miles Davis' group and Weather Report were using electric bass?

I just decided to tough it out. I had a lot of bad years financially. I worked around the city playing duo gigs when New York had the cabaret law, which didn't allow clubs to use drums. I went as long as six or eight months without working with a drummer. I did those duo gigs for years and learned a lot.

I never had it easy, and if things did seemed to be getting easy, I would make them hard. I'm always trying to push myself to get into something new without being trendy. I tell people I've never been in, but I've never been out. I've carved my own little niche in the business. I've always gone for the sounds in my head that I wanted to hear. Over the years I've been involved with some innovative groups that never got really famous.

 Can you name a few?

I was in one of the original fusion bands, Silverlight, with [keyboardist] Barry Miles. We were playing that kind of music when no one was doing it. I did two records with him. From '74 to '76 I was in Double Image with Dave Freedman and Mike DiPasqua. We recorded for the Enja and then ECM labels and toured all over the world playing major festivals. People used to think that the unique thing about that band was that it had both vibes and marimba. The instrumentation was kind of a gimmick; what made the band special was the compositional approach.

I played in Steve Kuhn's band with Sheila Jordan. That was an unusual group—it had a singer who wasn't the leader of the group and whose voice was used as another instrument. Around that time, Sheila and I began rehearsing our bass and voice duo.

 You've said that the bass and voice duo is one of your favorite combinations to work with.

Well, it is not just the instrumentation or that I love the sound of just bass and voice. It is working with Sheila specifically because she is a master in that setting. Many are skeptical about what we will do all night with just bass and voice, but we always end up getting encores and a standing ovation. People love it after they hear it. Something magical happens, we don't even know what it is—and don't try to find out. I try to be a bass orchestra by bowing, playing double stops, counter melodies, and scat singing.

 At one point, you considered yourself a composer, band leader, and bassist in that order. Do you still prioritize them like that?

I don't know now. When I said that I was really trying to get my band Urban Earth going [circa 1988]. The obstacles became too great. It wasn't that the people didn't like the music, the business wasn't too kind to me. That soured me on being a band leader. I just consider myself a musician now. A few labels have made offers for me to do records, but I'm enjoying doing a lot of different music. I get to play in so many styles—avant-garde, salsa, Brazilian, straight-ahead swing, and post-bebop jazz.

 What do you think has enabled you to become such an in-demand sideman?

I come into a band and give 100 percent to the music. If I don't feel I can do that, I turn down the job. I really try to add to the music—whatever the style. Sometimes people don't know where to put me stylistically. Those who heard me with Barry Miles, Double Image, or Steve Kuhn didn't know I could play bebop.

Kind of by accident I got on a gig with Derrick Smith, a swinging, straight-ahead pianist. I knew I wasn't his first choice, but when we played he loved it and I have been playing on and off with his quartet for 12 years. He jokes about it, saying he'd thought of me as an avant-garde player who would play all this weird stuff. He was surprised that I was into Duke Ellington and the roots of jazz.

A sax player, who will go unnamed, came and heard my duo with Sheila, and now will never call me. He thinks that I would play that way in his jazz group. But I always try my best to play whatever the musical situation demands.

 What would you tell those who want a career as a sideman?

First, you have to be open to a lot of styles—understand funk, Brazilian, rock, different jazz styles. When you come into a situation, you should identify what it is that the leader does, and figure out how to fit your playing in. You want to figure out how you can make the band sound better. If you come in thinking of how you can make yourself sound better, you will be a crummy sideman. Someone I played with told me she thought I had a way of playing with a band as if I was looking at it from an overview. If someone nods for me to take a solo, I may pass on it if I have just soloed on the three previous tunes. My attitude is to make the music go well overall, not to try and dazzle everybody with lots of solos.

 So you are most interested in sticking with the primary role on the bass?

Well, I'll take the spotlight and I'll give my solo 100 percent, but my objective is to balance the band over the evening and play with the right feel. It takes a lot of thought and experience. There are many bassists who have a lot of technique and can do a lot on the bass, but I don't feel they are adding much to the music.

 You have done a lot of records with guitarists. Is there something about the combination of guitar and bass that attracts you?

I never was that into guitar until I started playing a lot with Mike Stern. I would have him play a jazz tune in his own way on my early records. I encouraged him and he gave me a lot of great musical things in return. That got me really excited about the guitar.

There is kind of a "Boston guitar sound" that I wanted to explore. Pat Metheny, Mick Goodrick ['67], John Scofield ['73], John Abercrombie ['67], Mike Stern ['75], Jay Azzolina ['76], and Wayne Krantz ['76] all come from that style. I wanted to document it on my *In a Different Light* CD. I wanted to have some of these guitarists play in a context that they hadn't been heard in before. The record has the only recorded bass and guitar duets with Scofield to date. I had Stern really stretch out—something he doesn't do on recordings. It was a very exciting project.

After hearing that, the Japanese BMG/Novus label asked me to do a quartet album, *Arrival*, with two guitars. They told me to use Marvin "Smitty" Smith ['81] on drums—which was great because I had been playing a lot with him. They said I could pick any two guitarists, so I chose Mick Goodrick and John Abercrombie because they have played together for 25 years but had never recorded together.

I wrote a bunch of material because the record company didn't want standards. I wrote very open and free tunes because I wanted John and Mick to retain their personalities and not to just come in and read a lot of notes.

How do you think the future looks for acoustic bass since pickup systems are improved and younger players like Christian McBride are championing the instrument?

Acoustic bass is going crazy—all the electric bassists want to double on it now. It is incredible how many young bassists are really serious about playing it. I have heard some new players really playing some stuff. I remember playing with Pat Metheny before I had a good pickup system. He kept telling me to turn up, but I couldn't get any louder. Now the bass can really blast, volume is not a problem.

How varied is your schedule?

Well, in the summer of 1995, I did a little tour of Europe with Sheila Jordan, then I played on and produced a CD for saxophonist Leonard Hochman, I produced a Brazilian record that featured Michael Brecker and Toninho Horta. Pianist Randy Klein ['71] and I finished our duo album called *Love Notes from the Bass*. I recorded a trio CD with Haru, a fine guitarist/composer from Japan, and Danny Gottlieb, and the following day I played on a children's album. I was also playing Tuesday nights with a very good salsa band.

Given your experiences, are you quick to recommend the jazz life to your young students?

I can't recommend or not recommend it. I say look into your heart, and ask yourself if you want to do this or not. If you have to think more than two seconds, you should do something else. I don't have a choice, I can't do anything else—I don't want to do anything else. I spent a lot of years "livin' off nickels and dimes" as Joe Lee Wilson used to say. I was willing to get married a little later in life, to not have a family, to be broke and not own a car for many years to do my music. I didn't question it. I did it because it is me.

I would recommend that whatever you do for work, you should enjoy it or you will resent it. You may not be a great musician, but if you love it so much, if it is all that matters to you and you can eke out a living at it, that's fine. I may regret some strategic moves I've made, but I have never regretted choosing music for a career. I am still picking up new things and will never come close to learning it all. I feel like I am looking at the grains of sand on a beach, and so far I only have a handful. That is how it feels to me every morning when I wake up.

Al Di Meola

no mystery

Two decades after RTF, Al Di Meola '74 is connecting with jazz and world music.

FOR AL DI MEOLA, THERE HAS BEEN NO MYSTERY involved with either break-ing into the business or sustaining a career among the most respected guitarists in the music industry. It was simple. All that was required were killer chops, to answer "yes" when Chick Corea asked him to join his band without an audition, the ability to devour Chick's treacherous charts, and then to wow a full house at Carnegie Hall later that week. Al was only 19 when he left Berklee to join Corea's Return to Forever (RTF) band, one of the most influential '70s fusion acts.

Al earned acclaim initially for his warp-speed lines and the searing tone of his Les Paul in concert and on record with RTF. He topped *Guitar Player* magazine's polls after RTF's *No Mystery* album earned a Grammy in 1975. Upon leaving RTF to lead his own group, nine further honors from *Guitar Player* (including induction into their Gallery of the Greats) and accolades from other magazines followed. With the release of *Land of the Midnight Sun*, his first solo album in 1976, Al proved himself a bankable artist and has been recording and performing around the world with top names in contemporary jazz ever since.

Highlights among his 18 post-RTF albums are a pair of acoustic guitar trio outings with Paco De Lucia and John McLaughlin. Their live album *Friday Night in San Francisco* was certified platinum. Later efforts with his eclectic acoustic project World Sinfonia documented Al's rich musical collaboration with the late

masters of music

Argentine tango composer Astor Piazzolla. For the last half of 1995, Al toured extensively and recorded with Rite of Strings, another superstar acoustic collaboration with bassist Stanley Clarke and violinist Jean Luc Ponty.

I caught up with Al for this interview at his northern New Jersey home a week after the Rite of Strings tour ended, before his much-anticipated reunion with De Lucia and McLaughlin. Al's home reflects his fascination with his Mediterranean cultural heritage. Some sculptures, mixed media works (oil on canvas with polenta) by Italian painter Andrea Vizzini, and a Salvador Dali lithograph are displayed near photos of past generations of Al's family in the foyer of his Spanish villa-style dwelling. As reflects in his music, Al is energetic, straightforward, spontaneous, and accessible. He paused for a wistful look back and a glimpse at the present realities.

 What do you think enables someone as young as you were to develop amazing technical facility at 19?

In recent years I have wondered why some people play for 30 years and don't have the technique of those who have played for 10 years. It may be more than just practice that develops technique. I did a guitar festival in Martinique and there were several classical guitarists on the bill. I asked a few of them about this and they were convinced that bone and muscle structure has a lot to do with technical ability. We never talk about that in the jazz or rock world.

 Do you think that is true in your case?

It could be. The guitarist's right hand seems to be a more fascinating subject than the left hand. I was taught basic alternate picking from the beginning and I worked really hard on it. The choice of rhythms I make within the range of my improvisations has a lot to do with my sound and a Latin sensibility.

 Can you share some highlights of your time at Berklee?

I had wanted to leave high school to come to Berklee instead of finishing my senior year. There was a way to do it, but I came after high school instead. After my first year at Berklee, I left to play with Barry Miles for a year. Then I came back. For me, everything was beneficial—arranging and the guitar classes. The courses were well laid out, and everything was applicable to my instrument. It was inspiring to be around all the musicians and to go to clubs at night. I am sorry it had to end so soon. I was enjoying learning, but when I got the offer to play with Chick Corea I had to take it because his was my favorite group at the time.

I am asked all over the world about Berklee, and I always say it was an extremely positive experience for me. Berklee helped lay the groundwork so I could handle the demands of playing with Chick and Return to Forever.

 Exactly how did that opportunity to work with Chick come about?

I had seen RTF in Boston at the Orpheum Theater. I expected to see Bill Connors playing guitar, but Earl Klugh was playing instead. As good a player as Earl is, he seemed out of place in that group. They were playing these high-energy instrumentals and then each group member would get a solo spot. For his solo, Earl played a standard like "Shadow of Your Smile." It didn't work. I mentioned to a friend that I really wanted to play with that band. He took it upon himself to find Chick and bug him until he listened to a tape of a Barry Miles show I played in '72 or '73. The timing was perfect, they wanted to make a change. I got a call from Chick asking me to come join the band.

I packed my bags and left Boston and never saw my apartment on Burbank Street or my girlfriend again. I had about 10 difficult charts to learn. Then, after two days of rehearsal, we played a sold-out concert at Carnegie Hall. RTF toured about 10 months a year for a few years. After three albums, I launched my solo career.

 After making such an auspicious debut with RTF, have you found audiences willing to follow the new musical directions you have pursued, or did they want you to continue what they first heard you doing?

Some fans have stayed, some who would like to hear the older stuff have gone. I have also gained new fans from the music I have made lately. There is no doubt about it, when I pick up the solid body electric guitar, audiences go crazy. It blows my mind because I may have played some really interesting and intelligent music before that, but it almost doesn't matter as soon as I pick up the Les Paul.

 That is surprising—by now, nearly half of your records are acoustic.

If I am doing an acoustic show, I don't have to worry about it. But, many shows will feature both sides. When I bring out the electric, it is as if the audience says, "Thanks for playing that other stuff, now let's get down to business." It may not be where my head is at, but it is a part of my personality from a time in my life.

 On your records, you have explored a lot of styles, from fusion, to flamenco, Brazilian, world music, to Latin. Do you have one favorite?

World Sinfonia is one I am most proud of. In terms of esthetics and musical depth, I think that group shows more of the range of my musical personality. I have roots in that music—tango. The roots of the tango go back to Napoli where my parents came from. My own renditions of Astor Piazzolla's works reflect my inner feelings. What I found to love about his work was the jazz and classical harmony as well as the spirit and soulfulness of tango and Neapolitan music. I did my own thing by adding percussion and putting the guitar at the forefront. Guitar is always in the background in tangos. There is a more rhythmic approach. My own pieces on the two World Sinfonia records are a little more contemporary, but somehow reflect the same spirit.

 Will there be a third World Sinfonia album?

I would like to do another. *The Heart of the Immigrants* album is a deep record. That one takes you places and connects with sentimental feelings. If I can fulfill my jazz sensibilities, some classical and ethnic ones, and feel sentimentality in the music, most of what I want to deliver is there. My early fusion music had less ethnic influence or sentimentality.

 Does the recognition received by winning magazine polls translate into a career boost?

If the poll is in a reputable magazine like *Guitar Player*, it does help. Promoters love to have things like that in an artist's press kit to help in advertising your shows. The only problem with *Guitar Player*'s polls is that after you win five times, they put you in the "Gallery of the Greats." It should be called "Gallery of the Dead." What happens to an artist if they make the best music of their career after that? Then you have a situation like Charo winning in the flamenco category because all the best players were ineligible. When you see Neil Young, who is more of a singer, as a co-winner in the "Best Acoustic Pickstyle Guitarist" category with Tony Rice who is a good guitarist, you can see that sometimes it just doesn't work.

Did being a poll winner and carrying the title of reigning guitar hero add more pressure on you at your live shows?

No, it didn't really seem to matter. What does matter is when you are playing out there with high-caliber players, or having to do a solo guitar spot in the show as I did in Chick's band. If it wasn't for him, I don't know if I would have gotten over the fear of doing that. He pushed me to do it. I am forever indebted to him because it paved the way for me to play solo spots in the shows with Paco De Lucia and John McLaughlin. That was quite a challenge.

What are your thoughts on the anti-virtuosity feelings among alternative musicians? They don't want to hear great guitar solos.

I hear that music once in a while, and I know the feeling is that it is hip to be sloppy. It is difficult for young players to find role models. In this country, we glorify musicians with little talent who get lots of exposure on MTV. The role models should be those who can play, not those with lots of money. A couple of years down the line, those players will run out, and be out of work. The musicians who play very well are the ones who will probably have a career for the rest of their lives.

What do you see yourself doing in the next 20 years? Will you continue the pace you've been keeping?

masters of music

I get tired when I'm out on tour, so I wonder about later on in life, if it will be one tour after the other. I just finished a five-month tour. I sometimes tell myself I am going to come home and take six months off, and for at least two or three months have nothing to do with music. What usually happens within a day or two is that I am back into working on another project. It's just natural, I can't sit around.

Opportunities just keep opening up for quality work, collaborations, concerts. So many are interesting and I want to do everything. That means less time off. It is possible I could keep going as long as I want to. I don't want it to be just a business decision, I want to remain really interested. I am about to get into a new project with Paco De Lucia and John McLaughlin. That will be challenging musically.

 The last project you did with them was a milestone in your career.

I began playing with Paco in 1976 on my *Elegant Gypsy* album. That ended up selling two million copies. The cut we played together became a hit single in some countries—Spain was one of them. In 1980, when we added John and toured, it was a mega success.

We made a live album, which also sold about two million copies. We did three tours from 1980-83, but haven't played together since. There has been a lot of talk of our getting back together. Finally, we are all on the same label—PolyGram—and they really want to see us back together.

 As you look on the fusion movement which you were such a part of, what do you feel as you hear it now?

If you take the better records of that era, there are elements that are somewhat timeless. You don't hear that kind of excitement in the pop-jazz being played on radio today. You don't hear that music as much anymore. When I do hear it, for me it is exciting.

 Do you think there will be a renaissance of that music?

Radio could make a renaissance, but it doesn't look like it is going that way. They are more concerned with selling ad time. Radio would rather have Coca-Cola pay for an ad than take a chance.

 Why do you think powers-that-be backed it originally?

They had a huge crossover audience from jazz and rock. I still think it is there—not the same people, but there is a new generation. Personally, I think the "Wave" radio formats, whose existence is justified by surveys taken at malls and office buildings, don't reflect what the people on the street want to hear. I think in the '90s you could program exciting music—Peter Gabriel then Chick Corea, or Wynton Marsalis and then Sting. I don't think there would be a problem playing Jimi Hendrix and then Joe Pass. Instead you hear one form of music appealing to one little crowd.

 Like many American jazz artists, you have a large following outside the U.S.

It is really good in Europe and South America. In some countries, my group can fill an arena like a major rock group. The Latin aspect grabs them in South America. Some countries I have only recently started going to. They haven't had a lot of my music over the past 20 years; they have been waiting a long time. I play in Western Europe two or three times each year. It is good there; I can try things and they will accept it. Here, they are still stuck on the electric thing.

 You have stated that an artist needs to take a breather from touring and develop new ideas before going back into the studio for the next album. How do you recharge?

I try to find something musical that fires me to go and try to write. My association with Astor Piazzolla took me to that place a few years ago. I'm looking for that again right now. It is not easy, and I'm not going to rush it. Sometimes you have to research. I like things in the world music area, I usually look there for things that haven't been heard before. For my own records, it has to be special.

At the time I was going to Berklee, I was very influenced by a record of Julian Bream's called *20th Century Guitar*. That later influenced my album *Cielo e Terra*. That was a magic record in some ways. I did some duets with Airto Moreira. I am proud of that one.

 The concept for the *Rite of Strings* recording and tour was your idea. How did the idea of an acoustic string trio with Stanley Clarke and Jean-Luc Ponty come about?

It was my idea. I have played acoustically with Stanley before. Though most of what he's done is electric, I've always thought he was a very strong acoustic bass player. Jean Luc was the key. I had never worked with violin before, and I wanted to put something together for the European jazz festivals. Each summer they look for something unique and different featuring name players. I am pretty good at putting things together that they like. I thought Jean Luc would be interesting because he hasn't played the festivals or really collaborated with anybody in this way. He always works with his own groups. He hasn't played acoustically since the '60s. It took a lot of convincing to get him out of his element. He finally called me back after a year and a half of thinking it over.

There are elements of compromise in situations like that. We are all at different places musically. I would have liked to play some more complex music with this trio, maybe even some classically derived pieces or a "Return to Forever"-type medley. There were varying opinions about that. It is a shame we didn't make a live album, because by the end of the tour it would have been much different than the studio record.

 Having launched your career as a trailblazer in technically astonishing guitar playing, what are your feelings regarding the influence you have had on the direction of contemporary guitar?

I hope I have been an influence on some players in some way. I get my fair share of fan mail. When I read what effect my playing and music have had on people I am touched by it. I am always trying to grow, so if I achieve what I want, I could be more of an influence.

How do you feel when you hear players that have been influenced by you?

There are a lot that I like and some that I don't. I am not into the rock approach where technique and speed is all that matters. In jazz there are not many contemporaries that are going in my direction. My way of playing is more like that of a drummer or a percussionist playing guitar. I don't hear a lot of people copying it, so I am not afraid of teaching it. Rhythmically, my playing is very unorthodox.

 What are your feelings on the lifestyle of the recording and touring musician?

There are ups and downs. The downs are physical exhaustion and difficulty maintaining relationships. When you are a busy music professional, you are all over the world. There are obstacles that they don't teach you about at Berklee, but there are no schools for that. The realities of the business and how to maintain a balance in life should be taught.

The blissful part of the career is when everyone sees you onstage. I like traveling, sometimes it is very pleasurable. The people that you meet around the world are extraordinary, especially the different musicians you come across. Some of those you admire, you wouldn't get to meet if you weren't a traveling musician. On a flight back from London, Peter Gabriel was sitting next to me and we talked the whole way.

The adulation and applause is amazing, and it is a letdown when you come home from a tour. Something I am very sure of is, if you have experienced an audience giving you that warmth, that ovation, you must have it again. Applause is as addictive as a drug. That is why a lot of older jazz musicians don't quit; you need it later on...perhaps even more.

Alf Clausen

primetime tunes

Composer Alf Clausen '66 is riding high underscoring *The Simpsons*.

WINDING THROUGH COLDWATER CANON IN BEVERLY HILLS with Alf Clausen '66 on the way to a *Simpsons* spotting session, the conversation was wide ranging. By nature, Alf is good humored, erudite, and unpretentious to a point belying his status as one of Hollywood's top TV composers. The traffic lights that day illustrated the subtext of our discussion of his bio: Alf's arrival as composer was also not without inconvenient pauses. He recalled the celebrated series *Moonlighting* ending in 1989 after a four-year run and six Emmy nominations for Alf. He says it's part of the business-riding high one day and then, boom, unemployed for seven months. However, when one door closes, it seems a better one always opens for Alf.

His 18 years of persistent dues-paying while seeking his break as a composer is a lesson in forbearance. When he came to Hollywood in 1967, he freelanced as a teacher, a bassist, music copyist, ghost composer, arranger—whatever put food on the table and held the promise of a toehold in the business. It took nine years before he got his first solid break as an arranger. That ultimately led to his becoming music director and conductor for the *Donny and Marie* variety show. In 1985, when he began writing for *Moonlighting*, he was finally recognized as a composer.

Growing up in Jamestown, North Dakota, Alf studied French horn and piano. He sang in choirs and played in the concert band. After high school, he enrolled at

North Dakota State University as a mechanical-engineering major. Aware that insights to the entertainment industry are rarely uncovered on the Dakota prairie, Alf spent a summer in New York City with his cousin—a professional pianist there. The impact of Broadway shows, concerts in Central Park, and lessons with a professional French hornist convinced Alf to switch his major to music as soon as he got back on campus. Correspondence courses acquainted him with Berklee, and ultimately led to full-time Berklee studies after graduation from the university. He earned his diploma, taught at Berklee for a year, and then headed for Los Angeles.

To date, Alf has been composer and/or orchestrator, and/or conductor for 29 films, 24 TV series, and 24 movies of the week, and arranger/music director for several popular variety shows. He has received a total of seven ASCAP awards for composition, two Emmy Awards, and numerous other recognitions. Currently Alf's music is heard on *The Simpsons* weekly in 70 countries, and six nights each week in the United States. Rhino Records recently released a CD of Alf's *Simpsons* music. All this provides confirmation that Alf's contribution to popular culture is no joke.

 When did you know you would become a composer?

It was such a gradual growth that I can't remember one conscious decision to go into that profession. As a student at North Dakota State University, I found it difficult to get answers to questions I had about the entertainment industry. I remember getting a copy of Henry Mancini's *Sounds and Scores*, a popular book in the early '60s about arranging and how it applied to film. I found the book to be a revelation about movie music from the composer/arranger's standpoint. My instructors didn't have a handle on what this was about.

 How did you end up coming to Berklee?

While I was earning my B.A. in music theory, I was taking the Berklee correspondence course to learn about jazz and how to write big band music. One of my instructors took a new position at the University of Wisconsin, and suggested I come down there to work on my master's degree. Their French horn instructor was John Barrows who had been a New York studio player who played on the Miles Davis/Gil Evans records and others. I ended up hating it. The attitude there very anti-jazz. The jazz band wasn't even allowed to rehearse on campus. Barrows and I also knocked heads over a bunch of things. I became frustrated. I quit the university and came to Berklee.

 Q. What were your impressions when you first arrived?

Coming to the city was pretty intense for me, but having spent a summer in New York, I had gotten my feet wet. At that time, there were a lot of professional musicians who would come off the road for more schooling. The level of the musicianship was amazing. It was so inspiring to be caught up in that intensity. There had never been a French horn player at Berklee, so the minute they found I played it, I was put into every ensemble I could possibly play in to add new colors. Herb Pomeroy put me in his recording band and I am on some *Jazz in the Classroom* records. I played all the time.

 Q. Who were some of your favorite teachers?

There were a lot of magnificent teachers—Bill Maloof, Dick Bobbitt, John Bavicchi, Bob Share—each had his own strong suit. Herb Pomeroy had something that cannot be defined. It was a way of getting to the heart and soul of the music very quickly. I was fascinated by that. I remember him rehearsing some very difficult pieces with the recording band. It seemed like the music would never come together. Then we'd begin playing the piece and something would start happening in the room. You could feel this spirit start to rise up out of the music. I looked at the guy next to me and he was feeling it too. We got into it deeper and deeper, and the whole band was playing as one unit, going somewhere we hadn't been before. It was spooky, but moving. When we got done, everyone just looked around wondering what just happened. Herb had this smile on his face that said, "Yeah, that's what it is all about."

 Q. What was the first door that opened up for you in L.A.?

When I first got to town in 1967, I was doing a number of things—playing casuals, teaching, doing music copying. It took a long time to get hired as a writer. I did a lot of piecemeal ghost writing. I would write a number for a Vegas act here, a jingle there, perhaps an arrangement for a record. All these things together kept me going. The first real break I got was as an arranger with the *Donny and Marie Osmond* show in 1976.

I got a panic call from a pianist, Tommy Wolfe, who was a special material writer for the *Osmond* show. He said the music director Tommy Oliver needed a last minute chart by the next day. I stayed up all night and cranked it out. The next day around 11:00 a.m. I got a call from Tommy saying I did a great job. He asked me to be a writer on the show. Every week he gave me more and more to write. By the end of the season I was writing the show's finales, which were about 400 bars. It was one of the jobs with a one-day or a day-and-a-half turnaround. You'd be up all night and the copyists were picking up my chart at four in the morning.

I was asked to sub as conductor on the recording sessions for Tommy Oliver a few times and Wayne Osmond was always in the booth watching me work. The next season, Oliver decided not to come back, and I was asked to be the director for the show's third season. At the end of that season, the Osmonds decided to open their own studio in Provo, Utah. They asked us if we wanted to move up there. I didn't want to move, but said I'd help them make the transition.

For the last five shows, I commuted to Provo. I would start writing on Friday, catch a plane to Salt Lake City on Sunday. I would finish the writing over the next two days. When they first opened the studio, they didn't have enough experienced musicians to do the show, so we'd fly in guys from L.A. on a private plane on Wednesday morning. We would do the pre-records that day and then all fly back. I would take a day off and then begin the whole process over again.

 Q. A variety show must have been a great training ground for the various styles you write in for *The Simpsons*.

After the *Donny and Marie show*, I did a year of the *Mary Tyler Moore* variety series on CBS, and ghosted for other shows. Not only was it a great training for various styles, but it was the best place to learn to make changes on the stand. You might find out that the choreographer and rehearsal pianist want changes in your chart. You and all the musicians are in the studio with the clock ticking and you have to chop up the chart and still make music out of it.

So you learn to think on your feet and communicate with an orchestra. You are recomposing on the stand, and learning to work under pressure.

You had a hiatus after *Moonlighting* ended in 1989 before your hiring for *The Simpsons* in 1990. How did the new connection happen?

I was talking to a friend of mine lamenting my state. He gave me a tip about *The Simpsons*. I had been so busy with *Moonlighting* for years. That series was considered a classic piece of television; you come off of that feeling pretty good, and then the phone stops ringing. It is a part of the business we all have to deal with whether you are a cameraman, actor, or composer. You can get into the depths of self-doubt when it happens.

You must have seen a lot of changes in post-production technology over the course of your years in the business.

I don't think I could have done either *Moonlighting* or *The Simpsons* without Auricle [time calculation and synchronization software]. It is great for when changes need to be made. Before, if a last minute change happened, you would have to wait while the music editor physically put new streamers and punches on the film. Now, after a few keystrokes, they are in the right place and on you go.

Otherwise, I still work in an old-fashioned way. I write on an acoustic piano with a drafting board on the front, and pencils, erasers, and a straightedge. I have a monitor and a VCR that will play picture and time code hooked up to the Auricle setup. That's all I use.

What is your weekly schedule like?

Monday through Thursday from 8:30 a.m. to 11:30 p.m. I am writing. Friday morning, before I go to the spotting session, there is a brief recovery time, but sometimes I may still have cues to write if I didn't finish on Thursday. On Friday, the spotting is at 2:00 p.m., and the recording session goes from 7:00 to 11:00 p.m. I try to keep Saturday and Sunday off.

 How do you begin the process at the start of each week?

My procedure is to look at the spotting notes and figure out what kind of orchestra I need and if there will be any special instrumentation. I then let the contractor know what my needs are. Once I have the music editor's notes with time code and start and end points for each cue, I'll make a template for each cue in the computer. When I am ready to start a cue, I call it up on the computer. The start time and cue number are already entered, so I can get right to the creative process. So I will scan the cues, and pick a no-brainer to just get my heart started. This is very hard work for me. It is good to start out with something that is very obvious to get back into the routine. Then I know that I am sending out cues to the copy department at Fox and that the list of cues is starting to diminish as the hours go by.

 What comes first when you are composing: a melody, a texture, or a chord sound?

Each cue is different, so I can't say if I think of a melody or a harmonic structure first. Many times if there are determined cues—like if Homer is angry and marching over to someone's house—I will center the cue on the pace of his footsteps, and figure out the tempo and the groove. Next, I might approach it from a harmonic standpoint and think of what will illustrate his anger in that tempo. Many times the melody may come last. It is the mood of the cue that exists first, but sometimes a melody will come first. Each cue is different.

 Some of the cues on the show are simply a whole-note chord. Are these easy to come up with?

I have a large repertoire of single-chord emotions—happy, depressed, angry, hurt, sad—but they are never quite the same. The character might be a little less sad or whimsical and sad at the same time. There are times when I have spent two or three hours working on three bars of music. As I play the piano I might be thinking this is sad, but too much so, or this is angry but it's too nasty. It is a weird process of elimination in trying to find the right combination of notes to convey the emotion.

For some dark things I may want to write in flat keys, but string players don't like to play in flat keys and they play differently. If something is to be extremely jubilant and heartfelt, D major is great. This has a bearing on things too.

 Would you say you are discovering new things as you compose, that you are not just going over what you already know will work?

I discover things all the time. That helps to keep things fresh, and I work hard to keep it that way. I do fall back on some things I've done before from time to time, and there are good and bad sides to doing that. The down side is that duplicating yourself can get boring. The good side is that if you really found the best solution, and if it worked once, you can use it again.

 When you do research to write in a certain style of music—one episode called for a klezmer cue—how much time can you give that research?

About 20 minutes. Part of the charm of this job has been learning to distill the essence of a musical style in a very short period of time. Someone on the production team says they'd like a cue to be like a klezmer piece, but they might not know what that consists of. Production assistants get me clips or CDs and I will listen to three tracks and figure out what makes klezmer have that sound. Then I make a spur-of-the-moment decision about what makes it seem like klezmer to these people. It is a very interesting study because what klezmer means to you or me may not be the same as what it means to someone without a musical background. Having to compose something that is harmonically, melodically, and orchestrationally correct knowing that I still have 25 or 30 cues left to write makes me distill pretty quickly.

Q. What are some of the more unusual things you've been called upon to write?

The whole musical palette exists on this series. My background has prepared me for this in a very unusual way. My experiences—being a legitimately trained French horn player familiar with concert band and symphonic literature, loving rock and roll and r&b in high school, becoming a jazz bassist, working weddings, bar mitzvahs, and backing singers in shows, knowing thousands of tunes from playing trio gigs—give me a lot to draw on. It all comes back. In the spotting session today, they asked for a cue sounding like a society band playing at a country club. I knew instantly what I'd do for that.

As a copyist, I'd worked on projects for many great composers. Generally copying is not something you give a lot of thought to, but I find sometimes late at night as I am thinking about what to do on a cue, somebody's score that I copied 20 years ago will flash in front of me. I start remembering what Lalo Schiffrin did with the high strings, and soprano sax doubling the lead violin way above the staff and how it gave a real intense angst. Boom, my answer is there. It is weird how that happens.

Q. If you were to have the time and resources to write and record anything you wanted—as a purely artistic statement—what type of music would you choose to write?

I'd love to write a symphony, that would be thrilling. I might like to write a cappella choir pieces, perhaps Christmas carols like the Alfred Burt carols. I love vocal music. I would also like to write some more jazz band music too.

Q. Given the pressure on the TV series composer, what is it that makes you love this very hard work so much?

On a television job, the instant gratification part is amazing. You can write this relatively large amount of music, then record it and hear it the same week. I can take a piece of film with a certain emotion, and then I have the power to make that emotion go any number of ways through the music. If I am astute enough to pull out the correct emotion, and if my craft is good enough to enhance that emotion, it can make it 10 times as deep as it is on film.

When I take the music to the studio with the right players with the right feel in the studio, it can put goose bumps on your arm. It goes on tape like that and is preserved. Ten years later, I can listen to that cue and the goose bumps will happen in exactly the same place. You have contributed something meaningful and you can preserve it. I am very blessed, how many other jobs can you say that about? It makes all those years of playing casuals and copying music until 3:00 a.m. worth it.

 You exhibit a grace under pressure in the recording studio which enables you to get what you need out of the musicians while the clock is ticking. Has that evolved or is it just part of your nature?

Part of it is personality; each conductor is different in his or her demeanor with the orchestra. I gained a lot from teaching and working with players who can't play it right the first time. I learned a lot from Herb Pomeroy and John LaPorta—how patient they were! Herb had this far-vision view of what the piece was supposed to be and knew how to rehearse each section just the right amount of time to get everyone playing it pretty well before putting it all together. I learned that you have to pick things apart but be kind to the players. Some conductors are impatient or nasty to the players. I find that tragic, you are only here once, why not be gracious to your fellow man? I think that will make someone play better.

 What is next for you?

Who knows. The funny part about this business is that one phone call can change your life.

Groening's Secret Weapon

"For The Simpsons, I felt it was very important that the show be anchored with a full orchestral score. I wanted the music to underscore the emotions of the scene, not the joke. We get a bigger laugh out of a joke when Alf scores the drama of it. Then the audience can see the folly of the characters.

Alf understands the show and produces a voluminous amount of music in all different styles. He is our secret weapon. Sometimes the animation isn't as crisp as we'd like it, but it is anchored by his confidence-inspiring music, so a lot of the minor glitches in the animation are glossed over.

If you filmed The Simpsons in live action, it would be like filming a $75 million movie every week because of the things we do visually. Alf's music is the equivalent of scoring a movie at that grand level.

Alf meets whatever emotional needs we have for The Simpsons—we certainly don't take his needs into account when we're thinking of crazy stuff for the show! He takes whatever is thrown at him and comes back with something original, surprising, and fun to listen to.

For me, the most entertaining part of the show is coming to a scoring session. At that point, my job is over, and I get to sit there and have a free concert. Alf is one of the unacknowledged treasures of the show."

—Matt Groening, "The Simpons" Creator

Patty Larkin

a life in song

Tunesmith Patty Larkin '74: melodies and metaphors from American life.

THE GIFT AND BURDEN OF THE BEST SONGWRITERS is to create a deeply affecting moment within the confines of a three-minute song. Though crafted from the elements of everyday parlance and the centuries-old 12 musical tones, a great song makes the heart soar, sob, or smile.

Patty Larkin's unique gift is sculpting these transcendent moments from what many might regard as the unspectacular facets of contemporary living. She hears a metaphor where others might hear distracting sirens, finds spiritual reconciliation as a train's headlight illuminates a Colorado canyon, and can fully plumb the depths of a relationship in three verses and a chorus.

In an agile alto voice, sometimes throaty and powerful at the top of a chorus and then a fragile whisper by the end of the strophe, she reveals her life and imagination. Her adroit guitar accompaniments have brought accolades from numerous critics. Beyond rhythmic strumming, her guitar style incorporates state-of-the-art string tapping, bottleneck slide, finger picking, and Celtic-inflected bent notes. Her guitar work is the bedrock supporting the expansive fretted soundscapes she and producer John Leventhal have constructed on her last two discs.

Raised in Wisconsin in a family where music created generational bonds, Patty came to Boston via Oregon in the 1970s. After studies at Berklee, she launched her career busking in Harvard Square. Rising to prominence in the germinating neo-folk scene of the 1980s, she recorded three records for the Philo/Rounder label. Jumping to Windham Hill's High Street label in the 1990s, albums four, five, and six have preserved her folk stylings while packing enough punch to catapult her to the top of the adult, album, and alternative radio charts.

A veteran performer, she plays 150 concerts yearly and has appeared on several network TV shows. Her sardonic stage patter includes impersonations, terse social commentary, and spoofing on a range of societal foibles. Introducing her song "Angels Running" to the crowd at the 1996 Champlain Valley Festival in Vermont, she announced that Cher's latest album, *It's a Man's World*, features the tune. Patty basks in the irony of the person who sang "Gypsies, Tramps, and Thieves" learning her lyric. Offstage though, she sees it more a smile of fortune than a cultural collision, and confides that she really likes the sound of Cher's voice on her tune.

After her set at the Champlain Valley festival, we stopped at a nearby café. Over a bowl of broccoli soup, Patty spoke about where her music comes from and where it is headed.

 Are there any memorable experiences you had when you were young that made you decide to become a musician?

My grandmothers both played piano and when we would get together we would sing. My grandmother Larkin knew lots of tunes; she used to accompany the silent movies in Chicago. I remember being small and standing underneath the keyboard while someone was playing boogie woogie music and I felt like I had just seen God; it was a great sound to me. I knew that music was something that was fun to do and brought everybody together. I wanted to take lessons before I really could, and had to wait until I was seven or eight.

 Did you start on piano then?

Yes, classical piano, but now I'm clueless. I blocked it all out. I mostly play guitar these days, but I will play keyboard pads for preproduction. I started guitar in my preteen years—wanting to be popular. I went into the folk thing, probably because of camp. I started listening to Tom Paxton and Bob Dylan not even knowing who they were, but from hearing other people do their songs. A guitar made it into the house when I was about 11, and I was writing songs by the time I was 12 or 13. By the time I was in high school, it was part of my identity even though I didn't talk about it with anyone outside of my family. My sister was my critic.

 Q. How did you come to Berklee?

I earned a degree in English literature from the University of Oregon before I came. The whole time, I was doing music too. They had a really good folklore department and a lot of people were playing old-time fiddle tunes. I took fiddle lessons from a guy named Pop Powers and played some backup guitar for him. He was probably in his 70s or 80s at that point, and we would go out and play at nursing home picnics.

I got hooked into the coffee house circuit there and ended up working in a blues/jug band with a guy named Chico Schwall. His brother Jim was in the Siegel-Schwall Blues Band, so he knew a ton of old blues music.

When I was doing student teaching as an English major, I was in the library looking for material on *One Flew Over the Cuckoo's Nest* and I came across Bill Leavitt's *Guitar Method* [Berklee Press]. I had been curious about reading guitar music. I took the copy home and started realizing that the kind of stuff I had been playing on piano could be played on guitar.

One day I was talking with a friend Kathleen Hicks, who has now become a Hollywood actress. She asked me what I really wanted to do. I told her I liked English, but I really wanted to study guitar. She said I should just go to the music department and tell them I wanted to study guitar. I ran over there and asked an advisor about it; he thought it was very funny and said "we don't teach guitar." I was astounded later to find out about places like Berklee where you could study jazz guitar.

masters of music

I moved to Boston after my senior year and started taking jazz guitar lessons and enrolled at Berklee in the summer. I got a lot out of Berklee; it helped me get things organized. It was a huge hit of energy, paranoia, enthusiasm, and competition, but I learned that there was a structure and a way to study music.

 Q. Are there any courses that stood out?

I liked theory and arranging a lot. I was pretty terrible in my ensembles; I ended up feeling, okay, I'm a folk singer. There was one other person, a guy named Bob, who played acoustic guitar, while everybody was playing Fender Strats. I recently ran into him on a tour I did in North Carolina, when he came to my gig. He has switched to playing upright bass now, and is a teacher and jazz player.

I really thought ear training and learning to do record copies was very helpful. Just being exposed to that much music was very exciting. Trying to translate standards to guitar and learning that there was a way to read this music was great for me. I had no idea how the music business worked; it was a total mystery to me. I just knew that I wanted to play music. I thought if I could study music and read it, I would be much more versatile at what I did. I wanted to learn as much as I could because I didn't know how to do it as a songwriter.

I remember seeing Elvin Jones give a clinic when I was a student. I was sitting outside afterward with the other woman I knew from school. It was about 2:00 p.m., Elvin stopped and invited us out for a beer. We said, [putting on a girlish voice] "Oh no, we have to go practice." I thought about that a few years ago. Elvin Jones, the drummer for John Coltrane, what was I thinking? Go get a beer and some peanuts with the man! But we thought if we were guys he would not have asked—and we did have to practice.

I did a songwriter workshop at Berklee last year, and it was really fun to see so many young women in the class interested in music. It was good to see how vibrant the atmosphere is there now. There were very few women instrumentalists when I went to Berklee.

Q. After you left Berklee you played electric guitar in bands before coming back to your acoustic roots.

I continued to study jazz guitar with a guy named Chet Krule. He had an ensemble where some guitars played saxophone lines and one played rhythm guitar. I was playing rhythm guitar and was just graduating into the sax lines when I quit. But I had learned a lot about the George Van Eps chord style.

I was really drawn to Brazilian music because it was so melodic and I liked the rhythms. I put together a trio with flute and congas and we played some of the Airto and Flora Purim stuff, and wrote some things along those lines too. That group added a bass player and became a rock band in about 1981 and we played places like The Tam. It was really hard keeping an original rock band together. Players were always quitting to go for more lucrative deals or with someone they thought was going to make it. I had also found it hard to write things in a pop vein that people could dance to.

I had been playing and writing acoustic music all along and opening for acts like the Persuasions, Jesse Colin Young, and Loudon Wainright III at the Paradise Club. I was having more fun on my acoustic gigs so I broke up the band and went with Rounder Records.

The only problem with playing acoustic music then was the kind of places you started out in. I never played at a Ground Round, but I've played at worse places where people would come up totally drunk and want to play your guitar. I have a vintage 1946 Martin guitar, and I'd say, "No you can't," and the person would spit on the floor or something. I would become the English teacher again—"Okay, everybody sit down now, we're going to eat the popcorn now." Once I got my first album it helped a lot.

Q. How long have you been performing your own music?

I started out in 1976, I did the rock band in '78 to '79. After that I played at a place called the Idler where people like Suzanne Vega, Shawn Colvin, and even two of the members of the Cars played as a duo. It was the only place where we could play because we weren't famous folk singers.

 On your last two albums, *Angels Running* and *Stranger's World*, the backing tracks have been described in the press as "soundscapes." Did you and producer John Leventhal work them out collaboratively?

A lot of the guitar layering and texture was completely John's. I did some pre-production work at my own home and some ideas came out of that. John has an ADAT studio where we did about half the vocals live with my guitar for the *Stranger's World* album. Then he would putz around and come up with ideas to show me. We would try this or that and keep what we liked. A lot of the layering and texture was completely John's.

Jon is like a kid in a candy shop when he gets going. It is fun to see him work. He has about 35 different instruments; he collects them. He understands the feeling and mood of the song, and listens to the lyrics. He has an artist's sense about the music that I like.

When I left for a month and then came back, he had to get his new ideas past me though. He knew if I was hesitant, it wasn't ringing true.

 There is a lot of subtlety to the production; some parts are almost inaudible unless you are listening in headphones.

One reviewer I was talking with told me he had decided what he was going to write after listening the *Angels Running* album in his car. He got home and put it on his CD player as he began writing. He told me he wrote something completely different because he could hear so much more. The production is fairly subtle—maybe we need more Peter Frampton guitar slides?

 In your songwriting do you find lyric writing to be the hardest part?

It has actually gotten more difficult. I go between a real Zen approach of stream-of-consciousness writing and maybe just babbling poetry and writing it down to see how it comes out. Once I get the first verse or chorus I try to work with it. I read an interview with Leonard Cohen who said it takes him a year to write a song and some songs take a decade. When I first read it I thought, yeah, right. Now I am starting to believe it. He will fill a whole notebook with lyrics for one song.

I have one song that I have wanted to get on my last two albums but it's not done. One verse is done, and it's not even that great a verse. I just know where I want it to go.

 Are some of the personalities that come up in your lyrics imagined and some real?

There is a Helen's Restaurant up in Machias, Maine. I used to go in and have breakfast, while everyone else was probably having lunch. The lyric in the song "Helen" comes out of my imagination, impressions I got while driving around Down East Maine. The character from "Dave's Holiday" came from a real-life person who would come down to Cape Cod in the summer. He and his friends would just sit in lawn chairs all weekend with the bug zapper going. I don't know where "Mary Magdalene" came from. I think part of it is coming out of me. I tried to write from the viewpoint of someone who felt completely defeated. If she was alive today she might be on welfare living in a hotel on a highway strip with her two kids.

 Where is the balance between inspiration and perspiration in your songwriting?

It takes about a week of really bad writing, another week of thinking I'm getting somewhere, then in the third week something else might pop out. I think the craft is in going back to finish a song, not copping out or saying this is good enough. As I write for my next project, I realize that I will have to sing these songs for the next three or four years if I put them on an album, so I'd better believe in them.

Do you have notebooks with hundreds of song fragments in them?

I do have fragments. There are some that I have a verse and chorus for but no idea what I am talking about. I'll really want to finish them because it will be really fun. Others I come back to and think, nice try, but I'm not convinced. I know which ones I am curious about.

 I think it is really a gift for you to be able to put together lyrics that convey a big picture or scenario with just a few words.

My friend songwriter Cheryl Wheeler says there has to be a different way to say, "Oh baby, baby I love you." You can say that if you want but I think you should dig as deep as you can. That is why it is really hard sometimes. You can work for days on end and still not say what you want.

 You say that you feel very comfortable operating outside the pop mainstream. Could Cher's cover of "Angels Running" edge you closer to the mainstream?

I don't know how much impact having one song on an album will have, but it is something to talk about with my publisher and ASCAP. I remember when I wrote "Angels Running" I thought it sounded kind of pop, but I wanted to do it. If I can write songs that have integrity and some roots to them, I wouldn't mind.

On the last album, Windham Hill was saying that they needed a "hit." But you have to look at the record company, look at my track record, the circuit I play on, and how I write. On the last album there were about five songs that could have gotten pretty strong radio play, in my opinion.

The record company was sold toward the end of my tour. The people I knew were leaving and now there are only three people at the company whom I knew a year ago. It is completely different. Admittedly, they are in the business to sell records—so am I or I would just make and distribute them myself. I don't want to handle that. For me, it has to come from the writing, and I need to feel I am doing something new for myself, looking at the stone from a different angle.

My publishing company, BMG, is talking about me starting to cowrite with different people. I think there are advantages to writing with someone who has had cuts on other people's albums. At this point though, I just want to finish writing for my next project.

Mary Chapin Carpenter came out of the D.C. folk circuit, and I remember in 1987 when I went down to D.C., there were people who had been her supporters who were thinking she was going so country. To me it was just great music. She has done really well with her writing, walking the line between pop, country, rock, and folk. She has been able to succeed on her own terms.

 That is your goal too it seems.

Yeah, right now I am into the guitar and into writing. This new batch of songs I am demoing is all over the place—some Celtic, some bossa nova. Hopefully, it will all come together.

 Where your songs are so personal, is it hard to get up every night and get into the right frame of mind to go there?

I am very lucky sometimes because I can get to that place, I can get a sense of release. I can let a lot out—be it anger or joy, being loud, screaming, or being really soft and really sad. It is kind of like role playing when I do the song. Sometimes it is hard if it is really personal. I recently played a song I wrote for my friend Liz who died. When I looked up and saw her partner in the audience, it was almost too heavy, too sad to sing it.

 You play about 150 concerts annually. Judging from your itinerary, you must have played 75 of them this summer.

That is a little hairy, and is another reason I want to get more into the writing. With the new album out last year, I really pushed. Before I was doing so much nationally, I was touring in New England and that was a cool thing. There is something beautiful about playing locally, writing, practicing, and having a sane home life. [Jokingly] It is like my dream-come-true has become my nightmare... be careful what you wish for.

 You've won 11 Boston Music awards, have appeared on the major TV networks, and are drawing audiences to your shows all over the country. What do you see up ahead?

I want to expand what I've got going already. I see songwriting and the music publishing industry as a way to do that. I am ready for a left turn somewhere along the line. I have had some people talk to me about film scoring. That would be amazing if it happened. I think about playing a tour and not plugging anything in or writing a play based on my "At The Mall" characters.

To me it is amazing just to be able to play and record the songs I've written and have people be interested in them.

Steve Smith

a different drummer

For Steve Smith '76, rocking a stadium or playing a quiet jazz club, it's all the same-part of the American drumming tradition.

STEVE SMITH IS A DIFFERENT DRUMMER. His spectacular career, spanning the past two decades, has at times found him pounding out high-decibel rock tunes in 50,000-seat arenas with Journey or supplying sophisticated stickwork with Steps Ahead or Vital Information in the hushed ambiance of clubs like New York's Bottom Line. Unlike many 40-something musicians, Steve wasn't a rocker who matured into jazz; it was the other way around. Growing up in the sixties, the music of Hendrix, Led Zeppelin, and Deep Purple had a big impact on him, but drummers like Tony Williams, Elvin Jones, and Eric Gravatt were his musical heroes. His first break in the business came in 1976 with Jean Luc Ponty's band in the midst of both the fusion era and Steve's seventh semester at Berklee. Opting to continue his education on the road ultimately led to gigs with platinum rockers Journey and numerous top jazz artists.

For Steve, knowing the history and tradition of American music is as crucial as knowing where the downbeat is. He considers it part of his job to understand the history of drumming in America and to examine the paths down which popular music and jazz have traveled since the birth of the blues. At his home in Marin County, California, he has bookshelves lined with histories of the early blues and jazz legends, and CD cases stuffed with remastered historical recordings. Testifying to his own place in American popular music are 31 gold and platinum records on his wall. Most mark his achievements with Journey; others reflect his contributions to top albums by artists like Mariah Carey and Bryan Adams.

The hallway with the platinum records leads to Neverland, Steve's state-of-the-art studio, where he has recorded albums with his group Vital Information. With the celebrated reunion of Journey, and the greeting their *Trial By Fire* disc received, odds are Steve will have more platinum records to hang on this wall.

 Who were some of your most influential teachers at Berklee?

Drum instructor Gary Chaffee made a big impact. He helped me develop my musical voice. I thought his ideas were very radical and I really took to them. To this day I still work on the information he gave me and stay in touch with him.

Alan Dawson was also a very strong teacher in a different way. He stressed basic coordination and traditional techniques and the jazz tradition. Every week, I had to learn a standard tune well enough to sing the melody while playing his drum exercises. Unlike many drum teachers, he integrated music and drumming so that you learned the form and could improvise on it. He helped me build a vocabulary on the instrument.

 Were any fellow students important to your development?

At Berklee, I connected with bassist Neil Stubenhaus ['75] and pianist Orville Wright ['74]. We worked in a nightclub band called Ecstasy. Even though Neil is the same age as me, he had this maturity, and helped to mold me. He helped me develop a concept of groove playing and timekeeping that I didn't have before.

I later played with bassists Jeff Berlin ['75] and Kermit Driscoll ['78] and guitarists Mike Stern ['75] and Bill Frisell ['77]. Jeff got me an audition with Jean Luc Ponty. Playing Ponty's music was a reach for me. It was fusion with more emphasis on rock than jazz, and I hadn't played a lot of rock. The audition was a lot of reading and my reading chops for odd time signatures were really up. Ponty and I played a lot of duets, and with the freedom I felt as an improviser, I got the gig. Working with him really piqued my interest in rock. He got me to check out drummers like Billie Cobham and Narada Michael Walden, and convinced me to get a big set with double bass drums.

 After leaving Ponty, what shaped your decision to go with Montrose when you were offered a gig with Freddie Hubbard that same week?

After a year with Ponty, I had a lot of interest in following through with rock. I felt I had a weakness there. When I moved to L.A., I got an audition with Montrose, and it seemed the logical path for me to follow. Why not play with real rock-and-roll players and get the full experience? Their music was closer to the Jeff Beck Group's sound then—all instrumental rock. The offer to join Freddie Hubbard's band seemed like one I could probably get again. Montrose represented a doorway into another world.

 I guess it really was the doorway into the rock world for you.

Yeah, it was. Things worked out with musical experience and success in a way I'd never dreamt of, but my decision was strictly musical. I played with Montrose for eight months. On our first tour, the opening act was Van Halen. They had just put out their first record and no one knew them yet. Montrose would play second, and Journey was the headliner. Steve Perry had just joined Journey and was just getting introduced to the audience. It was an interesting point for Journey, because they had been primarily a four-piece instrumental rock band—only about half the songs had vocals. Ainsley Dunbar, Neal Schon, and Greg Rollie had come to hear me playing with Ponty in Cleveland and really liked what I was doing. They asked me to join in September of 1978. For me the hook to Journey was their musicianship.

 The most recent Journey CD, *Trial By Fire*, has a dramatic production concept and a big rock-and-roll sound. Your drumming really orchestrates ideas in the lyrics on several songs.

I used what is called a China Trash cymbal for the ride cymbal on "One More." People love that sound at every session where I've taken that cymbal out. On "The Rain," I used a flat ride with rivets and it got a rain kind of sound.

I've developed a concept that custom fits the band. I don't know that I would have come up with that if I had not joined Journey. Bassist Ross Valory and I work on the rhythms a lot. We tape everything at rehearsal. At the beginning, we are just trying ideas and improvising, but as we listen to how a phrase worked, we'll learn it and fine-tune other parts. By the time we get to the studio, we have rehearsed a lot. That is different for me; I am used to learning a song the same day I record it. In Journey, we are thinking more about the composition. The most creative process is in writing and rehearsing the song. When we take it on the road, we have to be true to the performance on the record. Listeners identify the guitar solo as a melody, and will air drum along with my fills; those things become part of the composition. This idea was really hard for me coming from a jazz background, but I realize a compositional approach is part of the role drums play in rock.

 Not too many members of major rock acts later become sidemen for top jazz artists. Do you have to alter your technique—matched grip versus traditional grip—for such different musical settings?

I use traditional grip about 90 percent of the time in either style. I don't change to matched grip for power; it is for the feel I am after. I don't think volume is much of an issue in rock drumming, it is more the sound. I let the mikes do the work. I don't play really soft or anything, but I am not excessively loud. It is the same with singers. They don't have to sing really loud, they need to get the right sound and let the mike pick it up. I want a good sound out of my snare, bass drum, toms, and cymbals, so drum size can be a factor, but you don't have to be excruciatingly loud.

 So when you are in big arenas, are you able to manage the stage volume?

It has been about 15 years since I played the arenas. In the old days we kept the stage volume down because the guitar amps were under the stage, although that was more for cosmetics than volume. Ironically, my own snare and cymbals were probably the loudest instruments because they were one or two feet from my ears. That caused me to have some tinnitus. Now I wear ear protection.

How did the Journey reunion come about?

We had always thought about it. I had discussions with various band members over the years, and they seemed pretty open to it. There were a lot of unresolved feelings after the breakup. John Kalodner, an A&R man for Sony, really pushed to get it to happen. He brought us together and helped us work through any hesitancy we had. Once we played together again, it felt good and the chemistry was right. We were inspired to make a go of it. We decided it was best not to do an unplugged version of our greatest hits, but to write material for a new record.

 Did the band write many tunes or just the 15 that appear on the disc?

Steve, Jonathan, and Neal got together and came up with ideas for some songs; they didn't do a lot with computers or drum machines. When Ross and I got into the rehearsal studio, we could develop our own parts. One of the problems that led to the breakup was that they wrote everything with drum machines and synth bass for the *Raised on Radio* record. They created our parts for us, which diminished the creativity for us. This time they came in with 15 to 20 very rough song ideas. We rehearsed for a few months fooling around with different chorus or verse ideas. We were working from 10 to 5 five days each week, and developed about 30 songs. We then focused on 20, and got those to completion. The music for a song might take a day to finish, but the lyric writing can take Jonathan and Steve a lot longer.

Kevin Shirley, the producer, picked 16 out of the 20 figuring we would use 12 on the record. We recorded them all, and then no one could figure which ones to leave off. The Japanese version of the CD has all 16 songs, the American version has 15.

Shirley and the record company were listening hard and giving us very critical feedback. In the old days, we never heard anything from the record company. We made the records and they put them out without heavy involvement from the A&R department. Now record making has developed into a big, high-risk business with the majority of the product being unsuccessful. The companies are cautious with their investment dollars, and want to make sure they are going to get a good return. They are more involved now and less trusting that a band will objectively create a successful record.

 After all of the hits Journey has had, this must add a new twist to doing your job.

Now the heads of the companies are younger than us and have grown up in a different era, and maybe don't understand as well as we do what we are doing. That was difficult, but we had to deal with it. They put us to the test, but the record debuted on Billboard at number three, the single became number one on the adult contemporary chart, and went up on the top 100 chart.

The producer did a great job. There are no fade-out endings on the record, every song ends. That wasn't planned. In the studio when we were playing the tracks, we would stretch out at the end of the tunes and have fun, then play an ending. Some of the endings were very spontaneous. After working on the record for a couple months, everyone got used to those endings, so they stayed.

 Frequently, in a fade ending you can hear the players start to loosen up and throw in some really cool ideas.

Sometimes you take a little more license because you think no one is ever going to hear it, so you have some fun and slap each other five during the playback. It should always be like that, but sometimes you get so self-conscious trying to make everything right that you aren't loose until the end of the song. I was glad that Kevin kept all of that stuff.

 When you shifted gears to go back into jazz after leaving Journey, was it a big adjustment?

In 1985, Ross Valory and I got fired from Journey. It's a long story, and it never should have happened. There were lots of regrets. So I made a decision not to try to form or join another rock band. I focused on jazz playing. The whole time I was in Journey, I played gigs around San Francisco and recorded with keyboardist Tom

Coster. I would also go back to Boston to play with bassist Tim Landers ['80] guitarists Barry Finnerty and Dean Brown ['77], and saxophonist Dave Wiltchesky. That evolved into Vital Information. I made the first three records with that band while I was still in Journey. So I had laid the groundwork for what I would do next.

I had a mountain to climb to get some credibility in the jazz world though. Festival promoters still saw me as Journey's drummer. Even touring with Vital Information wasn't bringing me the credibility needed to get hired. That came when I started playing with Steps Ahead. I was doing a drum clinic in Philadelphia with Peter Erskine and Lennie White. Peter told me he had just quit Steps Ahead, and Lennie told me he had just turned down an offer for the gig from Michael Brecker and would recommend me. The next day I got calls from Brecker and Mike Manieri both. They told me I didn't need to audition, just to come to New York and start rehearsing.

That was a transforming and healing experience after getting fired from a successful rock band. The players in Steps Ahead were musical heroes to me. For them to hire me and be really happy with what I was doing was what I needed. I learned a lot about music playing with musicians of their level.

We did a lot of touring—especially in Europe. I began winning the *Modern Drummer* polls. I made connections and gained recognition for having made the move from Journey to Steps Ahead. I went out of my way to meet promoters, agents, club owners, and record company people. That is how I got connected with the Intuition Records label. Eventually it became time for me to pursue my own thing, so I left the band after seven years to play more dates with Vital Information.

 What is your perspective on "fusion" music these days?

This is a good question. That term "fusion" has a negative connotation, and it gets applied to a variety of artists. At the San Francisco Jazz Festival, they billed Dave Sanborn as a fusion artist. I love his playing, but I don't think of him as a fusion player. Fusion had its heyday with Mahavishnu Orchestra, Return to Forever, and Weather Report. Like so many other eras in jazz—New Orleans jazz, big band jazz, be bop—I feel fusion has had its beginning, middle, and end. There were identifiable fusion artists, but it was really a band thing. I feel the last fusion band was the Chick Corea Elektric Band. There are other people playing great music in that vein—like John Scofield, Steve Coleman, or Mike Stern—but I feel the original concept has had its day. Smooth jazz feels very unrelated; it is closer to instrumental r&b pop like Booker T. and the M.G.s or King Curtis. What Fourplay, Bob James, or Kirk Whalom do in no way resembles the musicianship or intensity of Mahavishnu, nor does it have the depth of Weather Report's music.

Elements of world music, Afro-Cuban, Brazilian, and Caribbean sounds are coming into the music, but sometimes the vitality and musicianship are missing. I have a video of the original Mahavishnu Orchestra playing live. The dynamics and touch that they played with are amazing. About 70 percent of the time they are playing pianissimo, really saving the explosions. They weren't in your face all the time. As fusion developed, it got louder and louder.

The players that followed were people who grew up in the fusion era. If that is where your roots are, they are not very deep. The original fusion pioneers were primarily jazz musicians who grew up absorbing rock. When players grow up imitating a sound without understanding its source, the music is not as potent. That is not to say that the newer players are not good, but they don't come from as rich a background.

I enjoy playing with the people in Vital Information because they have jazz roots. It is a real challenge to come up with something that is unique and strong. With the band I want to look more into that and look less into trying to do something I think people will like.

 Q. As an artist whose records mix jazz and rock, do you think there is a future for this style?

I have to get philosophical. I don't see a big future for the genre. I do feel that if you look at different music that has had its beginning, middle, and end, there will always be representatives of that sound who will continue to work. For example, Louis Armstrong came out of the New Orleans tradition. Though styles changed, he was a representative of that school of music for the rest of his life. Count Basie, Stan Kenton, and Dizzy Gillespie didn't alter their styles too much in later years. Maynard Ferguson and Sonny Rollins continue to work. Brilliant players in any style will always find a market for the time and music they are representing. Jazz festival organizers love to have the living masters in to play.

 What do you think it takes to succeed in the business?

The playing is a major aspect of being successful, but another key element is to not get knocked down by disappointment. Some friends of mine who were great players didn't do well career-wise because they were hurt deeply by the business and never made a recovery from that. Those who persevered and processed what happened to them and used it to focus their resolve did better.

Whenever I lost a gig, got fired, or was told that I wasn't playing what the leader wanted to hear, I would get hurt and angry. But ultimately I would look at the situation to see what I could learn from it. I know a lot of people who couldn't weather the storms psychologically.

You also have to know how to develop personal relationships; that's what the business is based on. You have to keep in touch with people, be easy to get along with, and available.

In the time that I came up in, the concept of a getting a bio, a photo, and a demo tape together wasn't important, it was all word of mouth. In a way it is still the same. Those breaking out today do it with ability and a good attitude. Networking is a big thing. For me, the Berklee environment was key. The academics were helpful, but playing—inside and outside of the school—with other students was really important. We got together to play a lot, and I developed from those relationships. Networking got me into the business.

 Let's fast-forward 20 years. What do you see yourself doing?

I see myself going into the educational side doing clinics and master classes. Max Roach is a real inspiration as is Louis Belson, or Ed Thigpen. They are in their 60's and 70's and are still out there working a lot. I don't see any reason why I wouldn't want to do that. It is inspiring for me to go out to play and do clinics.

 Is there any one subject you are asked about frequently at your clinics?

Yes. I get asked about the difference between being a highly-schooled and self-taught musician. All really great players are self-taught in a way. You can be guided and taught the mechanics of your instrument, but the ability to actually play can't be taught. Playing your instrument well is different from playing music well. Getting together with other players and making the music happen is a self-learned process. To me that is really clear.

The total environment at a school like Berklee is more helpful than you would find at a school that teaches only drums, bass, and guitar. My main teachers now are not drummers, but bass players, keyboardists, sax players. They help me develop as a musician.

 You have had an unusual career in that you have straddled genres recording with successful rock artists and with top jazz artists.

Other drummers like Steve Gadd, Vinnie Colaiuta, Greg Bissonette, and Dennis Chambers have done this too. An aspect of that is relating to the different musical personalities and outlooks on a day-to-day basis. I got my initiation into that with Montrose. I find a way to relate to the musicians personally and musically. I have more of a camaraderie with the jazz musicians; there are some foundational differences with rock musicians.

Looking at the bigger picture, I see the music starting with the blues roots and the New Orleans sound—it is all American music. I see blues as the thread. So I feel comfortable with all of the branches of the tree because I have a good knowledge of the basics of the tradition. My listening and reading habits are oriented towards becoming well-versed in the entire history of U.S. music. I have done a lot of homework studying American music and the drumming traditions of the past 100 years. It helps me to address the music.

There are physical, intellectual, and intuitive or conceptual things to know about American music. The intuitive part comes to me because I am an American. It is not natural for me to play Afro-Cuban music, that is not my culture. I could intellectualize it, physically get behind it, and approximate it to a degree, but I will always have an American accent speaking that language. When Airto Moreira or Alex Acuña play a drum set, they have an accent. They sound like they are from South America, you can hear it. I am focused on my culture and what comes to me naturally. I perceive myself as a U.S ethnic drummer, so I have made a study of the history of the music from the blues to the present.

The slave trade and the African-American experience in this country is the foundation of this music. The blues has no history or tradition in Africa; it was the black people's response to the oppressive lifestyle they experienced here. That has become the wellspring for American pop, which has spread around the world. I have read a lot of books, and whenever there was a reference to an important Jelly Roll Morton, Original Dixieland Band, or Louis Armstrong recording, I would go and get it so I could listen to the first recording of the first recordings.

If you follow that history, it takes any mystery out of how I play with Journey or Steps Ahead. They are both branches on the same tree.

Aerosmith

rock 'n' roll survivors

Feelin' lucky, Brad Whitford '71 and Joey Kramer '70 go beyond *Nine Lives* with Aerosmith, the band that is living for 10.

NINE LIVES IS A FITTING TITLE for the latest CD by Aerosmith, one of America's longest surviving and greatest rock bands. The 1997 disc was the band's first under the terms of a deal (reportedly worth as much as $30 million) the band inked in 1991 with Columbia, the label which originally signed them in 1972. From the first notes of the title cut—Steven Tyler's scream, the snarling guitars of Brad Whitford ['71] and Joe Perry, and the thundering rhythm section of drummer Joey Kramer ['70] and bassist Tom Hamilton—it's clear that this quintet of 40-something rockers still possesses all the fire and energy it had 25 years ago.

Over the course of its two and a half decades, the band has claimed its own corner in the pantheon of rock icons. Aerosmith has played to packed stadiums around the world, sold over 70 million records, won countless awards (including three Grammys), and influenced numerous up-and-coming bands. They are also enjoying an unprecedented wave of popularity among a generation that wasn't even born when the band began playing. This wide fan base supplied the fuel that rocketed *Nine Lives* to the number-one spot on the Billboard 200 chart a week after its release.

Whitford and Kramer took a few minutes to speak with me as the band was gearing up for a Scandinavian tour to support the new disc. In their pre-Aerosmith days back in the early '70s, Whitford, from Reading, Massachusetts, and Kramer, from Yonkers, New York, had each come to Berklee at age 19 seeking to refine their musical skills. "My desire to become a better drummer drew me to Berklee," recalls Kramer. "I got discouraged, though, when I knew it wasn't going to happen. This was 27 years ago, when the primary focus at Berklee was jazz. My drum teacher wanted me to play with traditional grip, not matched grip like I had been doing as a self-taught, street-type of player."

Around that time, opportunity knocked for Kramer when Joe Perry and Tom Hamilton, who were putting a band together with Kramer's former high school buddy Steven Tallarico (a.k.a. Steven Tyler), came to Kramer's apartment on Hemenway Street to audition him for what would become Aerosmith. "I knew that I wanted to play," he says," and when I realized what was happening with the band, I left Berklee to go and do that."

Whitford, who studied at the college until early 1971, recalls, "Right after I finished the spring semester, I went to Nantucket to play with a friend's group. We also played some gigs up in New Hampshire, that is where I met the guys in Aerosmith. Their other guitarist wasn't working out and they came to see me play in Sunapee, New Hampshire. Later they asked me to join."

"We started out playing originals and cover tunes we wished we had written. The colleges and clubs in New Hampshire and Vermont didn't care that we weren't playing top-40 hits. In those early days we rehearsed in what is now the Berklee Performance Center. It was the Fenway Theater back then. We auditioned there for Frank Connelly, who became our first manager. He paid us each a hundred dollars a week—whether we worked or not—because he wanted us to have 'walking around money' until things happened. He had a vision of what this band could become."

Kramer recalls, "We were with Connelly, who was promoting big shows in Boston back then, until about 1972. He moved us up to the next level and got us with management in New York City."

The New York management team of Steve Leber and David Krebs helped Aerosmith get signed to their first recording contract with Columbia in 1972.

Soon, the band was set up in Boston's Intermedia Sound Studios to record their eponymous debut album, *Aerosmith*. Released in January of 1973, the album contained their first hit, "Dream On." Critics, in hindsight, now point to that song as the first power ballad.

It was a rags-to-riches scenario. The momentum of their growing popularity thrust the band into high gear. They released an album each year for seven years and toured almost continuously. Living with the spoils of the band's tremendous success, however, proved a more severe test of their mettle than attaining them did. Broken marriages, lawsuits over contractual issues, substance abuse of disastrous proportions, and a host of other hazards encountered in the fast lane dogged the band.

By 1979, morale and productivity had deteriorated to the point that Joe Perry left to front his own band. Whitford followed suit in 1981. Tyler, Kramer, and Hamilton hired replacements for the two guitarists, and Aerosmith continued touring and recording, but the magic was gone. On their own, Perry and Whitford discovered starting over was very difficult.

"We found that other projects didn't work," states Whitford. "All of the ingredients have to be there. It happens to a lot of people who don't appreciate the chemistry. That's what was behind Rodgers and Hammerstein, Lennon and McCartney, and Steven Tyler and Joe Perry. You can't explain that, it just is. When you take it away, it isn't—it is one of those God things."

The original band members reunited in 1985 after a five-year hiatus and released *Done With Mirrors*, their first album under a new contract with Geffen Records. They embarked on an extensive tour but had to cancel it midway through when continued drug and alcohol problems made finishing the tour impossible. The group's then-manager Tim Collins and the entire band checked into the Caron Foundation rehab center in Pennsylvania where each achieved sobriety through a 12-step program.

In control of themselves for the first time in years and with renewed vigor, the band started touring again and, over the next several years, recorded five platinum albums for Geffen. They earned their first Grammy Award for "Janie's Got a Gun" from 1989's *Pump* album, followed by Grammys for "Livin' on the Edge" in 1994, and "Crazy" in 1995.

After finishing a major tour and delivering *Big Ones*, their last album under the Geffen contract in 1994, it appeared the band could focus its energy on their long-awaited release for Columbia unfettered. Perhaps it was the intense pressure to come up with a blockbuster under the new multimillion-dollar contract, but the process of making *Nine Lives* was anything but easy. The trouble started early in 1996, soon after Alanis Morrisette producer Glenn Ballard started cowriting and recording with the band in Miami. The first casualty was Joey Kramer.

"This album was a crisis-in-progress from the time we started until we finished," states Kramer. "There were so many things that happened." Kramer was overtaken by a "blue funk," as he describes it, after receiving the news that his father had died.

"There were a lot of things going on in my personal life," he says, "and I went through a deep depression. I had to go away to take care of it." Kramer caught a flight to Boston in the midst of the sessions with no word of when he might be back. "My problems came right after preproduction and everybody had to deal with it. Going through that phase of the album I believe contributed to how it came out though. If things didn't go that way, we probably wouldn't have the album that we have today. I don't know if it is necessary to go through that amount of pain, but it seems to be that way for us."

With the agreed-upon September 1996 release date looming, the band decided to forge ahead with session drummer Steve Ferrone. But, as talented as Ferrone is, he didn't bring Kramer's brand of thrash to the sessions. Kramer returned within a few months and recut Ferrone's drum tracks. "That is part of what really helped me get back in touch with what it is that I do," he says. "It was very validating to see that an Aerosmith album couldn't be done without me. Steve is probably 100 times the musician that I'll ever be in terms of being a schooled player; he's just not a rock-and-roll drummer. It just shows you that there is room for everybody. He does what he does and I do what I do. I only specialize in one thing, but I am grateful to know that there are few who do it."

By June 1996, tension in the studio between Tyler and other band members began to mount. On the verge of splitting up, the band decided to stop working and check into a rehab center in California for conflict resolution counseling. They emerged 11 days later having decided they needed a change in management. Summarily, Tim Collins was fired, and Wendy Laister was hired.

The band had already completed half of the anxiously anticipated album with (Quincy Jones protégé) Glen Ballard producing when Columbia executives listened to the tracks and said it didn't sound like an Aerosmith recording. "It was difficult to hear that, being in the middle of it," says Whitford. "I remember going home and listening and thinking, they are right, this isn't the right sound. So we went into a studio in New York with another producer, Kevin Shirley, and cut everything over again. It worked out so much better because we ended up redoing some songs that we initially had decided weren't strong enough to be on the record. One of those was 'Hole in My Soul,' which I had thought was incredible when I first heard it, but some elements weren't gelling. The way we did it the first time, it was too light—like a pop-rock tune. Aerosmith can't make a record that sounds like that, people would wonder what happened. Our approach is more hard-edged, not neat and tidy."

Shirley, who has produced albums for Silverchair and Journey, took the band back to their rock-and-roll roots, away from the synthesizers, loops, and drum machines Ballard employed in his approach to the album. "Shirley said, 'you guys are a rock band, let's do this the way you do a performance,'" recalls Whitford. "We have done that for other records and there are a few ways to go at it. You can set up live and just fix up the solos later, or you can do a lot of fixing. Shirley didn't want to fix anything. He made sure the drum sounds going to tape were the ones that would be on the album. He wasn't going to use a sampled sound for the bass drum later—which we did on *Pump*, *Permanent Vacation*, and *Get a Grip*. Shirley wanted to move away from that and get an organic sound all the way through."

"On *Pump* and *Get a Grip*, we used a lot of sampled drum sounds," adds Kramer, "so the drums are right in your face. That was good for the time, and I still really like it. On this album, everything is mixed to form a big picture rather than as five separate things to be heard on their own. It is a band sound. What contributes to that is there are no sampled sounds—it is just straight drums. Also, the bass drum is not mixed out as far as before; it is blended in as a color in the picture. That is different for us, but it contributes more to the sound of the band."

The end result is an album that rocks as hard as anything Aerosmith ever recorded. And while it is a hard rock album, a very subtle stylistic nod toward the Beatles can be detected in some of the vocal harmonies, the orchestrations, and in the sounds of traditional Indian instruments blended with electric guitars.

"The [Beatles] influence has always been there for all of us in the band," says Whitford. "They were a huge influence on us, so at some point that was bound to come out in the music. I don't feel the music is derivative, but stylistically there is that influence. It is not easy to get that kind of magic on a record without copying them.

"On the song 'Taste of India,' we originally thought sitar would work. We met a guy in New York who knew a lot of Indian musicians and he suggested a sarangi player. We got him into the studio and just let him blow. It was fascinating, the initial stuff he played was incredible. In the end, we didn't need any other players, he really gave the whole flavor we were looking for."

Regarding the orchestrations, Whitford comments, "On our past albums, strings or other orchestrations were done as an afterthought, not as a part of the process of recording the song. We brought [arranger] David Campbell in very early to the sessions. We listened together and discussed what we wanted to do before the songs were completed. That made David a part of the process, and those parts became key elements of the songs—a much more integrated sound."

Once again bucking the odds, Aerosmith triumphed over adversity, rising phoenix-like from the ashes to make an album everyone is enthusiastic about. "I learned a great lesson from all of this," says Kramer. "God sometimes has a very weird sense of humor. As a band, we seem to function best under pressure and adversity. Without it, you don't move forward. Personally, there is a lot of strength between the five of us. I'm glad that I got to be a part of this album because there was a time when there was a possibility that I wasn't going to be a part of it."

Whitford muses, "It is as if obstacles keep coming up and we go, 'Oh yeah?' Like a fighter, when someone says we're all washed up, we go back, train harder, and come out fighting. You can't always get a record like this where you are very pleased with every aspect of it. On other albums, you might feel there is a weak link or a couple of tracks that you weren't one hundred percent behind. In a band, there is always a certain amount of compromise, but this album seems to make everyone in the band really happy."

The degree of commitment Aerosmith possesses as a band is seldom seen and is one good reason they are at the top of their form after 25 years. While it is not unusual for solo artists to have performing careers spanning 50 or more years, it is rare for a rock band's original lineup to have that kind of longevity. Whitford recalls, "When I was at Berklee, I didn't think I would be doing this when I was 45. It makes me think of Chuck Berry showing up to his gigs with his guitar in the back of his car and then working with a pickup band." When asked if he foresees Aerosmith still going at it when its members hit their 60's, he states, "I don't see why we wouldn't. We can certainly continue to make records, but we might have to modify personal appearances somewhat, but probably not a whole lot."

Kramer is more cautious. "We have seen a lot of things come and go and we are still here," he says. "There is a lot of energy in the band, but I choose to live one day at a time. I want to get through this tour and this record and see what progresses. I am happy with my part in all of this. I still really enjoy the playing. This band has never been about the money."

"I tell people we are the biggest fans," says Whitford. "We are right there and we aren't sure what makes it work. We know if we show up, it works. We go to see the show too. There is always something going on—good or bad. It is never boring. We keep coming back to see what will happen next. Our personalities are just driven enough that we keep at it, and are having a really good time doing it."

Looking back over the past 25 years, Kramer reflects, "This has been an education that goes beyond what you learn in college."

Howard Shore

subliminal scores

Many dream about scoring a movie, but top film composer Howard Shore '69 makes dreaming part of the scoring process.

IT'S A SULTRY SUMMER AFTERNOON when I knock on the door of the ivy-covered carriage house, headquarters for Howard Shore '69 and his Prince in New York Music company. Here, sequestered away in a sleepy community on the banks of Tuxedo Lake an hour north of Manhattan, Shore has penned scores for top films in a wide range of genres.

Some of his darker scores heighten the on-screen terror in The Silence of the Lambs, Seven, and Single White Female, while lighter strains add airiness to hit comedies like Mrs. Doubtfire, Big, and The Truth about Cats and Dogs. Shore's writing has netted him numerous awards and accolades including the Los Angeles Film Critic's Award, the Gotham, Genie, and Saturn awards, and BAFTA and Grammy nominations.

Shore answers the door and shows me around the facility. The operation covers several rooms where a receptionist and several staffers handle various chores at computer workstations. Shore's nephew Ryan Shore ['96], a Berklee film scoring grad, maintains the computers and performs music preparation duties in Finale® from his uncle's pencil scores. Shore works either in a small office with an upright piano and a desk, or in his upstairs studio fully rigged with a Synclavier, a computer, recorders of various formats, a mixing board, and signal processing gear.

When his first opportunity to score a film came up in 1979, Shore had little formal training in the technical aspects. His approach has always been heuristic, improvisational, and subliminal. He devises his own systems for pairing music with an image. One of his most creative approaches involves viewing the footage only once, then napping to let it seep into his subconscious before beginning to compose or improvise on the film's emotional undercurrents. He sometimes approaches a score as a single composition, which he later digitally edits into individual cues. This is a holdover from his youth in Toronto. He used to record a piece on his tiny Wollensack reel-to-reel recorder and experiment with editing various segments together.

That Shore's well conceived scores consistently deliver just what a film needs is evidenced by the number of prominent directors who call him back for subsequent projects. Eight of David Cronenberg's films feature Shore's music. The roster of other directors who have collaborated with Shore includes Martin Scorsese, Jonathan Demme, Sidney Lumet, Al Pacino, and Penny Marshall, to name just a few.

The directors' differing styles have led Shore to create a diverse body of work (45 scores to date) covering an eccentric variety of musical expression and instrumentation. His score to *Ed Wood* (which one admiring critic dubbed "a theremin and bongo fest") combined cues sounding like classic '50s horror movie music, Latin numbers reminiscent of charts from the Ricky Ricardo Band, and poignant string orchestra cues. The austere score to *Crash* is anchored by the sonority of six sizzling electric guitars, three harps, percussion, woodwinds, and strings.

Shore's phone rings continually with new offers, but his schedule mandates that he turn down many more than he accepts. When we spoke, he was in the middle of two films: *Cop Land*, a police drama starring Sylvester Stallone, and a psychological thriller titled *The Game* with Michael Douglas and Sean Penn. Though his career is a busy one, Shore always meets deadlines—with enough dream time figured in to the schedule to get the job done right.

 Did any teachers or experiences at Berklee influence your career?

Charlie Mariano was one of my instructors for improvisation. I was an alto saxophone player and a composition major, and he had a big influence on me. Hearing him play was a big deal back then. Joe Viola was also an influence in my not continuing with saxophone and learning to write. Teachers like Ray Santisi, Herb Pomeroy, John LaPorta, and John Bavicchi were also my mentors. They essentially taught me where to find the knowledge. They pointed me in the direction of the library and scores. When I came to Berklee, I needed a good foundation. I had studied harmony and counterpoint in high school, but there was so much that I didn't understand. I soaked up the material at Berklee like a sponge. It was the first time in my life where it all made sense. There was a great logic to music that I didn't know about before. The knowledge that I took away from Berklee in those years has been the foundation for everything that I do with music now.

 How did you end up as the first musical director for *Saturday Night Live?*

Right after Berklee, I went on the road for four years with a band called Lighthouse. It was a rock rhythm section with horns and a string quartet. We recorded for RCA. I did over 250 one-nighters a year for four years with them. We played in the Far East, Europe, and throughout the states and Canada opening for acts like the Jefferson Airplane and the Grateful Dead. We were able to play both jazz and pop festivals.

I came off the road and had settled down a bit in Toronto. From '72 to '75, I led my own group and wrote music for documentaries—nature films and shows about Canadian parks. I was also working on radio and TV shows for the Canadian Broadcasting Corporation, and worked with Lorne Michaels, whom I'd known since I was a kid. He asked me to do *Saturday Night Live* [*SNL*] when he became the show's producer. It was basically like a show we did in Canada called the *Hart and Lorne Terrific Hour*. SNL followed the same format, comedy and music.

Back in 1975, there was no rock rhythm section with a horn section on TV; it was a new thing. The whole concept for using music in that show was also different from anything that had been on. In the beginning, I wrote all the special music for the sketches, things for the guest hosts, and arranged all the charts for the band. Then I would perform on the show. It was an 18-hour-a-day, six-day-a-week job. I thought the show would last only a few months, but it kept going and I did 120 shows between '75 and '80.

 How did you move into films?

I started during the *SNL* years. I knew instinctually that a music director job was not what I was looking for. It became lucrative and allowed me to write movie scores, but I knew I didn't want to stay in television. The show became like a movie you had to keep coming back to week after week. I was interested in something that allowed me more creative musical freedom. My first film, *I Miss You Hugs and Kisses*, was an opportunity, and I took it. The next film, *The Brood*, directed by David Cronenberg, was the start of a long working relationship that has gone on for nearly 20 years.

All of Cronenberg's movies are a bit experimental, and so there weren't restrictions. *The Brood* had a 12-tone score that allowed me to do things I couldn't do on *SNL*.

 You frequently seem to employ unique instrumentation in your scores. Do you develop these ideas on your own, or does the director give you some input?

A director or producer won't give you much indication about what to do with it, the movie dictates it. The movie will tell you what to do if you are open and don't have preconceived ideas about what to do with a particular film genre or what the score should be. The sound of the score is less important than the composition itself, that is what comes first.

 The music to *Crash*, which is built on the sound of six electric guitars, is such an unusual score.

That was originally written as a chamber piece for three harps. *Crash* was done with a pretty small ensemble. The guitar idea came when I was thinking of making sound in a room with some volume. I tried to amplify the harps, but the piece worked better with guitars. I didn't want to have 14 acoustic instruments, I wanted to amplify something for a large sound.

We recorded all six guitars live, they were not overdubbed. There were two guitarists doubling each harp part, two percussion players, and three woodwind players. I used a string section for two cues, and I processed that sound quite a bit with reverb and delay. I spent a week manipulating what we had recorded, using it as samples and creating other things in the computer. I would lower things, change the direction of pieces, take out segments, and create new ones.

 How do you approach writing a score?

There are different stages of the process for me. One is to find the notes, meter, and tempo. Once I've gotten those, I think, who is going to play this thing? That's when you have to consider budget and time restrictions, and who you want to play. That is all part of the orchestration/recording phase. I will orchestrate based on the recording and the hall. I am not orchestrating a piece to be played at lots of different courts around the world like Mozart did. I am writing a piece that is going to be recorded once for a film. There is a lot you can do in a recording session that you can't do live, so I write for the recording studio.

Next is the postproduction period. You have written the composition, done the orchestration and recording. Now you have to figure out how it all fits into the film. This involves editing, mixing and other processes. For *Crash*, about 25 percent of the score was created after the recording session with editing and digital manipulation.

 Do you start playing along with the film or begin sequencing right away?

There were times when things were on a longer postproduction schedule and I could take weeks just to dream about the music. I would take long naps, wake up and write a cue. I was trying to watch it once and then dream about it for a few weeks. I didn't think about schedules, scoring, or numbers. Nothing technical was involved. Then I would sit down to play and recall a scene in my mind and intuitively think of something for that scene at the piano. I would then log it in a notebook and note that it felt like the scene on the fire escape or whatever. Over a period of two weeks, I would have logged in hours of improvisations and ideas on tape, sequencer, or paper that related to the movie in a subliminal, dreamy way. So I wasn't looking at the movie, I was just thinking about it. Having a jazz background, I write from an improvisational point of view.

Later, I would analyze the movie in detail, going through all the math involved. Then I would go back to my creative ideas and score the movie with them. I wrote maybe 20 or 25 scores like that when I had the luxury to do it. *Crash* and *Looking for Richard* were done that way. I saw *Looking for Richard* once, then I studied the play Richard III by Shakespeare. I wrote that music without really dealing with the movie. I wrote hours of material then fit it into the movie.

My scores are not meant to be up in your face and twirling around your eyes. They focus on a deeper subtext emotion. This is what I love about film music and why I was interested in doing it. A significant portion of what I've done can't be readily labeled, it has more to do with feelings. *The Silence of the Lambs* is like that. It is not a score that grabs you on record, but in the movie it has a power that you can define. You feel it more than you hear it.

 What is your philosophy on how music should fit a scene?

If you write too closely to the scene, you take away some of its power. You have to write to it without being too observant of it. The music has to relate to the sense of it, but you need a connection to the audience who is watching it on a much more subliminal level. You lose that subliminal effect if you approach it head-on. That is why I write so much music in advance—that subconscious kind of writing about a subject. Then I figure out how to put that with the subject without going right up against it. You don't want to be too obvious.

You can't apply this to all movies. Having been offered a lot of movies, I have been able to try different approaches. Comedies are tough because you don't want to write funny music. I will try to go for the emotion of a scene rather than the pure comedic aspect. When we would underscore scenes on *SNL*, we always focused on the drama, and let the comedy play off the music. We were always like the straight man.

 It seems that there are about 25 composers who do all of the major films in the United States. Do you ever think of how hard it would be if you were just starting out now?

I've never thought about it too much because I didn't plan this. But once you arrive in a group, you stay there as long as you are doing good work. I turn down about three movies for every one I take, and it is hard enough for me to do that many films.

I'm not interested in where I am in that group. How I got there was sort of coincidental. There was no planning or trying to get there. I was a relatively obscure person doing this, and then suddenly I was known. It happened in the '80s after I had done *The Fly, Big*, and *After Hours*—that's a Cronenberg movie, a commercial hit with Big, and a Scorsese movie. Then people figured I must be doing something good to work on those films. That placed me in another category.

 What drew you to film music initially?

The whole reason I got into this field was because this was a way to write music and get it recorded. I could have written music like the score to *The Brood*, but who would play it or have the budget to record it? I wanted to learn about orchestras. The only way I felt I could do it at that stage was through movies. I was always interested in movies, theater, and television, so everything went together.

Scoring movies gave me access to a recording studio even if only for a limited time. Having the London Philharmonic playing your music in Abbey Road Studios is cool. These are the reasons I was interested in this. I wasn't thinking of making money at it or becoming popular.

Do you get invitations from orchestras to conduct a suite of your film music?

I did a concert in Seville, Spain, in November, which was a retrospective going all the way back to my first movie, *The Brood*. The first hour of the concert was a suite of five pieces from David Cronenberg's movies. It included *The Brood*, *The Fly*, *Dead Ringers*, *Naked Lunch*, and *Madam Butterfly*. The second half featured themes from *Nobody's Fool*, *Big*, *Mrs. Doubtfire*, *Ed Wood*, *Philadelphia*, and then some darker pieces from *The Silence of the Lambs* and *Seven*. The concert ended with *Looking for Richard* with orchestra and choir.

We are talking about some future concerts. I am extending what I have done in movies, trying to take it somewhere else. I want to do a concert with Ornette Coleman of the music we did for *Naked Lunch*. I'd like to do some world premieres of new music. I'd like to play the *Crash* music live with that ensemble. It is almost like coming full circle. I started out as a performer, wrote all this music—now I'm performing and writing more.

 Your résumé says you did six scores in 1996. Your life must be straight out at times.

I did a lot last year—too much. I am trying to do less this year. I am also writing a piece for a record with the London Philharmonic and choir like the *Looking for Richard* music. The text will be from another historic piece. That could take a year or two.

The movie schedules keep me pretty tied up. You have to say "no" a lot, and then you have to put the time to good use since you said "no." The whole nature of being a freelance musician is to say "yes." You spend your whole life trying to get to the point where you can do the things you want to do. Whether you are starting in movies or playing an instrument, all you want is work. When you get there, you also want to do other things.

Q. Does that mean you are thinking that you may one day stop scoring movies?

I'm thinking about how someone might view the body of my work. I had a successful rock-and-roll career. I did eight records and toured for four years. I did live, network television for five years, and scored 45 films, then what? I am in that same state where I was earlier when I had done five years of television. How do you know when it is enough? The show [*SNL*] has been on 22 years. I could have done 22 years of network television. So I am wondering should I do 45 movie scores or 90?

Paula Cole

she's not so ordinary

With two hit singles under her belt and a third in the wings, life for Paula Cole '90 is becoming anything but ordinary.

IT HAS BEEN FOUR YEARS SINCE "I'M SO ORDINARY" appeared as the second track on Paula Cole's debut album *Harbinger*. If the lyric expressed her self-image at that time, today there is precious little that would identify Cole as the song's protagonist. The music on her second CD, *This Fire*, reveals that she is very comfortable with who she has become personally and as a writer, performer, and producer. Powered by two hit singles, "Where Have All the Cowboys Gone" and "I Don't Want to Wait," the CD has sold a million copies.

It was announced days before this publication went to press that Cole received an astonishing seven Grammy Award nominations in the categories record of the year, album of the year, song of the year, best new artist, best female pop performance, best pop album, and producer of the year. Cole is the first woman ever nominated in the nonclassical producer of the year category.

Even a casual listener would be drawn in by Cole's superb voice, but it is her songs that distinguish her from the legions of other great singers out there. Somehow there is a universality in her deeply personal lyrics. She is able to portray complex scenarios with a few carefully crafted metaphors. Like Picasso's ink drawings, Cole's songs, full in their minimalism, reveal her unique perspective. She depicts the emotional density of events in her life with an economy of strokes. During the 51 minutes of *This Fire*, Cole's songs rage, weep, psychoanalyze, and dance with concupiscence. Her lack of inhibition in the studio and on stage is an element connecting her with young audiences and beckoning her adult listeners' inner child. A solid conception of how to produce her music so that it comes across on radio is another.

Cole's identity as a performer was sculpted by hundreds of appearances, beginning as a backup singer for Peter Gabriel in 1993, and continuing as opener for Melissa Etheridge, Sarah McLachlan, and others. After headlining for much of 1997, she had to retreat when strep throat forced the cancellation of her year-end dates. She spoke to me before the holidays from her New York apartment where she said she was enjoying being an average citizen again and getting reacquainted with her cats. In conversation, I found her to be warm, eloquent, and honest.

Cole's young career continues to rise to heights unforeseen a decade ago when her voice was just one among 60 or 70 others in Berklee's gospel choir. It is written that where much is given much is required. Success of the magnitude Cole is experiencing produces expectations that an artist will scale even loftier peaks. If I was a betting man, I would wager that Paula Cole will reach them. Even among the brightest stars of the music world firmament, an artist who can write and perform music possessing the depth and visceral impact of Cole's is far from ordinary.

 What led to your coming to Berklee to study music after high school?

Growing up, I was a big fish in a little pond in Rockport, Massachusetts, singing in chorus and in plays. I had a silent dream that I wanted to be a musician, but it seemed so pompous to admit that or think that I could. For a dose of reality, I went to Berklee's summer program in 1985. I got a lot of encouragement from Bob Stoloff. He was very important and supportive of me at a crucial time. He told my parents that I had ability and that they should support my going into music. He also recommended me for a scholarship.

During my senior year in high school, I continued to study with him once a week. We did trumpet exercises, and read from drum books, and I tried to improvise vocally. Sometimes it seemed like esoteric knowledge, but ultimately I have used that in strange little ways on the stage.

This gave me confidence and motivation and helped me to fall in love with jazz and made me want to continue in music. I was a Professional Music major. [Laughing] I thought it was the easiest way to graduate from Berklee. It is just as important to think of what you will do after you are out of Berklee. You have to see beyond while you are there.

There were a lot of people whose egos were inflated by having celebrity status around Berklee, and that is a little dangerous. I think you need to remain humble and remember that it is a big, difficult world out there. I have learned that talent is very overrated. Your hard work and persistence are what create success in the end.

 What happened when you left Berklee?

After graduating in 1990, I stayed in Boston another year. I worked as a waitress at the MIT faculty club and sang at weddings and parties—just making a living as a musician. I think everyone's uniqueness is what is important. When I was singing jazz standards, as beautiful as they are, I thought the lyrics had a sexist point of view. Most were from musicals of the '50s and weren't too relevant to today's society. I also felt jazz—which I adore—was atrophying and becoming less and less a reflection of today.

I got depressed with my journey in jazz and wanted to express myself in words as well as music. I started writing, and it wasn't jazz. It was what it was. I'd gotten a lot of encouragement; GRP offered me a deal while I was still a student. That gave me tremendous confidence and hope even though I didn't take the deal. I figured if I could get one that easily, I should wait to go with a company that offered me greater artistic freedom. So I continued waitressing and being a G.B. [general business] musician while trying to become a better writer. I'm still trying to become a better writer.

I wanted to be in New York, but that terrified me, so I went to San Francisco. My sister was there. It was a strange place for me to be, I found it hard to make friends. I was holed up in my room writing songs furiously. I ended up getting a publishing deal with Famous Music.

 How did you get the offer from Imago Records?

After a few years in San Francisco writing, working in a bakery, and getting very humbled, I really wanted my dream to come to fruition. Kate Hyman at Imago was the first one who really believed in me and understood my art and did not want to change me. I felt then that a small company would be good for me. It is very easy to get lost in the shuffle of a large company. I felt if it didn't work out, it would be easier if I was dropped from a small label rather than being dropped by a bigger one.

 It seems like you may have avoided a couple of traps as you started out.

I have read a bit about the business and learned along the way, but signing with Imago hurt at times. In the beginning it was good. They got me out on the road opening for Sara McLachlan, Melissa Etheridge, and Counting Crows. That experience was very valuable, but it came crashing down when Imago died as a company and I couldn't find my record anywhere when I was out on tour.

 How did you get with Warner Bros.?

Warner Bros. people came to some of the important shows in New York and Los Angeles. They really wanted to sign me. They fought for me and ended up making a deal with Imago. I am still not free of the Imago shackles, but I feel like a Warner Bros. artist now.

 The clout of the big company has helped you to have two hits.

Yes. I worked very hard to make *This Fire* and decided to produce it myself. That was a tremendous personal and musical victory. I started the record with my former producer Kevin Killen. We did eight songs and spent $80,000. I didn't like it and knew I could not live with it immortalized in plastic. I can't promote things I don't believe in. That was my inner voice speaking, and one must always follow that voice. I approached all of these business people I had never worked with and said, "I want to throw $80,000 down the toilet. Will you let me produce this myself?" They said yes, and I will be forever grateful to them for believing in me at that moment.

I was very scared, but I had to do it. I knew I possessed the musicianship to be my own producer. I was tired of my vision being compromised, so I plucked up my courage and did it. I was making budgets and became a much better business person. Once we got into the music, it felt like freedom. I was making something I really believed in, so if it failed at least I would know it was my fault. When I turned it in, I got tremendous support; they felt they had a hit. I never understood what a hit was or felt that I could write one. I have never compromised myself trying to craft a hit. A song has to have a purpose for being and reflect life honestly or it will be empty.

I also understand how record companies are structured around selling records through radio. The production and the way a track sounds are important to radio. Now that I have visited countless stations across the country, I understand the nature of radio a lot more.

 Was it a great thrill to start hearing your songs on the radio?

At first you just giggle a lot. It feels like you have won the lottery. It is beautiful to feel supported and feel that what you are saying is reaching people.

 Many people feel they would enjoy the money pop stardom brings, but the fame is another story. How do you feel about becoming a public figure?

I hope I never consider myself a celebrity. I still walk out boldly. I hope to never lose that kind of freedom. I do see that people know who I am now. I have been eating dinner at a restaurant and had people come up to me. Once I was followed home by about 10 professional autograph seekers. It was actually kind of frightening. We had to get back in the car and lose them in traffic. Those experiences are a byproduct of success that I don't like.

About the money, everybody probably thinks I am a millionaire with two big hits. That is so untrue. I was told that my record has to go double platinum just to recoup the company's expenses. That is the reality. Once you have a hit single, MTV becomes vital and you must make a great video. That doesn't mean you have to spend a lot of money, but you usually do. My last two videos cost 380 grand each. That is a lot of money to recoup. I just try to remain positive.

 So becoming an established artist is a long-term project.

It is. I feel very blessed to have these hits, but my career isn't about those hits. It is more about me going out on the road and creating impressions through live performance.

 Does having hits put pressure on you for your next album?

That will be a new vantage point for me. I have to admit, I feel a little nervous about my next record, but I have to put that aside and just write honestly. My favorite music has always been honest music, not derivative of something where the players are trying to be hip or virtuosic. I keep reminding myself that all I can do is write from the heart because that is what made these two songs hits.

 Do you find that people who have loved your music and felt the emotions of the lyrics feel that they have had a dialog with you?

Absolutely. I think I am touching something important with young girls. I remember how it felt to be fourteen. It is hard to be a girl transforming into a woman. Suddenly the world starts treating you differently when you start sprouting breasts. There are a lot of young girls at my concerts, and it gives me incentive to keep working hard so that I may do some good in my lifetime. It is not me; it is the music that is touching them and giving them hope in a world that is hostile to women.

How do you go about writing a song?

There are different stimuli and they happen at different times in my life. Occasionally it is like a lightening bolt and feels truly like a gift from God.

The song "Mississippi" came that way. I could hear the song. I could see it as if I was a crow flying above and I could see the song below on the land. Sometimes they come by laboring at the piano or by reading journal entries that seem important. The music comes much more easily than the words. Having been on the road for a year, I haven't been writing because most of my energy is directed outward. Now that I am home, music is coming to me again. I never pressured myself in the time that I wasn't writing—I knew it wouldn't produce anything good. You must live life. Ordinary life experiences give you seeds that become songs.

Sitting at the piano feels like home, and that is where most of the ideas come to me. I have always gravitated to the piano even though I sometimes get ideas that are best for guitar. The piano represents a beautiful, sacred place for me. It is like beginning a Zen meditation, and ideas come. I have quite a few pieces that I hope will become songs for my next record, although most of them don't seem commercial.

 Your songs are written in many different keys. Do you choose a key because of its color?

The beauty of feeling comfortable with the language of music is that I can make those decisions consciously. Different keys have different colors, moods, and vibrations. I love the dark, flat keys. I have to restrain myself from writing in them sometimes. When I write a song in E major, I might decide that I won't play piano on it; the guitar will be the main sound. Your hands are like old dogs. They want to go to the same places. Forcing myself to write in a key I am not as fluent in brings out new ideas.

 You wrote your second hit "I Don't Want to Wait" in G-flat.

It is funny that when we made the songbook for the album, I wanted to keep all of the songs in the original keys. But most of the sales of songbooks are to beginner and intermediate musicians. The publishers didn't want to put that song in G-flat so it is notated in G. Most songs in the book are in the original keys.

 Q. Some of your early performances were done just with drums and piano. That is adventurous in terms of instrumentation.

I went through Berklee knowing how to play piano but never doing it because I believed I s*cked. You are what you think, so if you believe it you never get better. I was extremely diffident on piano. Before I made *This Fire,* I was in a relationship with a guitar player. We broke up and suddenly I didn't have my band anymore and my inner voice told me I had to stand up to my fears about being a piano player. My first performance was in front of 16,000 people, a gig with Sarah McLachlan, Patty Smyth, Lisa Loeb, and Aimee Mann. I just walked out and played four of five songs and was terrified. I had practiced the hell out of them, and that started to build my confidence.

I recorded *This Fire* with the piano and Jay [Bellerose '87] on drums. Later for overdubs, I brought in Tony Levin on bass and guitarist Greg Leisz. I realized that if I worked at it I could become a good piano player. It has been a liberation and taught me that with love and persistence, one can do anything at all.

 Q. Your band features players you met while you were at Berklee.

I play with my friends [guitarist] Kevin Barry ['87] and [drummer] Jay Bellerose ['87]. Sometimes I play with [bassist] Paul Bryant who also went to Berklee. I feel like I grew up musically with Kevin, Jay, and Paul. We played so many different kinds of music together, experimented, and grew.

 Q. It must be nice to tour with people with whom you have so much history.

When my first tour came along, I was encouraged at times to use other players. I thought the record company would know best, but in the end, I decided the best musicians were the ones I had always been with.

I have been playing with Jay for 10 years, and with Kevin for nine. Jay has been with me at every musical turn. I couldn't be here today without him. I've learned so much from him. Starting out as a singer at Berklee, I was just listening to the top of the music. Jay took me into the world of the bottom of the music so I would hear what the kick drum and bass player were doing. It affected me profoundly.

 Do you think women are making strides in the music business?

I feel that the [first] Lilith Fair created a great media sensation. I hope it directed mainstream attention toward the fact that women have to really fight hard to be noticed. My first album *Harbinger* was turned down by so many radio stations because they felt they already had too many female artists, like there was a novelty quota. For me, being inside a woman's body, I didn't feel like a novelty. This felt like discrimination.

I am glad that women in the Lilith Fair supported each other in unity not competition. No minority can be suppressed for long when they are united. There is a lot of work left to do. It is still very hard to find female drummers, bass, horn, and guitar players. I have only met one female producer and I've yet to meet a female engineer. In the record companies, you don't see women CEOs. Most of the women are in publicity positions. It originally started with women making parties for the employees and that became the publicity department.

The top-40 charts show a lot of women and radio has changed a lot in the past two years. Lilith Fair was so successful that they can't deny its validity. Consequently, radio has embraced me a lot more. I am grateful for that. I hope I am doing something that will inspire girls to want to play the drums or produce.

 It would be nice if one day simply the best person for the job gets hired.

I hope it happens too. That is who I hire, and they all happen to be white men! I go for who is best, and their personality matters. I don't hire anyone unless they are humble and kind and want to work. I have been on the tour bus for 10 months with 10 men. You have to be spiritually centered and stoic to endure that. I suppose Berklee prepared me for this too because there was about a 13-to-one ratio of men to women when I was a student. I really miss the company of women on the road.

 Do you think, now that you have established yourself in the market-place, it will be easy to maintain your spot or do you worry about the public being fickle?

I find the public has been my friend; they do know what good music is and when I'm being honest. I felt like I started cultivating a fan base by performing live. It was through my honest performances that I reached the public. I am proud of my live show. That is where you can determine if a performer has it or doesn't.

I know the record company would love for me to have another hit, and I would love it too. I've seen the momentum it gives an album and the excitement it brings into your life. I am not going to write consciously trying to have a hit though.

 What would you like to be doing in 10 years?

I will be 39 then. I hope I'll have several really creative albums under my belt by then. I would love to make a jazz album. I poured so much of myself into jazz, it must come to fruition so I can feel like I can go on. I recently sang "Autumn Leaves" with some great jazz musicians for the soundtrack of the film *Midnight in the Garden of Good and Evil*. It was so wonderful to just be a jazz musician again and not the businesswoman, the producer, the self-promoter shaking hands at radio stations. Somewhere in my future there will be at least one jazz album even if it will only sell 5,000 copies.

I would love to be involved in film. Acting is a challenge that beckons me. I would love to have a foundation of success so that I can loan myself to help some causes. Success could afford me to have a few years between albums so I could have children, a home, a dog. I see my early life as a time to work hard and lay the foundation for a lasting career. In my middle life, I want to be a mother.

 Is there anything we didn't touch on that you want to say?

Yes. As much of an oasis as Berklee was for me, you can find yourself pursuing the narcissism of your own virtuosity there. I was doing that. I had been concentrating on becoming as virtuosic a singer as possible. It was a little bit of a distraction; it helped me, but it wasn't my true path.

Musicians need to find their unique point of view. In the natural world, the more unique a species is, the better the chance it has of surviving. It is the same way with your artistry. Don't try to mold yourself to the standards of others. You can become homogenized by the process. Look within and reveal your thoughts as uniquely and honestly as possible. That means not trying so hard to sound like other people. The influence of others can help you become comfortable with the language of music, but ultimately you have to honor your own voice.

Neil Stubenhaus

"a team" player

Neil Stubenhaus '75, one of L.A.'s top studio bassists, explains the rules of the game and gives his forecast for the future.

IT IS A SUNNY FEBRUARY MORNING and composer Jimmy Haskell is recording his soundtrack for a Disney animated project at Capitol Studios in Hollywood. Haskell has gathered several of the eagles of the Los Angeles studio scene for the gig. There are about 30 cues to record in a three-hour session that the Disney representatives behind the glass are hoping won't go overtime. There is little time for rehearsal, less for goof-ups.

Veteran session players Neil Stubenhaus (bass), Tim May (guitar), Randy Waldman (keyboards), and Alex Acuña (drums) are in the hot seats, but they are not even close to breaking a sweat. Watching them nail each cue on the first or second take makes it immediately apparent why these players are continuously in demand.

The union steward calls a break, and I follow Stubenhaus outside while he checks progress with the man detailing his car in Capitol's parking lot. Before the session resumes, he heads for the phone—the lifeline of a session player.

Stubenhaus has been a Los Angeles "A Team" player for two decades. He jokes that the first thing he did after receiving his union card was to stand in picket lines during the musicians' strike that many hoped would bring changes to L.A.'s music business in the '80s. To date, Stubenhaus has played on hundreds of albums (60 certified gold or platinum), 40 Grammy-winning songs, over 200 film scores, and

80 television themes. Among the superstars he's worked for are Whitney Houston, Elton John, George Benson, Quincy Jones, and many, many more.

Equally impressive is the roster of lesser-known masters, like Milton Nascimento and Bill Watrous, with whom he has recorded. When it has been worthwhile financially and professionally, he has taken to the road. Barbra Streisand's 1994 tour is a case in point.

Stubenhaus has remained a busy double-scale player in a fiercely competitive, ever-changing market where superlative musicianship is the coin of the realm and affability and mutability are musts for the kind of career longevity Stubenhaus has enjoyed. Having logged 20 years as a top studio bassist places him in a class with few peers and begs the question: will he do it for another 20?

After finishing the session with Haskell, Stubenhaus gave a candid interview about his past and future and a unique insider's assessment of the studio business in L.A.

 Let's start at the beginning. When did you begin playing music?

I started playing drums when I was very young, and took drum lessons until I was 10. At 11, I was already playing with bands. I used to sit in at clubs and resorts I went to on vacation with my parents. I picked up guitar, and was playing that pretty well within four months. In the bands I was in, I would teach the bass players their parts, and eventually just decided to play bass. I really took to it, and was able to play whatever I heard on records. I knew there was a demand for bass players and knew I was good at it.

 Some bassists who started out on guitar overplay, forgetting the groove. You have obviously not gone that way.

I may have done that a bit in the beginning, just for experimenting. That was a long time ago and I've learned to home in on what the bass is supposed to do.

What originally shaped your decision to study at Berklee?

I had been touring with the old soul group Little Anthony and the Imperials for a while. I hoped it might lead me to a better situation musically and financially, but the circuit we were on wasn't leading anywhere. I had fun and met some people, but I figured that the intelligent thing to do was to come to Boston and learn more about music. I watched some of my friends from Connecticut—John Scofield and Chip Jackson—go to Berklee, and it sounded great to be where a lot of musicians were. It was a good move. It worked for me.

 Were there any teachers at Berklee who helped to shape your outlook or career?

Steve Swallow was my electric bass teacher. I loved talking with him and being around him. Pat Metheny was on the faculty then, too, so I got to know him and Jaco Pastorius who visited Berklee frequently back then. I liked Jerry Cecco, who was my arranging teacher. He knew how to relate to everybody and nailed everything down for us.

Todd Anderson, an arranging teacher and sax player, had an incredible nine-piece band that played Latin-influenced jazz-funk. I joined that band and it was a great musical experience. Todd's material was fantastic and the players were great.

 Did you become friends with fellow students who also went on to great careers?

Yes. I met [drummers] Steve Smith ['76], John Robinson ['75], Vinnie Colaiuta ['75], [guitarist] Mike Stern ['75], and [bassist] Jeff Berlin ['74]. I wanted to meet the really good drummers, so I introduced myself to Steve Smith. We were walking through the halls one night and heard a great drummer practicing. Steve said, "That's Vinnie Colaiuta, he's scary." I became friendly with Vinnie and we have been friends ever since. He is in Sting's band now.

How did you end up living in Los Angeles?

I later started teaching at Berklee after Steve Swallow recommended me for the job. I taught there for two years. At night, I had a band with [faculty member] Orville Wright playing keyboards. As the routine of teaching five days and playing six nights was getting old, Mike Stern, who was playing with Blood Sweat and Tears at the time, called me up and said the band had just fired its bass player, and I was in. I was thrilled, and went on the road with Blood Sweat and Tears. That ended abruptly after the saxophonist died when we were in Europe and the band went on a long hiatus. I took a job with Gap Mangione, Chuck's older brother. He had an album out that had been produced by Larry Carlton. While touring with Gap, we ended up in Los Angeles, and I auditioned with Larry Carlton and he hired me. I had no interest in L.A. at the time because I wanted to be in New York. It is funny how things work out because I don't think I would have been happy in New York.

 That must have been a great connection—Larry Carlton was very popular then [1978].

Larry had his first album out and was getting started as a solo artist. I was in his first band for his solo outing. It was not the best time to join his band. Later, as he developed a following, the gig paid better and was more settled, but the timing was good for me.

 Did Larry help to open doors for you in L.A.?

When the band was idle, I pressed Larry to make a few calls for me. He called two friends: composer Mike Post and jingle writer Don Pieistrup. Those two connections were all I needed. I still work for Don. He is one of the most brilliant musicians I have ever worked for. There was a lot of business back then, and things could snowball. At one of Don's sessions, I met a contractor who called me for some obscure record sessions. Those led to other record dates with more powerful contractors, and my name started to spread. On a Mike Post date, I met Tom Scott who later started calling me to play on his records with great studio players like Steve Gadd, Rick Marotta, Jeff Porcaro, Hugh McCracken, Richard Tee, and Eric Gale. Slowly it turned into a lot of work.

 Was your reading a strong point enabling you to do well on TV and movie sessions?

I was a confident player, but not a fluid reader when I came to L.A. Reading a part in the studio is not like going to a gig with a big band where you sight-read one chart after the other. There was usually enough downtime on a session with people getting sounds and doing other things for me to look at any tough passages—like cramming for a test. By the time we needed to record, I'd have it down. Everyone thought I was a good reader, and actually, that perception was more important. The way I look at it, doing the gig is easy; it is getting the gig that is hard.

 Is it your philosophy to get the job first and then deal with delivering once you are there?

Impressing people enough to get hired is the name of the game. Look at the acting business. There is an amazing number of people who could rise to the occasion and do what Brad Pitt or some of the other young stars are doing, but they are not going to get the opportunity. Of course once you are there, if you fall on your face, nobody wants to hear about you ever again, but if you do well, it can lead to other gigs. There are people who are capable, but who don't get the opportunity for one reason or another.

 Is that where luck comes in?

There is some luck involved, but you must have the talent. Who can assess what the balance is? Does the luck come because the talent is there and you have confidence in your abilities? Everyone has a different story. For the person who didn't make it, was the bitterness there from the beginning, or did it come because he or she didn't get the gig?

 How has technology changed the face of session work in your view?

masters of music

When drum machines hit it was the beginning of the end for the necessity of live playing. There was a time in the mid to late '70s when there were at least 60 record sessions filed through the Los Angeles musicians union every day. That number could be as low as five a day now. That is not to say that there aren't more than five record sessions going on, but there is not as much business today. People are falling in love with their demos with drum machines and synthesized bass and string parts.

I wouldn't want to be trying to break into this business now. For instance, television used to provide a decent chunk of work for musicians who primarily played on records and represented a bulk of the work for guys who did mostly motion pictures. I had a lot of fun playing TV sessions for Tom Scott, Pat Williams, Alan Silvestri, and other great writers. Now this work has diminished by about 90 percent and television budgets have decreased by 70 to 80 percent. Very few composers are inclined to hire live players any more. The composer is now given a "package" fee and pays all of expenses himself.

To make matters worse, the quality of the music is not close to what it was then, and the TV audience doesn't seemed to have noticed. Unfortunately that comes as no surprise. Why should TV producers pay $20,000 for a great orchestrated score like they used to if someone can go boink boink on a synthesizer for a sitcom and use string pads for dramatic stuff? It seems to be working just fine. Letters aren't pouring into the studios complaining about the music. So technology has played a role in eliminating a lot of peripheral work that used to fill holes in a session player's schedule.

 So when TV music changed, your business changed too.

It certainly has changed somewhat. Jingle work has also been affected dramatically by synthesizers. Fortunately, for me, record and film work has been plentiful, but it was always a secure feeling to have TV and jingles there for variety and as a supplement. Synthesizers went from being a tool with which composers made demos to being "good music." In a commercial or a television show, the music is not the event. It just enhances the scene. In records, the music is the event.

Do you prefer calls for records rather than TV or film soundtrack work?

For the most part, yes. But film scores are challenging and good musicians are on the sessions. When I feel I can contribute, I am thrilled to be there. Films are actually more lucrative at this point. If it is a big movie with a big budget, they think nothing of having the musicians there for three or four days. If it is an orchestra, they could be hired for 10 days. For records, that is a rarity.

Years ago, I used to work five days on every record. Today they do everything piecemeal and call me to work on a few songs at a time. Even if I played on the entire record, I could do it in two days. You can't make a living just doing records the way you could before. People want to do things frugally You can't blame them for that, but they don't get the kind of creativity that happens when six great musicians play together in a room and spend three or more hours on each song. If I get called for a film, I feel that the work booked is secure.

 Are there any film composers that you particularly enjoy working with?

Sessions with John Williams are by far the most challenging. I did a score with him for the films *Rosewood* and *Sleepers*. Neither of these films did particularly well in first release, but the music was unbelievable and very difficult to play.

 Why do you think producers and contractors hire you for their sessions?

It could be any number of reasons. Having a good sound and the ability to do the job well is a given. They call the people who they are comfortable with. Nobody is going to hire an unknown who might not be able to do it. Their decision might be based on the type of music they will be recording. I get calls from people who have used me for years and know that I am comfortable in a range of styles. There is nobody new breaking into the business these days. The competition I have for gigs has been the same for the past decade.

Q. No one new is breaking in these days?

I have a theory on that. I am part of a rock-and-roll generation which is still alive and well. Years ago, the older musicians were phased out. A musician in his late 40s or 50s was considered too old or dated. That is not the case these days. Musical styles popular when I was 20 remain popular and current today. So there aren't many musicians breaking into the arena that I work in.

However, there are still several other circles of musicians in this town, and there is a whole new circle of younger musicians that the established studio musicians know nothing about. There are people doing rap and alternative rock records here or in other parts of the country, and it is routine for them. The same amount of work is there for us while new music is being created by a new generation of musicians elsewhere in the business.

Q. Do contractors try to pair you with drummers with whom they think you work well?

For the most part, yes. There are several drummers to choose from.

Q. Have you ever been paired with a drummer who feels time in a different way than you do?

It happens, but we can always make it work. In a perfect world, if I knew in advance exactly what the music on a session was going to be like, I could suggest the perfect drummer to work with me. I'm sure drummers could suggest bass players too. We could tailor things perfectly according to style or offer a few options to leave it flexible.

The first-call drummers are all so good that there is rarely a problem making the music feel good. You are really in trouble if you can't lock in and groove with a drummer like John Robinson. He lays down a rhythm that is impeccable. He already has made it feel great for you. Any musician will tell you that it is easy to overdub to his tracks. There are a few really fabulous drummers in this town. John is one, Vinnie Colaiuta is one of the most advanced and grooving drummers. He covers the widest range of styles. He plays with jazz greats as well as basic rock and rollers. Harvey Mason has a unique feel and is very creative. He is a joy to play with. It is easy to make music with these guys.

Some of the Japanese and Latin record companies want to make records quickly. They might hire us for six hours and they want us to get five or six songs. If the music is on paper, we can do it that fast. Good session players can make something sound like it has been well rehearsed in just a few minutes. With a lot of this music, they are not trying to make history, it is a simple record, there is a formula. We know that. We go in there, make it right, and cut it quickly. That is what they want. Musicians with less experience will try to turn it into something it is not and end up agonizing over it. We won't. We'll make it really really good, and the producer will be thrilled. People don't understand that this is really what they want. They are not looking to change the face of radio.

 Can you point to any session that has been especially magical?

There have been many. I can honestly say that all of the sessions I've done with Quincy Jones have been magical. Oddly enough, some of the obscure artists whose sessions took just three hours of my time during a particular year have been a real joy and pleasure. I hold some of the records that I played on years ago with Gino Vanelli and the group Pages near and dear to my heart because they were very creative and musical. That is not as common these days.

 Why is that?

It is the nature of the business and the nature of the music. There are different attitudes towards the music that let it go in directions that are unexpected. I had always assumed that rock and popular music would get more sophisticated over time, but the reverse is true. I have played on some things recently that I enjoyed, like the record by an artist named Adam Cohen. It was a youthful rock-and-roll record.

 Do you get called as a specialist for any styles?

Overall, I think I get called because I can cover a variety of styles, but I do get called for a lot of r&b and pop ballads. A racial factor plays in the r&b world, so I may not always be considered for a share of that work.

 On the Quincy Jones *Juke Joint* CD there were many great black artists, but you and John Robinson played on most of the tunes.

That gives you an idea of what Quincy Jones is all about. He is an equal opportunity employer who just wants the job done right.

 You have done studio work now for about 20 years. Do you think you will go another 20?

It's possible but not probable. I think I could go another 10. I hope to venture into other parts of this business so I can be less dependent on the phone ringing on a day-by-day basis. I would like to get into producing, composing, songwriting, any number of things. I have seen music change, and I know anything can happen. Five years from now I could be in demand for more work than I can possibly imagine or I could be waiting month to month for another phone call. The potential for becoming a studio musician is not terrific now, but that may be different in five years.

 Would you tell young musicians that becoming a studio musician today is a hard career choice?

This is what I tell young players: learn and make the best music you can make. A variety of opportunities will come to you. Don't restrict yourself. You may end up in the next Beatles, or the symphony, or find yourself composing jingles and enjoying it. You might become a studio musician in a big or a small town. A whole new crop of work may come up that is just right for you. It is important to stick with the music you like to play—don't get too far away from that. Time passes too quickly. Twenty years later you may wake up and say what did I just do... and why?

Bill Frisell

unwitting iconoclast
Without intending to do so, Bill Frisell has changed the image of jazz.

MORE THAN ANY OTHER PLAYER IN THE NINETIES, Bill Frisell has redefined jazz guitar. His broad vision has prodded many others to widen their view of what jazz is. Evidence of this was in the 1998 annual *Down Beat* critics poll where Frisell was named the top guitarist and his *Nashville* CD was voted "jazz album of the year." *Nashville*, the ultimate dark horse candidate in that race, bested efforts by jazz mainstays like Tom Harrell, Joe Lovano, and Herbie Hancock. The music on *Nashville* is a delightful improvisational amalgamation of bluegrass, jazz, and pop elements featuring Frisell and some of the Music City's top acoustic studio players.

Part of what makes Frisell's playing so unique is his unabashed blending of dreamy pedal steel effects, psychedelic howls, folky acoustic textures, blues riffs, and avant-garde noise—sometimes in the same tune. Frisell's music, often hailed as a new bit of Americana, takes listeners on a picturesque journey to the outskirts of jazz.

With imagination unrestrained by style or genre, he has written new soundtracks for two classic Buster Keaton movies and two for animated features by his friend, cartoonist Gary Larson. His records have showcased his own compositions, masterworks by Aaron Copland and Charles Ives, songs by Neil Young, Bob Dylan, and, of course, jazz standards. He shows up live and on record with such diverse artists as Elvis Costello, Marianne Faithful, Ginger Baker, Jim Hall, David Sanborn, Lyle Mays, Allen Ginsberg, and Gavin Bryars.

"Raised by deer in Colorado" (according to one unverifiable source seeking to explain the guitarist's ultra-gentle personality), Frisell was lured as a teen to the guitar by the sounds of '60s pop and blues. Though he later became enamored with jazz (he still puts Miles, Coltrane, Bill Evans, and Monk on a pedestal), he hasn't lost or tried to hide his affection for other musical forms. That honesty and lack of pretense is a factor in the widespread appeal of Frisell's music.

 When was it apparent to you that you had to become a musician?

When I was 10, I started playing clarinet in the school band, and a few years later I started playing guitar just for fun. I just loved it so much. Sometime during high school I got serious about it. I had a great teacher, Dale Bruning, in Colorado. He really exposed me to Miles Davis, Thelonious Monk, and Sonny Rollins. Bruning is an amazing, unsung player. He is starting to get out a little more now.

 How did you end up at Berklee after high school?

I came to Berklee in 1971 for one semester. It was all too much. The big city, after living in Colorado, kind of scared me away. But I got a taste of Berklee. I went to study a little with Jim Hall and then went back to Colorado for four years. I returned to Berklee and went through the diploma program. Coming back later, I knew how to maneuver, and got myself right where I wanted to be.

 A lot of your peers at Berklee have ended up doing well in the music business.

There are so many memories I have from when I was in Boston at Berklee. I played with Mike and Leni Stern ['75 and '80], Tiger Okoshi ['75], Neil Stubenhaus ['75], Randy Roos ['78], so many people. Actually, I met [bassist] Kermit Driscoll ['78] my first day at Berklee and I have been playing with him ever since. Coming from a very small scene in Denver, where there were just a couple of people to play with, to Boston was amazing. You could be walking down the street and see someone carrying an acoustic bass and say let's go play. Everyone in Boston was ready to go and play.

 Was there any teacher who helped you find your direction then?

Well, I was a little older than the kids coming there straight out of high school. A few teachers were just what I needed at that time. Studying with guitar teacher Jon Damian was incredible. I got so much from him. Mike Gibbs was great, and I took all of Herb Pomeroy's classes. He is such a heavy musician. I wish I could take all of those classes again or pick his brain when I get in a situation where I have to do arranging.

 Is there any singular event that you consider to have been your first break?

There are all of these little steps that I kept taking. I went to Belgium for a year with Kermit and a few others that I met at Berklee. We played there with a Belgian saxophonist named Stephan Houben ['77], and a drummer named Vinnie Johnson ['75].

After that year, I moved to New York. That is where things started to happen after a few years. The only people I knew there were those I'd met earlier in Boston. I went to jam sessions and gradually started getting a few gigs. For me, when Paul Motian called me in 1981, that was a big turning point.

 The first album I heard you on was *Fluid Rustle* with Eberhard Weber.

That was an earlier break. I was in Belgium at the time. I had played in Mike Gibbs' ensemble at Berklee. Mike had planned a tour of England with incredible players like Eberhard, Charlie Mariano, and Kenny Wheeler. Philip Catherine ['72] was going to play guitar, but at the last minute couldn't make the gig. Mike knew I was close by and that I had already played his music in the ensemble at school. That tour was where I really hooked up with Eberhard. He introduced me to Manfred Eicher and Jan Garbarek. So that gig was one that opened a lot of doors.

Q. What have you been working on recently?

Last week, I was in New York doing a project of music written by Elvis Costello and Burt Bacharach. They wrote 12 new songs together and are recording a new album with orchestra. They asked me to take the tunes and make an instrumental jazz version of the same music. So they are doing their version of the record and I am doing mine. None of us heard what the others were doing with the music, and the records will come out around the same time.

 Q. What kind of an ensemble did you use for that project?

There was Don Byron on clarinet, Billy Drewes on alto sax, Curtis Fowlkes on trombone, Ron Miles on trumpet, Brian Blade on drums, and Viktor Krauss on bass.

 Q. Although the instrumentation of this group isn't too unusual, some of your groups have been unconventional. I'm thinking of the bassless trio with Joe Lovano and Paul Motian, or the group from your *Quartet* album featuring violin, trumpet, trombone, and guitar. What draws to you those unusual combinations?

I am just looking for new sounds, but there are also non-musical things that influence these choices too. That quartet had to be a small group so I could travel easily with it. I wanted to have sort of a micro-orchestra though. I thought of the violin as the string section, the trumpet and trombone as the brass section, and I filled out the other areas on guitar. More than anything, though, it is the personalities of the people that causes these groups to come together.

I am always trying to find a different slant. The quartet was a great group to write for—a small group of people offering a lot of colors. Sometimes the instrumentation is a set up for me to play the guitar more, as in a trio with bass and drums.

 Q. Music journalists have a hard time labeling your blend of blues, rock, country, and jazz, but ultimately categorize it as jazz. Is it all jazz in your mind?

It seems that in the last 10 years, jazz has gotten a more formal definition. I am coming from jazz and was influenced by teachers like Dale and artists like Thelonious Monk, Sonny Rollins, Miles Davis, and Bill Evans. I believe I am thinking the way they thought. Deep in my heart, I feel I am coming from jazz although I don't know what it is any more. Charlie Parker used all of the musical information that was around him at the time. He used to listen to Hank Williams, Stravinsky, or whatever. He was open to all that and it came through in what he played. Now 40 or 50 years later, that is jazz. So I am trying to let whatever I have experienced in my life come through. Having grown up with the Beatles and Jimi Hendrix, it almost wouldn't seem honest to not include that. In the end it doesn't matter what people call it.

 On your *Nashville* album and others, the solo wasn't the *raison d'être* of the individual songs. Sometimes you got into just creating textures. Where does the solo fit into the hierarchy of your music?

I have always been a fan of accompanists as well as soloists. When I would listen to Miles' records, I was always fascinated by what Herbie Hancock was doing behind Miles' solo. I have always been interested in the mechanics of how the instruments work together. The idea of a soloist out in front of a band playing all of his stuff is becoming less and less interesting for me. In my groups, everyone is accompanying everyone else all the time.

Working on the project I did with the Costello/Bacharach music, I was halfway through when I realized that there weren't any places where the music just opened up and people played on the chord changes. It didn't really matter if everyone was playing a melody or supporting a melody. To me, melody is very important too. Sometimes in jazz there is an attitude about playing the melody as fast as you can to get rid of it and start playing everything that you have learned. That can be a drag.

 A lot of jazz musicians play the same ideas over and over again.

Right. I think it is the melody that puts a tune in its own individual world. That keeps you within the architecture and makes each song individual. It is really a way for people to find their own voice in a way. Instead of discarding it and playing what you have learned, the melody stays in there and connects with your own voice.

Lately I have been learning bluegrass tunes, and it amazes me how good bluegrass players improvise around the shape of the melody. Maybe the melodies stay within one scale, but they are so active. Trying improvise and keep that intact is one of those mysteries that I don't think I'll solve in this life.

In the music of my favorite jazz players, I have always heard this approach. No matter how far Miles went, I could always hear that the melody was affecting what he was playing. Monk played the melody all the time.

 You have always included nontraditional ways of playing the guitar in your music. I am thinking of the various scrapes and taps, strums behind the nut and bridge, or rubbing a drumstick over the strings. When did you first start doing that?

Just prior to coming back to Berklee in 1975, I had been studying with Jim Hall. I was really conservative and just wanted to play bebop. There were a few years when I could only see music as what happened from Charlie Parker through the early 1960s. I couldn't see anything else. Then something snapped and I realized that I had cut myself off from all of the music that had led me to that point. So I tried opening myself up to anything, and a light went on. I have tried to keep that attitude ever since.

 On the guitar, there are probably only nine keys that permit really guitaristic playing with open strings and natural harmonics. Does that make you feel limited in the music you can write?

I hate to admit it, but my music comes so much from the guitar. One thing I got from the classes I had with Herb Pomeroy was a little bit of a handle on writing away from the guitar. I have done that quite a bit. I will just write on paper without having a keyboard or guitar. A lot of great things come from that. I am just following my ear or something that I'm hearing in my head.

It could come from either place. I might write a melody on paper in a sort of stream-of-consciousness style, whatever comes into my mind. It could start in any key and modulate anywhere. As soon as I get my hands on the guitar, it becomes more idiomatic. I start using the open strings and everything. I still don't play piano. A few years ago I tried to take a few lessons and I learned a lot, but I wish I'd spent more time at it. When I took those piano lessons, it was wild to feel that I wasn't boxed in by the intervals that the guitar seems to play by itself.

 Some of your music has a sweet and down-home sound, but other pieces have pungent dissonances. Do you use dissonance to create contrast or are the darker tunes entities unto themselves in your mind?

I am not sure that it is a conscious decision that I make. The tunes seem to come out fully formed. Some may stay in a really consonant tonality and that is enough, I don't feel the music has to go anywhere else. Sometimes I will need some contrast. It may start out really dissonant and I'll want it to resolve or the reverse. As I am writing a tune, I don't have a preconceived idea of what it will be, stuff just comes out. Later on you can analyze whether it is happy, sad, fast or slow.

 In your recordings, you have explored many musical avenues, but the *Nashville* album was probably the most unexpected turn to date. It is also your biggest seller. How do you interpret that?

After that album came out, some critics in local papers here in Seattle said I was selling out and trying to make money, playing it safe. For me it was one of the most avant-garde and risky things I could have done. Going down to Nashville to play with people I'd never met before, I had no idea what was going to happen. I don't know if that has anything to do with it being successful.

I had to figure out some kind of music that I thought we could play really quickly. We had no rehearsal and only a few days in the studio. I had never played with banjo or mandolin players in my life. For me, it was kind of terrifying. They were scared to play with me too. They didn't know whether I would bring in Charlie Parker tunes to see if they could read them. Nobody knew what was going to happen. When we started playing, it felt so good there was a rush of good feelings. I hope that came through in the music somehow.

 Did you bring in lead sheets for that material?

Yeah, but the players didn't really read the charts. Usually, for my own band, I will write out scores or lead sheets and everything starts from that point. The Nashville players were really ear-oriented. I'd play the tune, and they would learn it that way. They were frighteningly fast.

A lot of old bluegrass and country tunes seem simple on the surface because there are only two or three chords, but there is a whole bunch of other stuff in there that can get pretty complicated. There might be two beats of this chord, five beats of that one, and six beats of another. It is amazing how those players can really play on those bizarre forms.

 Dobro player Jerry Douglas plays with so much finesse on that record.

I don't know how he does it, he's really frightening. We had him overdub on the Neil Young tune ["One of These Days"]. He said he'd just like to listen to it and then go play it. We put the tune on and then everybody in the booth started talking about something like baseball. When it finished, he said he was ready and went in did it in one take. I don't know how he could even listen to it while we were talking.

 What was the project you did with orchestra?

Steve Mackey, who teaches at Princeton, composed a piece called "Deal" featuring Joey Baron and me as soloists. We played it with the Los Angeles Philharmonic New Music Group with Esa-Pekka Salonen conducting. We played it in Los Angeles, San Francisco, and then at Carnegie Hall with the American Composers Orchestra conducted by Dennis Russell Davies. It was a concerto for guitar and drums. We didn't have any actual pitched notations, just indications of where we were supposed to play and where not to play. So our parts were improvised and we got to play with an incredible orchestra. I never thought I'd ever get to play in Carnegie Hall.

 It seems like you have no constraints placed on what you do musically by Nonesuch, your record company. Does that amount of freedom make you have to dig deeper when you are approaching a new album?

I am always trying to dig deeper, I put pressure on myself. I feel so lucky that my records haven't been really big sellers because there is not pressure to come up to the previous one. It would be so hard to get a huge record deal where they give you all this money and then if your record doesn't do well they just drop you. That happens all the time in jazz and pop music. When someone has one big record and there is pressure to come up to it again. I feel like I am blessed to have this amazing record company that will let me do what I want to do when I want to do it.

My records sell well enough that I can keep doing it. My whole life has gone like that, like a snail's pace. There hasn't been one big break, but a lot of important moments, little steps all along the way. Some of my records sell better than the previous ones did, but the motion is incremental. This way I feel stable, I am not counting on the next recording to make or break anything. I have built up momentum after trying to play for over 35 years.

 If rock artists win a few Grammy Awards one year, they can go out and play a stadium tour, but then if the follow-up album doesn't receive the same amount of notice, they will be back to playing smaller halls. There can be a lot of fluctuation.

Things have been very steady for me, although I am still playing in small places. That's fine though. I don't need to play in a stadium.

You have a very distinctive voice on your instrument. With so many people playing the guitar these days, how could a young player develop his or her voice on the instrument?

That is a hard question. I am not aware of it in my own playing, but people tell me about it. All of the musicians that I really love have their own sound. The only thing I could say for sure is that you have to be true to where you are coming from and don't be embarrassed about whatever music you grew up with. It just never works if you try to pretend to be somebody else. You're not somebody else, so you'll never develop your own voice that way.

I spent years trying to be Jim Hall and it was valuable because I learned a lot, but it wasn't me, because I'm not him. Whatever music has been part of your life should come out. People tell me I have found my own voice, but deep down inside I feel the same way that I did in 1963 or whenever I started to play guitar. Music is an area where you will always feel that you don't have it together.

 There is always so much more you can learn, which makes it fun and a challenge.

If you could figure it all out, there wouldn't be any reason to keep doing it. When I was in college in Colorado, I remember an incredible moment when I got to meet Bill Evans. There was a little jazz club in Denver where Bill was playing for the week. I went with my friends every night. The last night, we were leaving the club and saw Bill wandering around outside. I guess he missed his ride back to his hotel. We offered him a ride. I was flipping out because I was giving Bill Evans a ride. In the car he was so bummed out, saying how he felt he hadn't play well that night. I couldn't believe I was hearing this. At the club, I had been listening to what I thought was the most amazing and magical music, and he was feeling he didn't play anything! I thought you got beyond that at his level. I realized then that there will always be nights like that.

Rob Mounsey

lots of monkey business

Busy composer, arranger, producer, and session keyboardist Rob Mounsey '75 sees his work more as a careen than a career.

A TINY ELEVATOR CHUGS UP EIGHT FLOORS to deliver you from the street into Rob Mounsey's Flying Monkey studio in Manhattan's Flatiron district. (The company's Flying Monkey moniker comes not from the airborne apes in the *Wizard of Oz*, but from Chinese mythology, according to the outfit's principal primate.) Here, surrounded by an array of digital and analog recorders, sound processing gear, samplers, and Mac-based editing equipment, Mounsey has worked on projects for Aretha Franklin, Carly Simon, Tony Bennett, Gloria Estefan, with producers Russ Titelman and Phil Ramone and others. This is where he produced his latest disc, *You Are Here*, his fifth as a leader and second outing with guitarist Steve Khan.

A wall of gold and platinum records testifies of Mounsey's successes elsewhere with artists like Paul Simon (*Graceland*), Natalie Cole (*Stardust*), Bill Joel (*The Bridge*), Steve Winwood (*Back in the High Life*), James Taylor (*Hourglass*), and Donald Fagen (*Nightfly*). Grammy nominations for various projects (including Local Color, his first duo effort with Khan) and an Emmy Award for composing theme music for the "Guiding Light" soap opera share a nearby shelf with a pile of ethnic instruments Mounsey has acquired over the years.

With characteristic wit, Mounsey says it is safe to say that he has worked on "less than 1000 albums but more than 12" during his 23 years as a top New York session keyboardist, arranger, producer, and composer. While probably only a small number of record buyers know his name, the extent of Mounsey's monkey business is well known to the movers and shakers of the industry. Last year alone he was part of three Grammy-winning productions and was music director for the NARAS-sponsored MusiCares show.

Starting at age 11, Mounsey taught himself to read in all clefs by studying mini orchestral scores he inherited from his older sister. After poring over Mozart, Berlioz, and Beethoven, he became determined to write his own orchestral scores. "There was no one around to tell me that I couldn't, so I just started doing it," he says. By the time he was 17, a score he penned won him a BMI contest for young composers. He came to New York for the first time to receive the award at a reception attended by contemporary composers William Schuman, Norman Dello Joio, and George Crumb.

After high school, he turned his attention to jazz and came to Berklee. From there, he moved to New York to become a key player on numerous chart-topping recordings. Multifaceted talent, adaptability, and affability have kept Mounsey swinging among the branches of the taller trees in the music business jungle for over two decades. There is every indication that his brand of monkeyshines will continue to elicit squeals of delight for decades to come.

 How did you end up coming to Berklee?

In high school, I had started to become interested in jazz and popular music and was losing interest in classical or serious music. I had heard about Berklee from some musician friends and wanted to go to school there.

My interest in jazz was growing. I liked the idea of improvisation or spontaneous composition and was also interested in jazz composition. That is kind of an arcane world, but it was so exciting to me. I was listening to music by Gil Evans, Stan Kenton, Tadd Dameron, Claire Fischer, and Duke Ellington. They were constantly stretching the idiom this way and that, exploring the European, African, and Latin musical heritage.

Were there any courses or teachers you had that were particularly influential?

The material Herb Pomeroy taught was very mind-expanding. There are many people who I remember almost daily for the things that I got from them. Phil Wilson is one of those. I used to play in his Dues Band. When I won Berklee's Richard Levy composition prize, I had to write a whole concert program that was played by the Dues band.

I had Gary Burton for a small band ensemble. He had very little to say, but it was extremely pithy, concentrated wisdom. He taught us how to play in a small group to make the whole sound better, not to make yourself sound better. That is something that I still try to do all of the time. I also loved analyzing Beethoven string quartets in John Bavicchi's classes. He got some young kids who were very green about that kind of music to really concentrate.

 How did your career unfold after Berklee?

I took a semester off before graduating to go on the road with the Tommy Dorsey Band. After only two weeks, I gave my notice. I couldn't take it. Traveling on a bus doing one-nighters is a very young man's job. I was only 21, but I was already too old for it. The band was a bunch of kids in their twenties with a leader who was 75 and a few guys in their forties. The older players had been on that bus for 20 years. I knew I didn't want to do that, so I stayed around Boston playing gigs and doing copy work.

Ralph Graham, a singer I was working with, got signed to RCA in 1976. I became good friends with Leon Pendarvis who produced Ralph's album. I commuted down to New York to the old RCA studio on 44th Street that summer for the sessions. I played keyboards and ended up writing some string and horn arrangements too. Afterwards, Pendarvis told me he thought I should move to New York. He said he'd book me to play second keyboard on his dates, so I moved down in the fall on my 24th birthday.

Q. How long was it before things started to open up for you?

Through Leon and a few other people I met, I started working quite a bit. I was lucky to get here at that time because there was a big boom happening in the record business. Everyone was making a disco record. We used to just crank them out. I have a few gold records from that era for working with Ashford and Simpson and the Michael Zager Band.

Back then, production teams were putting out an album each month. There was a large pool of players who always worked. There would be a lot of players in a room with a bunch of mikes. An arranger would come in and put out the parts and someone would turn on a tape machine. The recording business hadn't significantly changed in 30 years.

The scene that existed in the late '70s was all turned upside down by MIDI, drum machines, and sequencing by the mid '80s. Technology turned the whole business into something else. I am not saying that is all bad, but the work I do today is very different than what I did then. The scene is now completely fractured. You rarely work with a large group except for film work.

Q. As a keyboard player, it must have been easier for you to join the technological revolution than it was for other instrumentalists.

It was. I didn't really want to get into electronic music originally, but it was unavoidable. My first synthesizer was an ARP 2600 with all those spaghetti patch cords. I'd bring it to the studio and people would say, "You know how to work that thing?" After a half-hour of fooling around with it I'd make it go "doink" and everyone would say, "Wow, did you hear that? It went 'doink'!"

Q. Were you working mostly as a keyboardist on sessions when things started changing?

Primarily, but it was a hard adjustment as an arranger and producer too. There were some moments of serious vertigo. I produced three albums for Michael

Franks starting around 1982. The *Passion Fruit* album still stands up musically. We did that one the old way where we had a band for a week. I did simple overdubs on my Roland Jupiter 8 synthesizer and Michael sang. A lot of people liked that record. On the next two, we were struggling to incorporate all of the new electronic technology. We wanted to use the new tools, it was fun to make music with them, but there was a moment when we wondered where to start. It is a little easier now.

There are so many ways to build a recording. All of the technology is a big help but if you don't keep your ears and your tastes alive, it is easy to go seriously astray. You need to step back, see the big picture and take in the whole gestalt. You can get too obsessed with tiny details today because the technology allows you so much control.

I have always loved music, but I have especially loved recording. These days, you can play these crazy tricks on a recording. If I want to write a piece where all of a sudden 2,000 flutes start playing at the chorus, I can do that. You can create all of these illusions of things happening that didn't happen that way.

 Can you give me an example of a project where you've done something illusory like that?

With Phil Ramone, I worked to create a recording of Tony Bennett and Billie Holiday singing a duet on "God Bless the Child." It came from an old film Billie had done with Count Basie and a septet—four rhythm section players and three horns. We took this noisy, low fidelity recording and got it to sound pretty clean with multifrequency noise gates. I took that and built a new click track all the way through, setting every click manually. I transcribed the whole arrangement exactly as originally played and then we played it along with the old track. The final tape had the old track, the new instrumental tracks, and Billie's vocals, which we could fade up or down. Then Tony added his vocals.

It is amazing that it really works. Unfortunately, I wasn't credited on the album. How would you describe a credit like that anyway?

How does your work go these days— how much arranging, how much playing, and how much producing do you do?

It is hard to say. I tell everyone that I don't have a career, I have a careen. It all changes from week to week and year to year. Sometimes I may do a lot of TV commercials to pay the bills. I always get calls to write an arrangement or just to be a player—which is a lot of fun. Playing a session is pretty low-pressure compared to writing an arrangement and feeling the responsibility for how well a session turned out.

It had been quiet, but all of a sudden I started producing a lot of records at the end of last year. I did one with T. Monk and have another coming up with Bobby McFerrin. He wants to do another record with a choir. He improvised all of these pieces to multitrack tape and my job will be to organize them and arrange them for the choir. After he makes the record he wants to take the music around the country and perform it with college choirs.

I also recently released my own record *You Are Here* on Siam Records with Steve Khan. Siam has asked me to produce a CD by bassist Bakithi Kumalo. He is from South Africa and played on the *Graceland* album with Paul Simon. I expect I will end up cowriting some of the material and playing on it too.

I am also reaching out into the film music world again. I have worked on a few films, *Working Girl* with Mike Nichols and *Bright Lights Big City* with Donald Fagen. I did some episodic TV last year. The show, *Central Park West*, was terrible but it was a lot of fun.

 When you are asked to write something like the great arrangements you did for Sinead O'Connor's *Am I Not Your Girl* CD, are you given parameters or can you just let your imagination go?

I am pretty free. That project was also produced by Phil Ramone. He has been a good friend and supporter over the years. We all met and talked about things and told them my ideas. We went over the road map of the song, how long it should be, and what lyrics Sinead was going to sing. We also made some minor changes on the session. When a lot of nuances are written out for everybody, there is a limit to what you can change on the session. Sinead really wanted to make an old-fashioned sounding record with big band and, in some cases, strings.

It must have been a very different approach when you wrote charts for James Taylor or Donald Fagen.

Donald will usually have one really strong line that he knows he just has to have in the song. He will sing it to you. For other places he would tell me just to fill it in. It was really nice to get called for the latest James Taylor album because I love his music madly. Mike Brecker was on that session. James had asked him to improvise some lines and then harmonize them himself. Mike told James he should call me because I could do it faster. So I came in and sang James some lines and then harmonized them in two or three parts. Mike played all three lines on tenor sax. We called him "the three tenors."

Do producers call you for a certain style or are you considered a general practitioner?

That is a good question and a big topic. When I was growing up, I always aspired to be a complete professional. Henry Mancini was my hero. Everyone would depend on him to deliver the greatest stuff and he always did it. He could write great songs, lead the orchestra, and write scores. Who else could write both "Moon River" and "Peter Gunn"?

It is funny, you can work so hard all of your life to try to get to that place, and one day, you look around and feel like you have arrived more or less. You really are a pro. Unfortunately, in the music business, you find yourself in situations where the aura of professionalism is almost a liability. It depends on whom you are with. That is incredibly unfair and a misunderstanding of what it is all about. That is how it is a lot of the time.

The etymology of the word "amateur" indicates that it is derived from the word "lover." An amateur is someone who does something out of love. A professional is someone who can profess something; they have learned the discipline and now they can teach it. I think we all have to struggle to be both things at once. We need all of the professional skills and still have the amateur spirit. Some people think that in a pro, the amateur spirit is dead and that you can't experience music holistically. They think if you know what you are doing, there is not enough street in your music and that you have no edge. I have seen some incredible mistakes because people thought they should hire someone who didn't know what he was doing and so the music would have that edge.

Unfortunately, some people feed that notion. They get caught in a certain spot—like finally being able to play 64 notes in every bar. Then they do it on everything.

 Is the music on your own records the style that is closest to your heart?

It is hard to say, there are so many things close to my heart and I haven't gotten to do them. I may not get to do them all. I have three or four other ideas for records. I would like to make a phantasmagorical album for surround sound. It would be a compositional recording created specifically with surround sound as part of the concept. I would also like to arrange a reunion of an old band I had called Joe Cool. It was a quartet with Jeff Miranov [guitar], Will Lee [bass], Christopher Parker [drums], and me. I'd love to do an album of retro sixties r&b with them—just for fun. I'd also like to investigate the African music scene in New York a little more. There are a lot of African and Brazilian musicians here.

 What was one of the most memorable sessions you have been on?

When I worked on Steely Dan's *Gaucho* album, I was just getting used to the idea of completely obsessive-compulsive studio guys making themselves crazy in pursuit of perfection. We were trying to do the title track. Most of it was written out by Donald. I was playing piano, Victor Feldman was playing electric piano, Steve Khan was playing guitar, Anthony Jackson was on bass, and Jeff Porcaro played drums. We worked on that one song for about 12 hours starting at noon. The track is complex and long—six or eight minutes. We had gotten four complete takes.

To all of the players, all four takes sounded perfect, none of us could hear anything wrong with any of them. Donald and Walter were sitting in the booth looking like they had just tasted a rotten egg. They felt it wasn't really working. It was frustrating to us. All of the players loved Steely Dan's music so much. We were really happy to be on the record and were working very hard and being so patient. At midnight, Becker and Fagen said, "We're just not going to get this one, we're going to throw out the song." Then they split. The players were depressed because we hadn't made them happy. [Producer] Gary Katz stayed and Victor went back to his hotel. The engineer, Khan, Anthony, Porcaro, and I stayed from midnight until 4:00 a.m. We did seven more takes, and all seven sounded perfect to us. We were exhausted and went home.

Becker and Fagen came back in a few days later and listened to all of the takes. They called us to thank us for staying and doing all of the extra work and said, "I think there might be something here that we can use." They sat with Gary and started cutting the two-inch multitrack tape. According to Gary, there were at least a dozen edits between the various takes. Once they had done that and they had this two-inch analog tape with all the cuts, they erased everything but the drums! All of this was to get a drum performance that they really liked. Walter came in and replayed the bass part and I came back in and redid the acoustic and electric piano tracks. Steve Khan came in and redid the guitar tracks and they were on their way.

 That sounds like such a painful way to make a record.

Very painful. After *Gaucho* and *Nightfly*, Donald took a long break. This process that was the only way he could satisfy himself, but it was so painful to go through that he couldn't stand it. Maybe there is something wrong with the picture when it gets to that point. I don't think it is supposed to hurt that much.

 Do you have any thoughts for the young people wanting a career in the music business?

The best advice I can give is to keep the most open mind you can. You should realize when you go into this field that the music business is never going to make any sense. It is totally unpredictable and completely illogical. You have to be able to work well with a lot of different kinds of people. There are some brilliant ones and some that need a lot of hand holding because they don't know which end is up. Sometimes those who don't know what they are doing won't listen to you. There are others who are brilliant but really tough to work with. You just accept them because they are great and you know they have the stuff.

There are a lot of musicians who are really gifted though not educated who really have a lot that you can learn from them. They are going to be coming from a very different place than someone who studied at Berklee.

When I was younger, I had to learn to have respect for people who didn't have the education I had, but who genuinely had a lot to communicate. You can learn so much from people like that and if you have skills that they don't have, you can be a tremendous help to them. It doesn't necessarily matter that someone doesn't know how to read music or can't tell you what key his or her song is in. If they can do something beautiful that communicates with a lot of people, they have something for you to absorb.

Conversely, there are people who know all about scales and chords, but what they do does not communicate. That is missing the whole point. They might not be playing any wrong notes, but their music feels like a trigonometry textbook. If you are not communicating an emotion, the joy of making music, or the rhythmic excitement, what is the point? This is a good life lesson. It took me a while to learn it.

Vinnie Colaiuta

talking drums

Words fall short of describing the playing of Vinnie Colaiuta '75
—it's best just to let his drums do the talking.

VINNIE COLAIUTA IS ONE OF THOSE PLAYERS who has never needed to call attention to himself to get noticed. His drums do that job. Vinnie's virtuosic and highly personal style has been causing even casual listeners to do double takes since his days at Berklee. As his career unfolded, Vinnie began to attain legendary status among drummers. The buzz has spread to ever-widening circles, owing to his work on countless recording sessions with some of the brightest lights in the industry. Touring and recording as a member of Sting's band from '90 to '97 brought him name recognition internationally.

Back in 1978, moved by the kind of youthful optimism that frequently overrides common sense, Vinnie boarded a westbound bus in Boston with his drums and $80 in his wallet. He got off in Los Angeles and started gigging in jazz clubs. Soon, he landed the drum chair in Frank Zappa's band after running the gauntlet during an audition process that withered his competition. For two years, he toured with Zappa and appeared on vintage Zappa recordings *Joe's Garage*, *Tinseltown Rebellion*, and *Shut Up 'n Play Yer Guitar* before setting his sights on the L.A. studios. His creativity, astonishing chops (checked by good taste), and stamina to handle a punishing schedule made him a natural for session work.

Since the '80s, Vinnie has been one of L.A.'s busiest studio drummers. He's worked with pop artists like Madonna, Ray Charles, Barbra Streisand, Jewel, and

Joni Mitchell, and jazz luminaries like Chick Corea, John McLaughlin, David Sanborn, John Patitucci, and Allan Holdsworth, to name just a few. He also did stints as house drummer for television programs such as the *Joan Rivers Show*, and played on countless jingles, TV themes, and movie scores. In 1990, after more than a decade in the studios, a desire to stretch out musically prompted his decision to take a hiatus and join Sting's band.

While he is grateful for his success, he did not want to dwell on the accolades, the poll wins, and the number of hits and Grammy-winning songs he's played on during our interview. Vinnie possesses a humble attitude about his career. "I am a very strong believer," he said. "I thank God for my gifts and feel that without the Lord, I would not have anything."

Vinnie has not spent much time analyzing what makes his playing compelling and unique. The "Vinnie Stuff," as it is admiringly termed, includes much more than his facility with polyrhythms and odd meters, those wild fills, and the ability to lock into a comfortable groove no matter what the time signature. In the final analysis, whatever "Vinnie Stuff" is, it has had an impact on contemporary music and a generation of drummers.

 What led you to Berklee?

I came from rural Pennsylvania, a place called Brownsville, about 50 miles outside of Pittsburgh. When I was young, I started playing gigs all around the tri-state area [Pennsylvania, Ohio, West Virginia]. As I was starting out as a musician, I was hearing about Berklee. A trumpet player named Paul Lanzi ['74] from the stage band at my high school had gone there. One summer, Lin Biviano's big band passed through my area and played a gig at a local playhouse. Steve Smith ['76] was playing the drums in the band. I first met him there. He told me about Berklee.

 When you came to Berklee did you run into him again?

Yes, and we became really good friends. It is amazing to think of who was around Berklee in that time period. Neil Stubenhaus ['75] was teaching bass then. I also met [guitarist] Mike Stern ['75], [drummer] John Robinson ['75], and [bassist] Jeff

Berlin ['74]. Music was starting to change at that time and fusion was starting to emerge, and things were really fresh for people who wanted to be involved in jazz. It wasn't only the classes, but the people that I met and got to play with that made it a very exciting time.

The people you get involved with in an atmosphere like Berklee's really shape you as a player. They really helped me. What I learned during my time there has stayed with me and enabled me to write music and understand what is going on in the formats that I work in. It was practical information that I could apply in the real world.

 What was your next move after Berklee?

I hung around Boston for a few years, studied privately, and played whatever gigs I could get just to stay in that environment. Al Kooper hired some Boston musicians for a six-week tour and I did that. Tim Landers ['80] played bass, Stanton Davis ['69] played trumpet, Gary Valente played trombone. That led to some work on a record that Al produced for a guy named Christopher Morris. I went to California for a few months to work on that. It came out but got no promotion, so it didn't go far.

As a result of recording at the Record Plant, I got to see what it was like out here. Afterwards, I went back to Boston and was thinking of moving to New York, but a lot of my friends were in L.A. It was during the blizzard of 1978 that I just got on a bus and came out here to live.

I roughed it for a while playing in bars for beer money. I heard that Frank Zappa was looking for a new rhythm section. I was a Zappa fanatic in high school, so I found out who the manager was and called up and hounded him. I thought it would be a perfect gig for me. The auditions were at a big movie studio and it was like a huge cattle call, but I got the gig. That enabled me to become established here. In between the Zappa tours I would work in clubs.

After about two and a half years, I knew that if I wanted to be involved in the recording industry, I would have to stay in town. So I just tried to play around town and let my playing do the talking instead of trying to talk a big game about myself.

Finally, I got a chance to record with a band called Pages. Neil Stubenhaus was the bass player in the group. Richard Page and Steve George were in it too. The record was going to be produced by Jay Graydon. At the same time, I found out about an opening with Gino Vanelli. This was in 1981, and Zappa was beginning to rehearse for another tour. I had worked with him since 1978, so I told him I wanted to become a studio musician and that I couldn't do the tour. He was very understanding.

I ended up working simultaneously on the Pages album and Vanelli's *Nightwalker* record. I would record with Gino from noon to 6 p.m. and then zoom over to Dawnbreaker studios in San Fernando and record until midnight or 2:00 a.m. with Jay Graydon. That went on for a month. I earned enough money to hang out for a while playing clubs until another opportunity came along.

By the grace of God, people started hiring me for their projects. I was doing jingles and did a big band record for a writer named Patrick Williams. He was also writing for television and motion pictures at the time. The musicians on the Williams record included Robin Ford and top horn players like Chuck Findley. I was the new kid in town trying to read those charts and not make any mistakes around those players. I learned how to play with a click on the job.

 How hard was it for you to break in as a studio musician?

Little by little things came up. I worked with Williams on a TV show, I did more work with Gino, and Tom Scott started using me. I played some jazz gigs with bassist Larry Klein. He was involved with Joni Mitchell at the time and called me to play on her record. Next thing I knew, Joni and Larry were getting married and I was the best man. Afterwards Joni's band went on a world tour. After that, I started doing more and more studio dates. Business built up to where I was doing sessions all day and playing clubs at night. Between '83 and '87, things really started escalating.

By the end of the '80s, I was doing up to four sessions each day. I was doing television, motion picture soundtracks, and records. I had drums at studios all over town but would still have to borrow a set from my cartage company at times. I would do a TV date from 9 a.m. to 1 p.m., then a jingle for an hour and a half, then a record date from 3 to 9. I remember one time I was driving home at 9:30 at night after doing three dates that day. I was right around the corner from my house. My cell phone rang and it was Bobby Womack saying "Hey man, I've got a session for you." I asked him when it was, he said, "Now." I turned around and went to his session until 4:00 a.m. Things got crazy, but you don't want to say no when the phone is ringing all the time.

 Weren't you also the house drummer for the *Joan Rivers Show* at that time as well?

Yeah, I was hired to play the *Joan Rivers Show* on weekdays. At the beginning, I thought it would just be a couple of hours each day. With driving and everything else, it started eating into the time I needed for studio calls. I started to sub out from that gig to do record dates. It was loose enough to do that and still come back to the show when I wasn't as busy. I did that show for about a year, but I was subbing out a lot in the last six months.

Even though I was doing all of that work and my schedule was full, I didn't feel I was getting to actually play a lot. There would be a lot of sitting around on some sessions—like movie dates. Some of the other players wouldn't even talk about music. It seemed like they couldn't wait to leave the session to go play golf. I didn't want that. I would end up coming home and practicing for an hour even if it was midnight. I started thinking that I needed something fresh, I wanted to get into a band situation again. I decided that I would even go out on the road with the right artist. Then out of the blue in 1990, I got a call from Sting. I got on a plane the next day and went to England to join his band.

 You were a perfect choice for drummer in Sting's band. Songs like "Love Is Stronger than Justice" [from *Ten Summoner's Tales*] has the verses in seven and a chorus that goes into a country two-beat. He tapped your Zappa experience, fusion roots, and pop session expertise all in one song.

Thanks. It goes beyond diversity and just being able to play odd times or suddenly change styles. It comes down to how you do that, which has to do with your identity and how malleable you are while still being yourself. Concept is so important. When you play a groove, you have to understand its character.

 Were you worried about being away from Los Angeles for long stretches with Sting?

When I took the gig, I knew that I was taking a big chance. I figured it would either kill my studio career or enhance it. Thank God it enhanced it.

 How long were the tours?

The first tour was 14 months, a long time. Artists at his level go out and stay out. I had traveled before, short hops to here and there, but I worked all over the world with Sting—even in Vietnam. You start to get to know people—especially when the band comes back through an area again. The people know who all the band members are, not just Sting. Today, in most pop situations, the backup band is much more anonymous.

Sometimes the act is just a product by a couple of guys with machines. I saw an example of that when I was on the English TV show *Top of the Pops* with Sting. The first time we went, there was this act with a girl singing her hit tune, flanked by dancers. When we went back on the show another time, the same act was there. The singer and the dancers were different, but the name of the act was the same. You see that a lot.

 Were you treated like royalty in that band?

Everyone thinks a gig like that is glamorous all the time—like being with King Farouk—but it's really not. We spent a lot of time secluded on tour so that we wouldn't be dogged by the paparazzi or others. We would leave after the gig and stay in the next town or in a place people might not think of.

When we first started doing the gig we did a few Amnesty International festivals in Uruguay and Chile. We would get invited to dinner at an ambassador's or a diplomat's house, so you do rub shoulders with people you didn't expect to.

Was the travel schedule intense?

Sometimes there were four or five gigs in a week and then a full travel day to get to the next place. The gear goes in a truck and you can't get to your instrument. I would practice on a pad, or if I was in a town where I knew some musicians, I might find a place to go and sit in.

What I hoped would happen in regards to my studio career did happen. I would find myself with a few days off in a city and I would get calls for a session. One time when I was in London, Warren Cuccurullo [former Zappa and Missing Persons guitarist] called to ask if I wanted to play on a few tracks on a Duran Duran album. When people found out that I was in town I would get calls. I fit in sessions for Everything But the Girl, The The, and others.

Did the sidemen contribute a lot to the creative process of putting the music together?

Yes, but they were still Sting's tunes. I had a certain degree of creative leeway. When he first went solo after the Police broke up, he hired some players from Weather Report. He became known for the musicians he was working with, and the job was thought of as a "player's gig." It was the only gig with a pop star where you got to really play. Sting comes from more of a jazz background than any other pop stars.

You haven't toured with Sting for a few years, have you been touring with any other artists recently?

It is all studio work these days. Sometimes that involves short-term travel, a few days here or week there. I am based in L.A., but I move around.

What kind of music are you generally called to play?

It varies. I work for a lot of different people. Mostly, I do records and sometimes a motion picture or a jingle. Last year, I worked on a motion picture project with Sting. I recently played on a score by Burt Bacharach for a picture that will come out in late summer or early fall. I get calls to work with new artists and those who are well known. In L.A., I play mostly pop music since that industry is pretty much centered here. Sometimes I will do instrumental projects that are pretty adventurous, but they don't get the visibility that the pop records do.

Do people call you for sessions hoping that you will bring something very different to their record?

I still get calls where people want me to come and do some "Vinnie stuff," but I can't just force that in out of context. If there is a great song and I am playing a nice track on it, I might not do things that people can identify with me. That is the way it should be; playing something else would be out of context. I can hear a track back and think that I could have done this or that, but you have to learn to make decisions like that on the spot.

I have had people tell me that if they hear one bar where I played a cross-stick, they can tell it is me. I am not doing anything but playing the way I do. I can hear one bar of Steve Gadd playing time and know who it is. What is it that he is doing that identifies him? It is just the way he plays, how he touches the drums, where he puts the time. Those are hallmarks as much as anything. I did not start out with a bag of tricks, saying these five or six things will be my trademarks. I don't even know what it is that makes people recognize my playing. If I had contrived something, I might have defeated my own purpose.

It is as simple as this. Let's say you and I both like coleslaw, but you like it with less mayonnaise then I do. It is just what you like. In music, players gravitate toward what they like. Drummers find they like certain stickings better than others, or they play a little thing on the high hat. Those little things become a style.

For instance, when I play in 5/4 time, I prefer breaking the beats in the bar into groupings of two and three versus three and two. It takes longer for the back beat to lay. It is just something I gravitate to. I didn't say, "I'll be the guy who plays 5/4 in groupings of two and three." It is just what I prefer. As you start developing musically and building a vocabulary, you just instinctively lean towards doing things a certain way. If you don't interfere with your development by thinking that you should emulate someone else and try to be something that you aren't, who you are will come out. You just have to let it happen.

 Is there a favorite style of music that you would pursue as a recording artist in your own right?

I am passionate about post-bebop jazz. I like music that is rhythmically funky and has an interesting or beautiful harmonic structure.

 On your first solo album [titled *Vinnie Colaiuta*] you explored a wide range of contemporary instrumental styles with guest players like Chick Corea, Herbie Hancock, John Patitucci, Pino Paladino, and Sting.

I feel blessed that I could call them up and ask them to come and play. I had a lot of great people working on that album. I was not interested in writing throwaway tunes; I wanted a context for my playing. I didn't want to just chops out over the tunes or rip it up. To me that is like having a tasteless car with a 600-horsepower engine and a crappy interior.

Since I did that record, I haven't had a chance to go back and do another one. As for what the future holds, one really doesn't know. I would like to carry on doing this work and writing, and maybe do another project for myself. I want to play more in diverse situations. Some people expect that you have to ask for more, as if you are reaching for something better than what you have. I am very grateful for what I have, and it is only logical that I would want it to continue. There is always something to look forward to. I am a very strong believer, and feel that without the Lord, I would not have anything. That is my stance. I thank God for my gifts.

Q. What do think of people wanting to imitate your style of playing?

That tells me that I am doing something that hits them in a certain way. As far as someone trying to fully absorb my style goes, people can learn a lick I have played, but they don't know how I think. It can be healthy to learn about someone's style if the person you are emulating has some value to you. But let's face it, people are going to call me if they want to hear my style of playing. I'm still here. You have to be yourself and ultimately you will be better off for it.

I had gotten stuck emulating people and it took me a long time to get certain things out. Every once in a while it is okay. I might say, I wonder how [the late studio drummer] Jeff Porcaro would have played this. If I play in that spirit, it is a way that he will live on. It is a way to note that he contributed something to me that was very valuable. I think that is different than imitating someone in a competitive spirit.

Q. In the Summer 1998 issue of *Berklee Today*, there was a piece written as a tribute to a young drummer named Chris Yeoman who died in a car accident. Apparently, you were his musical hero, and he said to a friend that if he got to meet you, he could die a happy man. Apparently, you two did meet briefly in Nashville a few days before the accident last year.

That whole thing is beyond sad. I remember meeting him outside the studio when we were taking a break. I invited him to come in. I don't know if he got to see any of the session. It is very touching to me if I represented something that was meaningful to him. I am happy that we had the opportunity to meet. To touch somebody to that extent is success for me. It means a lot more than saying, "I'm the guy who plays on all of the dog food commercials."

Q. In the coming years, will you keep up this pace as a session player or look into other avenues in the business?

I think about other avenues, but I am a player and I want to continue that. Writing interests me more than producing does. Producing is interesting work, but it is a whole different thing. Mainly, I just want to continue to grow in my playing and writing and see where that goes.

 Looking back at your career, is there anything that you regard as a high point?

That is not something that I can fairly assess. I have been blessed to be in so many situations that were awesome. I've been very blessed in my career. My involvement with Sting has been really stellar, and I was there with Frank Zappa—a legend—and Joni Mitchell. These are people who helped to define music. How much better can it really get?

ANDREW TAYLOR
Co-author of MASTERS OF MUSIC

Andrew Taylor was the founding editor of *Berklee Today*, the alumni-oriented music magazine of Berklee College of Music, where he directed the structure, design, content, and production of the award-winning publication. Currently, he is assistant director of the Bolz Center for Arts Administration, a graduate teaching and research center at the University of Wisconsin-Madison. An active author, lecturer, consultant, and researcher, Andrew specializes on the impact of electronic communications on the management, promotion, support, and distribution of the performing arts.

MARK SMALL

Co-author of MASTERS OF MUSIC

Mark Small is a widely published music journalist. He has been editor of *Berklee Today* magazine since 1992 and has penned articles for *Guitar Player, Acoustic Guitar, Jazz Educators Journal*, and *Drums and Drumming*. An alumnus of Berklee College of Music, he also holds degrees from New England Conservatory of Music and California State University.

He has also released four classical guitar CDs with the Mark Small/Robert Torres Duo, performed throughout the country, and published numerous compositions and arrangments for guitar. (See www.ojoweb.com/smalltorresduo/ for more information).

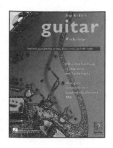  

Complete Guide to Film Scoring
by Richard Davis

Learn the art and business of film scoring, including: the film-making process; preparing and recording a score; contracts and fees; publishing, royalties, and copyrights. Features interviews with 19 film-scoring professionals.

50449417 Book.....................................$24.95

The New Music Therapist's Handbook – 2nd Edition
by Suzanne B. Hanser

Dr. Hanser's well respected *Music Therapist's Handbook* has been thoroughly updated and revised to reflect the latest developments in the field of music therapy. Includes: an introduction to music therapy; new clinical applications and techniques, case studies; designing, implementing, and evaluating individualized treatment programs, including guidelines for beginning music therapists.

50449424 Book.....................................$29.95

Masters of Music Conversations with Berklee Greats
by Mark Small and Andrew Taylor

An impressive collection of personal interviews with music industry superstars from *Berklee Today*, the alumni magazine of Berklee College of Music. Read about how these luminaries got their breaks, and valuable lessons learned along the way. Paula Cole talks about navigating through the recording industry, George Martin on technology's effect on artistic freedom, Patty Larkin considers the creative process, and Alf Clausen discusses scoring *The Simpsons*. Get the story from these stars and many others.

50449422 Book.....................................$24.95

Melody in Songwriting
by Jack Perricone

Learn the secrets to writing truly great songs. Unlike most songwriting books, this guide uses examples of HIT SONGS in addition to proven tools and techniques for writing memorable, chart-topping songs. Explore popular songs and learn what makes them work.

50449419 Book.....................................$19.95

Music Notation
by Mark McGrain

Learn the essentials of music notation, from pitch and rhythm placement to meter and voicing alignments. Excellent resource for both written and computer notation software.

50449399 Book.....................................$16.95

Managing Lyric Structure
by Pat Pattison

This book will help songwriters handle lyric structures more effectively. Equally helpful to both beginning and experienced lyricists, this book features exercises that help you say things better and write better songs.

50481582 Book.....................................$11.95

Rhyming Techniques and Strategies
by Pat Pattison

Find better rhymes and use them more effectively. If you have written lyrics before, even professionally, and you crave more insight and control over your craft, this book is for you. Beginners will learn good habits and techniques and how to avoid common mistakes.

50481583 Book.....................................$10.95